HARCOURT

Math

Reteach Workbook

Grade 5

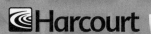

Harcourt

Orlando Austin Chicago New York Toronto London San Diego

Visit *The Learning Site!*
www.harcourtschool.com

Printed in the United States of America

ISBN 0-15-336491-2

1 2 3 4 5 6 7 8 9 10 022 10 09 08 07 06 05 04 03

CONTENTS

Unit 4: DIVIDE WHOLE NUMBERS AND DECIMALS

Chapter 9: Divide by 1-Digit Divisors

Chapter 10: Divide by 2-Digit Divisors

Chapter 11: Divide Decimals by Whole Numbers

Chapter 12: Algebra: Use Multiplication and Division

Unit 5: NUMBER THEORY AND FRACTIONS

Chapter 13: Factors and Multiples

Chapter 14: Exponents and Prime Numbers

Chapter 15: Fraction Concepts

Unit 6: OPERATIONS WITH FRACTIONS

Chapter 16: Add and Subtract Fractions

Name ______________________________

LESSON 1.1

Understand Place Value

The number 391,568 may be easier to read and write if you use a place-value chart.

Thousands				Ones		
Hundreds	Tens	Ones		Hundreds	Tens	Ones
3	0	0	,	0	0	0
	9	0	,	0	0	0
		1	,	0	0	0
				5	0	0
					6	0
						8

Standard form: 391,568
Expanded form: 300,000 + 90,000 + 1,000 + 500 + 60 + 8
Word form: Three hundred ninety-one thousand, five hundred sixty-eight

---

Write the number in the place-value chart. Then write the number in expanded form.

1. 716,583

Thousands				Ones		
H	T	O		H	T	O

2. 78,056

Thousands				Ones		
H	T	O		H	T	O

Use the place-value chart to help you write the value of the **bold faced** digit.

3. 5**8**,346

4. 7**2**3,308

5. **4**68,005

6. 420,**8**22

Name ______________________________

Millions and Billions

You can use a place-value chart to help you read and write greater numbers such as 721,306,984.

Millions				Thousands				Ones			
H	T	O		H	T	O		H	T	O	
7	0	0	,	0	0	0	,	0	0	0	seven hundred
	2	0	,	0	0	0	,	0	0	0	twenty-one million,
		1	,	0	0	0	,	0	0	0	
				3	0	0	,	0	0	0	three hundred six
					0	0	,	0	0	0	thousand,
						6	,	0	0	0	
								9	0	0	nine hundred
									8	0	eighty-four
										4	

Standard form: 721,306,984
Expanded form: 700,000,000 + 20,000,000 + 1,000,000 + 300,000 + 6,000 + 900 + 80 + 4
Word form: seven hundred twenty-one million, three hundred six thousand, nine hundred eighty-four

---

Write the number in word form.

1. 2,267,025,142

____
____
____
____

2. 702,326,500

____
____
____
____

Write the number in standard form.

3. 600,000,000 + 50,000,000 + 9,000,000 + 800,000 + 40,000 + 3,000 + 700 + 1

____

4. three billion, eight hundred six million, four hundred eighty-six thousand, two hundred twenty-six

____

Name ______________________________

Benchmark Numbers

A **benchmark** number helps you estimate a number of objects without having to count them.

Look at the jar on the left. It has 50 jellybeans. The benchmark number is 50.

The jar on the right is full. It has about 10 times as many jellybeans as the jar on the left.

A good estimate of the number of jellybeans in the jar on the right is 10×50, or 500, jellybeans.

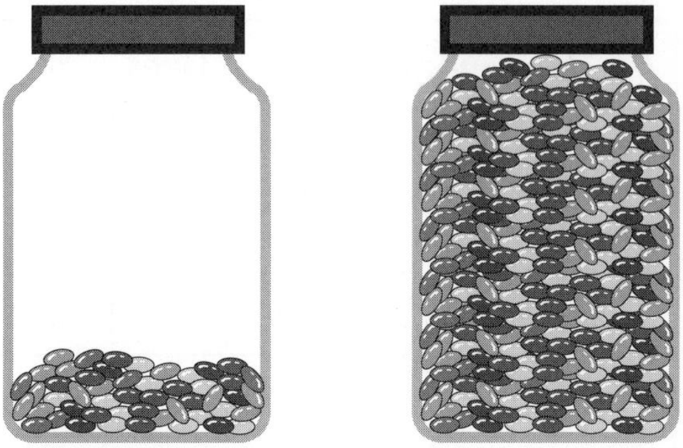

50 jellybeans

Use the benchmark to decide which is the more reasonable number.

1. golf balls in bucket B

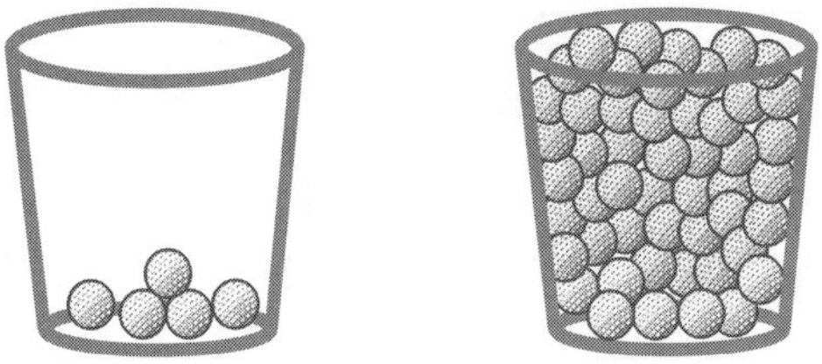

A **B**

Think: The number of golf balls in bucket B is about ______ times the number of golf balls in bucket A.

Are there 50 or 250 golf balls in bucket B?

____

2. coins in container B

A
500 coins

B

Think: The number of coins in container B is about ______ times the number of coins in container A.

Are there 1,000 or 2,000 coins in container B?

____

Use the benchmark to find a reasonable estimate.

3.

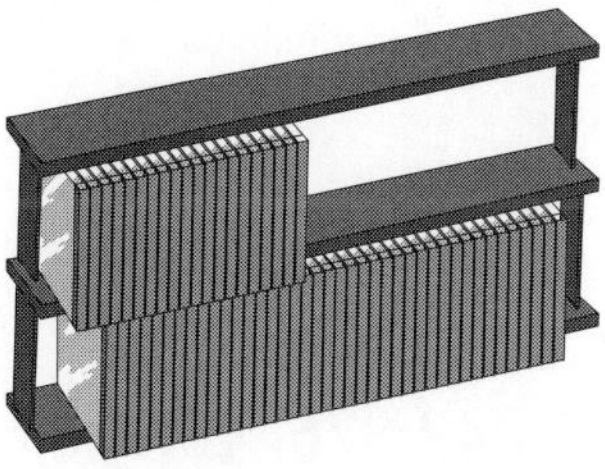

20 DVDs

____

4.

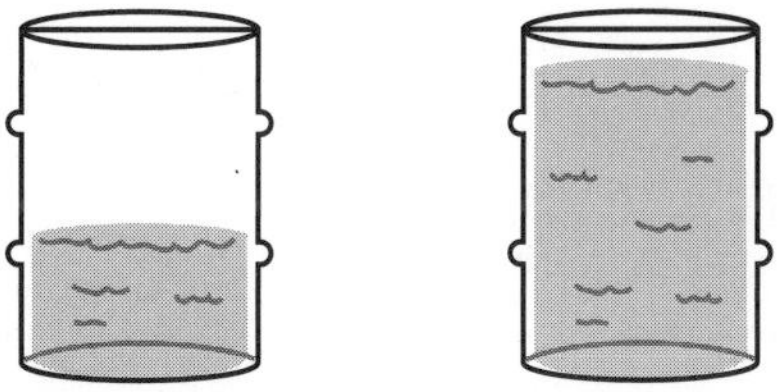

100 gallons

____

Name ______________________________

Compare and Order

You can use a place-value chart to compare and order numbers. Compare the digits from left to right.

Thousands			Ones		
H	T	O	H	T	O
3	2	2	6	7	8
3	4	2	1	9	8
3	2	2	5	0	1

↑ ↑ ↑ ↑
same 4 > 2 same 6 > 5

So, 342,198 > 322,678 > 322,501.

Since 4 > 2, 342,198 is the greatest number.

Continue to compare with the remaining two numbers.

Since 6 > 5, 322,678 > 322,501.

Complete the place-value chart. Write <, >, or = in each ◯.

1.

Thousands			Ones		
H	T	O	H	T	O

375,841 ◯ 367,841

2.

Thousands			Ones		
H	T	O	H	T	O

677,860 ◯ 677,860

3.

Thousands			Ones		
H	T	O	H	T	O

467,935 ◯ 476,935

4.

Thousands			Ones		
H	T	O	H	T	O

986,496 ◯ 986,495

Order the numbers from greatest to least.

5. 26,988; 28,688; 28,986

____

6. 144,421; 144,321; 145,221

____

7. 532,124; 58,124; 532,876

____

8. 45,342,523; 45,342,876; 49,123,563

____

Name ______________________________

Problem Solving Skill

Use a Table

Tables help organize data so you can make comparisons.

Suppose you want to compare the sizes of four planets. You could make the following table.

THE PLANETS	
Name	**Diameter (miles)**
Mercury	3,030
Venus	7,517
Earth	7,921
Mars	4,222

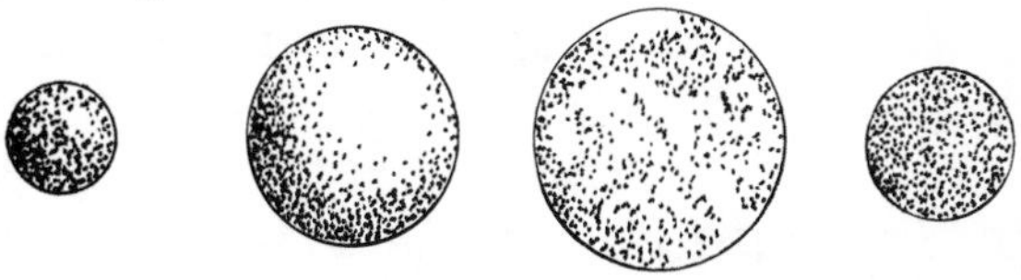

- Look at the diameters. Compare the digits from left to right.
- The smallest planet is Mercury. The largest planet is Earth.

Use the tables to answer the questions.

1. This table shows the sales for a popular music store chain. Which type of music had the greatest sales amount? the least sales amount?

____

____

MUSIC SALES	
Music Type	**Sales (in dollars)**
Alternative Rock	1,345,850
Classical	548,290
Country	1,930,000
Light Rock	425,830

2. This table shows the areas of some of the world's oceans. Which of these oceans has the greatest area? the least area?

____

____

OCEANS	
Name	**Area (square miles)**
Indian	31,507,000
North Pacific	32,225,000
South Pacific	25,298,000
North Atlantic	18,059,000
South Atlantic	14,426,000

Name ______________________________

LESSON 2.1

Decimal Place Value

A place-value chart can help you find the value of each digit in a decimal.

	Ones	Tenths	Hundredths	Thousandths	Ten-Thousandths
Decimal:	2 •	3	6	5	1
Read:	two	three tenths	six hundredths	five thousandths	one ten-thousandth
Write:	2.0	0.3	0.06	0.005	0.0001

In *Standard Form:* 2.3651
In *Expanded Form:* 2.0 + 0.3 + 0.06 + 0.005 + 0.0001
In *Word Form:* two and three thousand, six hundred fifty-one ten-thousandths

---

Record each decimal in the place-value chart. Write each decimal in expanded form and word form.

1. 1.51

Ones	Tenths	Hundredths	Thousandths	Ten-Thousandths
•				

Expanded form: ______________________________

Word form: ______________________________

2. 4.973

Ones	Tenths	Hundredths	Thousandths	Ten-Thousandths
•				

Expanded form: ______________________________

Word form: ______________________________

3. 7.0458

Ones	Tenths	Hundredths	Thousandths	Ten-Thousandths
•				

Expanded form: ______________________________

Word form: ______________________________

Name ____________________

Equivalent Decimals

Equivalent decimals are different names for the same number or amount.

2 tenths = 20 hundredths

0.2 = 0.20

In the place-value chart, both numbers have a 2 in the tenths place.

Ones	Tenths	Hundredths	
0 •	2		← 2 tenths
0 •	2	0	← 20 hundredths

The zero to the right of the 2 does not change the value of the decimal. So, 0.2 and 0.20 are equivalent.

Write the numbers in the place-value chart. Then write *equivalent* or *not equivalent* to describe each pair of decimals.

1. 2.5 and 2.50

Ones	Tenths	Hundredths
•		
•		

____

2. 0.73 and 0.703

Ones	Tenths	Hundredths	Thousandths
•			
•			

____

Write the two decimals that are equivalent.

3. 3.05
3.050
3.500

____

4. 1.110
1.1
1.11

____

5. 0.180
0.0180
0.018

____

6. 7.77
7.707
7.770

____

Write an equivalent decimal for each number.

7. 0.05 ____________________

8. 2.100 ____________________

9. 2.875 ____________________

10. 0.040 ____________________

Name ______________________________

Compare and Order Decimals

You can use a place-value chart to compare 6.741 and 6.742.

Ones	Tenths	Hundredths	Thousandths
6 •	7	4	1
6 •	7	4	2
↑ same	↑ same	↑ same	↑ $2 > 1$

So, $6.742 > 6.741$.

Write the numbers in the place-value chart. Then write $<$, $>$, or $=$ in each ◯.

1. 2.45 ◯ 2.54

O •	T	H
•		
•		

2. 6.23 ◯ 6.230

O •	T	H	Th
•			
•			

3. 72.648 ◯ 72.658

T	O •	T	H	Th
	•			
	•			

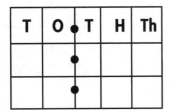

4. 564.876 ◯ 564.786

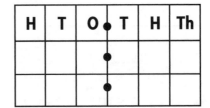

H	T	O •	T	H	Th
		•			
		•			

Write $<$, $>$, or $=$ in each ◯.

5. 3.21 ◯ 3.210

6. 721.460 ◯ 72.146

7. 6.275 ◯ 6.257

8. 468.036 ◯ 468.136

Order from least to greatest.

9. 16.54, 16.56, 16.55 ______________________________

10. 3.400, 3.004, 3.040 ______________________________

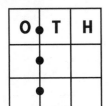

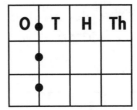

Name ____________________

Problem Solving Skill

Draw Conclusions

Michael exercises at 4:00 P.M. daily unless he is sick. The table shows the number of hours Michael exercised last week.

Can the conclusion be drawn from the information given? Write *yes* or *no*. Explain your choice.

HOURS MICHAEL EXERCISED	
Day	**Hours**
Monday	1.8
Tuesday	1.5
Wednesday	0
Thursday	2.2
Friday	1.6

Michael usually eats dinner at 5:30.

Michael was sick on Wednesday.

Can the conclusion be drawn from the information given? Write *yes* or *no*. Explain your choice.

During a kickball game between two gym classes, the final score was 25 to 22. Each team had 15 players.

1. There were more boys on the winning team than on the losing team.

2. There was a winning team.

3. Each player kicked a homerun.

4. More than 40 points were scored in the game.

Name ______________________________

Round Whole Numbers

You can round whole numbers by using the rounding rules.

Step 1: Underline the digit in the place to which you want to round.

Step 2: Compare the digit to the right of the underlined digit to 5.
Round Down: If the digit to the right is less than 5, the underlined digit stays the same.
Round Up: If the digit to the right is 5 or greater, increase the underlined digit by 1.

Step 3: Rewrite all digits to the right of the underlined digit as zeros.

A. Round 43,658 to the nearest hundredth.	B. Round 9,309,587 to the nearest million.
Underline. 43,658	Underline. 9,309,587
Compare. 5 = 5 Round up.	Compare. 3 < 5 Round down.
Rewrite. 43,700	Rewrite. 9,000,000

Round each number to the place of the **bold-faced** digit.

1. 3**8**,761

Underline. 38,761

Compare. ____ ◯ 5

Round ________

Rewrite. ________

2. 719,4**3**2

Underline. 719,432

Compare. ____ ◯ 5

Round ________

Rewrite. ________

Round 2,409,485 to the place named.

3. hundred thousands

Underline. 2,409,485

Compare. ____ ◯ 5

Round ________

Rewrite. ________

4. hundreds

Underline. 2,409,485

Compare. ____ ◯ 5

Round ________

Rewrite. ________

Name ______________________________

Round Decimals

The same rules you learned for rounding whole numbers can be used to round decimals.

Step 1: Underline the digit in the place to which you want to round.

Step 2: Compare the digit at the right of the underlined digit to 5.
Round Down: If the digit at the right is less than 5, the underlined digit stays the same.
Round Up: If the digit at the right is 5 or greater, increase the underlined digit by 1.

Step 3: Rewrite all digits to the right of the underlined digit as zeros. An equivalent decimal can be written by leaving off trailing zeros.

A. Round 5.643 to the nearest hundredth.			B. Round 0.8287 to the nearest thousandth.		
Underline.	5.6$\underline{4}$3		Underline.	0.82$\underline{8}$7	
Compare.	3 < 5	Round down.	Compare.	7 > 5	Round up.
Rewrite.	5.640 or 5.64		Rewrite.	0.8290 or 0.829	

1. Round 4.**1**872 to the place of the **bold-faced** digit.

Underline. 4.**1**872

Compare. __ ◯ 5 Round ____.

Rewrite. ______________

2. Round 82.64751 to the nearest thousandth.

Underline. 82.6475

Compare. __ ◯ 5 Round ____.

Rewrite. ______________

Round each number to the place of the **bold-faced** digit.

3. 7.**3**25 ________

4. 9.0**2**87 ________

5. 108.1**0**8 ________

6. 2**6**.3199 ________

Round 12.8405 to the place named.

7. hundredths ________

8. ones ________

9. tenths ________

10. thousandths ________

Name ______________________________

Estimate Sums and Differences

Jonas earned \$55.87. Kevin earned \$20.94. About how much did they earn in all? About how much more did Jonas earn than Kevin?

You can estimate by rounding to the nearest dollar and then adding or subtracting.
You can also use front-end estimation and add or subtract using only the first digit of each number.

A. Estimate by rounding.	B. Use front-end estimation.
\$55.87 → \$56 \$56 + 20.94 → + 21 − 21 \$77 \$35	\$55.87 → \$50 \$50 + 20.94 → + 20 − 20 \$70 \$30
Jonas and Kevin earned about \$77. Jonas earned about \$35 more than Kevin.	Jonas and Kevin earned about \$70. Jonas earned about \$30 more than Kevin.

Estimate by rounding.

1. \$63.98 →
+ 5.29 → + ______

2. 7,542 →
− 2,958 → − ______

3. 380 →
− 122 → − ______

4. 8.604 →
− 6.71 → − ______

5. 26,457 →
+ 11,351 → + ______

6. 56.8 →
+ 8.592 → + ______

Estimate by using front-end estimation.

7. 423 →
+ 1,015 → + ______

8. 8.25 →
+ 0.385 → + ______

9. 9.52 →
+ 1.29 → + ______

10. 74,908 →
− 15,259 → − ______

11. 5.128 →
− 1.56 → − ______

12. 5,013 →
− 4,804 → − ______

Name ____________________

Add and Subtract Whole Numbers

You can add or subtract to find an exact answer.

Estimates will help you determine if you have a reasonable answer.

A pilot flew his plane 4,859 miles from Salem, Oregon to Tokyo, Japan. A year later, he flew 2,311 miles from Little Rock, Arkansas to Caracas, Venezuela. How many miles did he travel together?

Add. 4,859 + 2,311

First, estimate.

$$\begin{array}{rcr} 4{,}859 & \rightarrow & 5{,}000 \\ +\ 2{,}311 & \rightarrow & +\ 2{,}000 \\ \hline & & 7{,}000 \end{array}$$

The answer should be close to 7,000.

Then, add to find the exact answer.

$$\begin{array}{r|r|r|r} \scriptstyle 1 & & \scriptstyle 1 & \\ 4 & 8 & 5 & 9 \\ +\ 2 & 3 & 1 & 1 \\ \hline 7 & 1 & 7 & 0 \end{array}$$

7,170 is close to the estimate, so the answer is reasonable. He traveled 7,170 miles.

Find the sum or difference. Estimate to check.

1.
$$\begin{array}{r|r|r|r} 5 & 4 & 9 & 2 \\ +\ 4 & 0 & 7 & 8 \\ \hline & & & \end{array}$$
→
→

2.
$$\begin{array}{r|r|r|r} 7 & 9 & 0 & 6 \\ -\ 4 & 2 & 3 & 4 \\ \hline & & & \end{array}$$
→
→

3.
$$\begin{array}{r|r|r|r|r} 2 & 9 & 5 & 3 & 6 \\ -\ 1 & 0 & 8 & 1 & 9 \\ \hline & & & & \end{array}$$
→
→

4.
$$\begin{array}{r|r|r|r} 6 & 8 & 4 & 4 \\ +\ 4 & 7 & 3 & 9 \\ \hline & & & \end{array}$$
→
→

5.
$$\begin{array}{r|r|r|r} 1 & 3 & 7 & 6 \\ - & 4 & 3 & 2 \\ \hline & & & \end{array}$$
→
→

6.
$$\begin{array}{r|r|r|r|r} 3 & 6 & 7 & 4 & 8 \\ +\ 1 & 4 & 2 & 4 & 7 \\ \hline & & & & \end{array}$$
→
→

Name ______________________________

Add and Subtract Decimals

To add or subtract decimals, line up the decimal points in the numbers. Estimate the answer first. It will help you determine if your answer is reasonable.

Subtract. 18.04 − 5.76

Estimate.

18.04	→	18
− 5.76	→	− 6
		12

The answer should be about 12.

Subtract.

			9	
		7	~~1~~~~0~~	14
	~~1~~	~~8~~ .	~~0~~	~~4~~
−		5 .	7	6
	1	2 .	2	8

12.28 is close to the estimate. So, the answer is reasonable.

Find the sum or difference. Estimate to check.

1.

1.58 →	
+ 4.53 →	+ ____

2.

18.52 →	
+ 3.73 →	+ ____

3.

6.39 →	
2.18 →	
+ 7.85 →	+ ____

4.

8.76 →	
− 5.23 →	− ____

5.

16.32 →	
− 4.8 →	− ____

6.

6.28 →	
− 3.96 →	− ____

7. $5.86 + 8.79 = n$

____

8. $14 - 2.87 = n$

____

Name ______________________________

Choose a Method

There is more than one way to find the sums and differences of whole numbers and decimals. You can use mental math, a calculator, or paper and pencil.

- Use mental math for problems with fewer digits or rounded numbers.

43,000	1.22	$10.00
+ 7,000	− 0.82	− 5.50
50,000	0.40	$4.50

- Use a calculator or paper and pencil for larger numbers.

6,716,678	$237.18	3.1045
+ 5,014,209	− 164.77	+ 14.7298
11,730,887	$72.41	17.8343

Ramon wants to buy a football that costs $19.95. He has saved $11.00 from his after-school job. How much more does he need to buy the football?

- In this case, you could use mental math. You don't need a calculator to know that Ramon needs $8.95 more to buy the football.

$19.95
− 11.00
$8.95

Choose a method. Find the sum or difference.

1. 6,577 − 3,538	**2.** 900 + 450	**3.** 18.517 + 29.023	**4.** $157.23 − 100.00
5. 761,250 + 488,329	**6.** 66,645 − 33,193	**7.** 70.05 + 20.05	**8.** 348.625 − 251.083
9. 2,329 − 687	**10.** 880,000 − 520,000	**11.** 1.4416 + 0.7285	**12.** $150.00 + 80.00

13. 7,000 − 2,500 __________

14. 52,405 + 65,323 __________

15. 12.613 − 5.8708 __________

16. $95.50 + $30.05 __________

Name ____________________

Problem Solving Strategy

Use Logical Reasoning

A table can help you with logical reasoning.

Elizabeth, Alan, Calvin, and Marie each ordered a different ice cream flavor. The flavor choices were vanilla, peach, chocolate, and strawberry. Neither Alan nor Marie ordered vanilla. Calvin had a brown ice cream stain on his t-shirt. Marie is allergic to strawberries. Which flavor ice cream did each person order?

- Calvin had a brown stain on his t-shirt. Put a *yes* in the chocolate column for Calvin and a *no* in each empty box in that row and in that column.
- Marie is allergic to strawberries and she did not order vanilla. Put a *no* in those boxes. Put a *yes* in the remaining box, peach, and a *no* in the remaining boxes in that column.
- Alan did not order vanilla. Put a *no* in that box. That leaves strawberry.
- So, Elizabeth ordered vanilla. Put a *yes* in that box.

	vanilla	peach	chocolate	strawberry
Elizabeth	*Yes*	No	No	No
Alan	No	No	No	*Yes*
Calvin	No	No	*Yes*	No
Marie	No	*Yes*	No	No

Use logical reasoning and the table to solve.

1. Rishawn, Julie, Kevin, and LaTia each have a different favorite subject. Julie likes to use paint and chalk. LaTia enjoys using numbers. Science is not Kevin's favorite subject. What is each student's favorite subject?

	art	math	music	science
Rishawn				
Julie				
Kevin				
LaTia				

Name ____________________

Expressions and Variables

An expression has numbers and operation signs. It does not have an equal sign.

Use these words to help you write expressions.

Addition: more, sum, plus, added, gave

Subtraction: less, minus, loss, difference, spent, left

John had 12 marbles. He won 7 more.

Translate this into an expression.

Clue Word: more $12 + 7$

Mary had $10. She spent $3.

Translate this into an expression.

Clue Word: spent $10 - 3$

An expression may have a variable. A variable is a letter or symbol that can stand for one or more numbers.

Peter caught 2 fish in the morning. In the afternoon, he caught some more.

Translate this into an expression.

Clue Word: more $2 + n$

Susan had 4 sharpened pencils. Then she broke the point off of some of them.

Translate this into an expression.

Clue Word: left $4 - n$

Write the clues. Then write an expression using *n* for the unknown number. Explain what the variable represents.

1. The temperature dropped 7 degrees and then went up 4 degrees.
   Clue Words: ____________________

   ____

   ____

2. When the train stopped, 5 people boarded and 2 got off.
   Clue Words: ____________________

   ____

   ____

3. Steven wrote 8 pages for homework. The dog ate some of them.
   Clue Words: ____________________

   ____

4. Gabriel collected 7 stones. John gave some more stones.
   Clue Words: ____________________

   ____

Name ______________________________

Write Equations

An equation is a number sentence that shows that two quantities are equal.

You can use variables to stand for numbers you do not know.

Peter had 10 books. After his birthday party, he had 16 books. How many books did he receive for his birthday?

books he has plus books received = total books

10 books + books received = total books

$10 + n = 16$

Write an equation with a variable for each. Explain what the variable represents.

1. Joseph had 7 paper cups. There were 22 students in the class. How many more cups did he need to serve punch to all his classmates?

   cups he had + cups he needed = total cups for punch

   ____

   ____

   ____

2. Mary Beth loves chocolate chip cookies. Her mother took a sheet of 12 out of the oven. Mary Beth ate some. Now there are 8 left. How many did she eat?

   total cookies − number eaten = number left

   ____

   ____

   ____

3. Jennifer had spent $32 for a new jacket. She had $12 left. How much did she have originally?

   original amount − amount spent = amount left

   ____

   ____

   ____

4. Monica had a collection of stickers. She bought 7 and had a total of 21. How many did she originally have?

   number in collection + number gained = total amount

   ____

   ____

   ____

Name ______________________________

Solve Equations

When you solve an equation, you find the value of the variable that makes the equation true.

In an equation, the amounts on both sides of the equal sign have the same value. It is like a balanced scale.

$n + 6 = 10$

To solve, ask, "How many counters would I need to add to the left side of the scale to make it balanced?" Use mental math to find the missing addend.

The solution equation will be

$n + 6 = 10$. Think: what number plus 6 equals 10?

$n = 4$

Check your solution. Replace n with 4.

$n + 6 = 10$

$4 + 6 = 10$

$10 = 10$

Use mental math to solve. Check your solution.

1. $n + 5 = 15$ ______________

2. $n - 6 = 6$ ______________

3. $n - 10 = 20$ ______________

Solve the equation. Check your solution.

4. $15 + n = 22$ ______________

5. $n - 8 = 12$ ______________

6. $25 - n = 22$ ______________

7. $n + 10 - 6 = 7$ ______________

8. $22 - n + 7 = 18$ ______________

9. $14 - 8 + n = 13$ ______________

Name ______________________________

Inequalities

An inequality is a number sequence that can have more than one solution. The solutions to the inequality are the values that make the inequality true.

$x > 5$ means that x is a number greater than 5. Some whole numbers that satisfy this inequality are 6, 7, and 8.	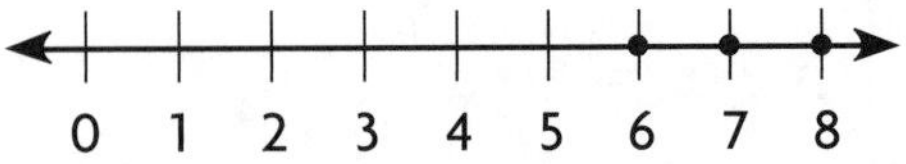
$x \geq 5$ means that x is a number greater than or equal to 5. Some whole numbers that satisfy this inequality are 5, 6, 7, and 8.	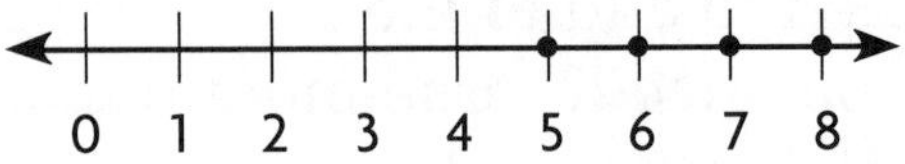
$x < 5$ means that x is a number less than 5. Some whole numbers that satisfy this inequality are 0, 1, 2, 3, and 4.	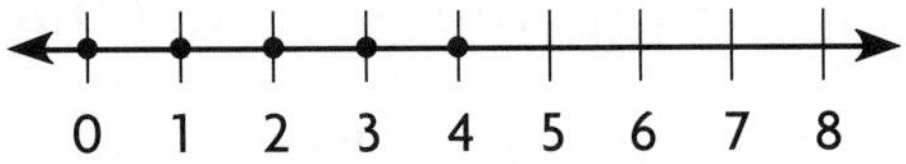
$x \leq 5$ means that x is a number less than or equal to 5. Some whole numbers that satisfy this inequality are 0, 1, 2, 3, 4, and 5.	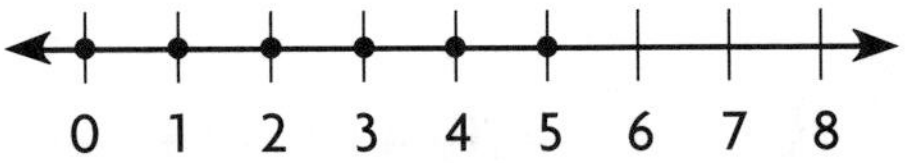

Find which of the numbers 1, 2, 3, and 4 are solutions of the inequality $x + 3 < 6$.

Think: Which of the numbers plus 3 are less than 6?

$1 + 3$ is less than 6.
$2 + 3$ is less than 6.
$3 + 3$ is **not** less than 6.
$4 + 3$ is **not** less than 6.

Of the values 1, 2, 3, and 4, only 1 and 2 are less than 3.
So, $x = 1$ and $x = 2$ are solutions of the inequality $x + 3 < 6$.

Which of the numbers 4, 5, 6, and 7 are solutions of each inequality?

1. $x - 3 \geq 4$ ____________

2. $x + 1 < 7$ ____________

3. $x - 4 \leq 4$ ____________

Locate points on the number line to show the whole-number solutions from 0 to 8 for each inequality.

4. $x > 3$

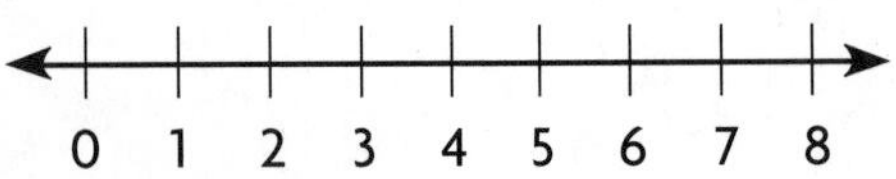

5. $x + 2 \leq 6$

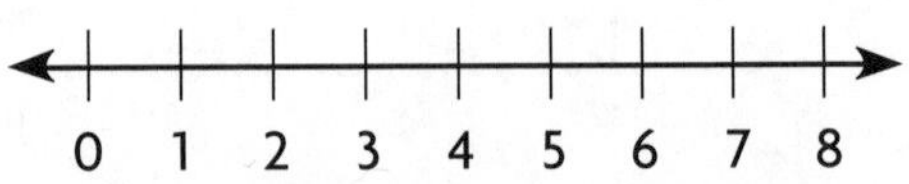

Name ______________________________

Mental Math: Use the Properties

You can use the properties of addition to help you solve problems.

The **Associative Property** states that you may group addends differently without changing the value of the sum.	$7 + (8 + 4) = (7 + 8) + 4$ $7 + 12 = 15 + 4$ $19 = 19$
The **Commutative Property** states that addends may be added in any order without changing the value of the sum.	$6 + 5 = 5 + 6$ $11 = 11$
The **Zero Property** states that you may add zero to any number without changing the value of the number.	$5 + 0 = 5$

Sometimes you can use a strategy called **compensation** to help you find sums and differences. These are examples of ways to use this strategy.

To make it easier to add, make one addend a multiple of 10.	To make it easier to subtract, make the second number a multiple of 10.
$19 + 17 = (19 + \mathbf{1}) + (17 - \mathbf{1})$ $= 20 + 16$ $= 36$	$42 - 18 = (42 + \mathbf{2}) - (18 + \mathbf{2})$ $= 44 - 20$ $= 22$

Find the value of *n*. Identify the property used.

1. $200 + n = 100 + 200$

____

2. $78 + (5 + n) = (78 + 5) + 7$

____

3. $4 + n = 7 + 4$

____

4. $0 + 88 = n$

____

Use mental math strategies to find the value.

5. $(5 + 9) + 1$ ________

6. $6 + (4 + 8)$ ________

7. $7 + 8 + 2$ ________

8. $19 + 15$ ________

9. $53 - 19$ ________

10. $26 + 29$ ________

Name ______________________________

Problem Solving Strategy

Write an Equation

You can **write an equation** to help you solve a problem.

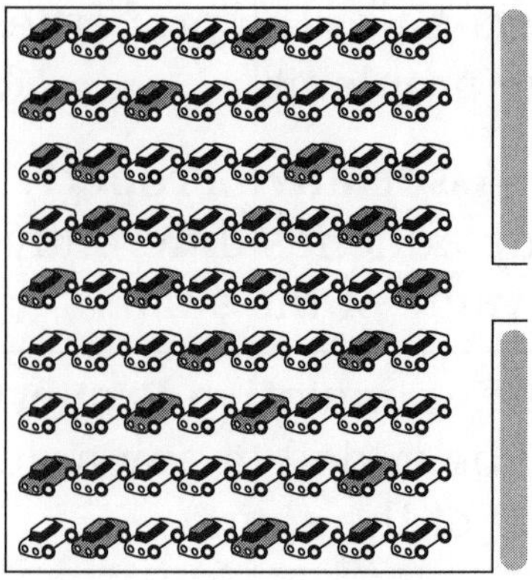

Felicity and Alex were in charge of parking cars in the small parking lot at the State Fair. The lot was filled with 72 cars in all by noon of the first day. The cars were organized into 9 equal rows of cars. How many cars were in each row?

Write an equation to find the number of cars parked in each row.

Think 9 times what number equals 72.

So, each row had 8 cars.

total cars in lot	=	rows of cars	×	number of cars in each row
72	=	9	×	c
72	=	9	×	8
c	=	8		

Write and solve an equation for each problem. Explain what the variable represents.

1. Jacob has to stack boxes in the grocer's storage room. The room is 96 inches high. Each box is 12 inches high. How many boxes can Jacob stack on top of each other?

____

____

2. The shelves that the grocer stacks the canned goods on are 30 inches high. The grocer stacked the cans 5 high. How tall is each can?

____

____

3. Chelsea has to line up 48 chairs in 6 equal rows. How many chairs should she put in each row?

____

____

4. Troy made a striped blanket for his bed. The blanket was 54 inches wide with 9 equal stripes. How wide was each stripe?

____

____

Name ____________________

Collect and Organize Data

When you are gathering information about a group,

- the whole group is called the **population**,
- and the people surveyed are called the **sample**.

In a **random sample**, everyone in the population has an equal chance of being surveyed.

Example 1
A new toy store is polling people in order to name the new store. Would a random sample of 100 students represent the population?

No, a random sample of 100 students leaves out adults.

Example 2
The survey asked the following question: "Isn't 'Toys 4 All' a better name than 'The Toy Shoppe'?" Is it a good survey question?

No, the question favors the name 'Toys 4 All.' It is a *biased* question.

TOY STORE NAME SURVEY	
Store Name	**Number of People**
Toys 4 All	卌 卌 卌 卌 卌
The Toy Shoppe	卌 卌 卌 ||||
Play World	卌 卌 卌 卌 卌 |
Funtown	卌 卌 卌 卌 卌 卌

Example 3
Survey results are often displayed using a tally table and a cumulative frequency table. How many people were surveyed?

Each 卌 represents 5 people surveyed. The cumulative frequency table shows that 100 people were surveyed.

TOY STORE NAME SURVEY		
Store Name	**Frequency (Number of People)**	**Cumulative Frequency**
Toys 4 All	25	25
The Toy Shoppe	19	44
Play World	26	70
Funtown	30	100

---

1. A soft drink company wants to test 2 new drinks. Would a random sample of 100 teenagers represent the population? If not, explain.

____

2. This question was asked during a taste test: "Doesn't soft drink B taste better than soft drink A?" Is this a good survey question? Why or why not?

____

3. How many people are represented by 卌 卌 ||| tally marks? ________

Name ______________________________

Find the Mean

Tom has taken three tests. He wants to know his average score for the three tests. The type of average Tom is looking for is called the **mean.**

TOM'S TEST SCORES			
Test	1	2	3
Score	80	70	90

Step 1

Add the three test scores together.

$80 + 70 + 90 = 240$

Step 2

Divide the sum by the number of tests.

$240 \div 3 = 80$

So, Tom's mean test score is 80.

Write an addition sentence for the sum of each set of numbers.

1. 3, 5, 4, 1, 7 **2.** 20, 15, 10 **3.** 22, 26, 28, 32

______ ______ ______

Write how many numbers are listed in each set of numbers.

4. 3, 5, 4, 1, 7 **5.** 20, 15, 10 **6.** 22, 26, 28, 32

______ ______ ______

Write a division sentence to find the mean for each set of numbers.

7. 3, 5, 4, 1, 7 **8.** 20, 15, 10 **9.** 22, 26, 28, 32

______ ______ ______

10. One month later, Tom took 5 more tests. His scores were 80, 70, 90, 90, and 100. What is the mean of these test scores? Show your work.

____

Find the mean for each set of data.

11. 9, 11, 13, 13, 9 **12.** 33, 28, 35, 33, 26 **13.** 105, 112, 133, 118, 102

______ ______ ______

Name ____________________

Find the Median and Mode

Sam takes tests to see how many words he can type in a minute. The data in the table show his first 7 tests.

NUMBER OF WORDS TYPED IN A MINUTE							
Test	1	2	3	4	5	6	7
Score	22	16	18	14	16	34	20

You can find Sam's median score and the mode of the data.

Step 1

List the scores from least to greatest.

14, 16, 16, 18, 20, 22, 34

Step 2

To find the median score, cross off a number from each end until there is only one number left in the middle.

~~14~~, ~~16~~, ~~16~~, (18), ~~20~~, ~~22~~, ~~34~~

The number 18 is the **median** score.

Step 3

Find the score that occurred most often.

Sam scored 16 twice.

The number 16 is the **mode**.

Sometimes there is more than one mode or no mode.

Arrange the numbers from least to greatest. Circle the median number.

1. 13, 12, 11, 11, 9, 8, 16, 17, 19

____

____

2. 24, 32, 28, 45, 19, 23, 16, 51, 32

____

____

3. 103, 98, 105, 101, 99

____

____

Arrange the numbers from least to greatest. Find the median and the mode.

4. 9, 7, 5, 11, 11

____

median: ______

mode: ______

5. 14, 12, 12

____

median: ______

mode: ______

6. 3, 7, 2, 9, 6, 5, 3, 1, 3

____

median: ______

mode: ______

Name ____

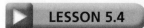

Problem Solving Strategy

Make a Graph

Mr. Schwartz recorded the number of newspapers he sold in his store every day of the week for two weeks. Newspapers sales were 60, 65, 66, 71, 71, 72, 74, 75, 76, 77, 79, 80, 81, and 83. Is the number sold usually in the 60's, 70's, or 80's?

You can make a stem-and-leaf plot to organize the data by place value.

Make a column of the tens digits of the data, listing them in order from least to greatest. These are the **stems.**

Stem	Leaves
6	
7	
8	

Beside each tens digit, record the ones digits of the data, in order from least to greatest. These are the **leaves.**

Stem	Leaves
6	0 5 6
7	1 1 2 4 5 6 7 9
8	0 1 3

The stem-and-leaf plot shows the greatest number of leaves are on the 7 stem. So, the number of newspapers sold is usually in the 70's.

Make a graph to solve.

1. Lynnette's golf scores are 72, 74, 74, 78, 80, 82, 83, 87, 88, and 91. Does she usually score in the 70's, 80's, or 90's?

____

2. The coach of the Tigers recorded the number of parents that attended each home baseball game. Parents' attendance was 16, 17, 23, 24, 29, 30, 33, 36, 36, and 38. Is parents' attendance usually in the 10's, 20's, or 30's?

____

Name ________________________________

Analyze Graphs

Graphs help you to draw conclusions, answer questions, and make predictions about the data. Study the following graphs to answer the questions.

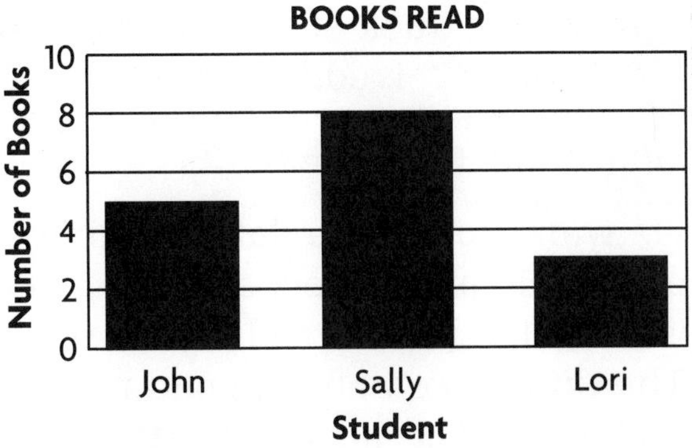

1. A **bar graph** is useful when comparing data by groups.

   Which student read the most books? the least?

   ____

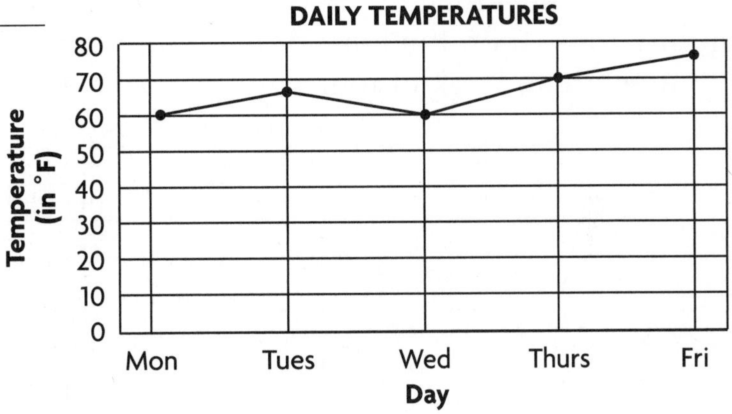

2. **Line graphs** are helpful to see how data changes over a period of time.

   What happened to the temperature as the week passed?

   ____

   ____

   ____

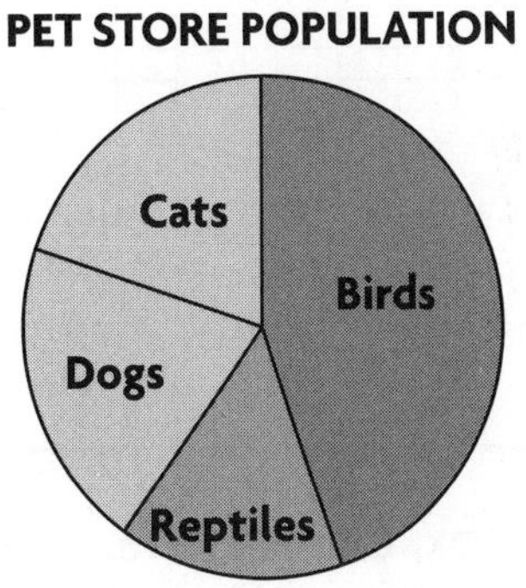

3. A **circle graph** shows how parts of data relate to each other and to the whole.

   About one half of the animals in the pet store are what type of animal?

   ____

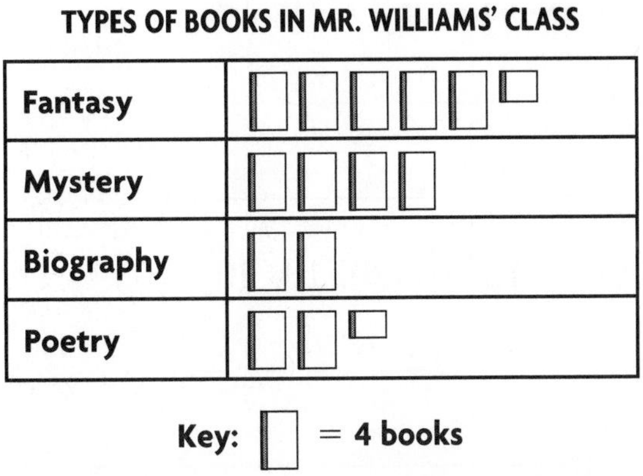

4. A **pictograph** displays countable data with symbols or pictures. Pictographs have a key to show how many each picture represents.

   How many books does Mr. Williams have in his class? ________________

Name ______________________________

Choose a Reasonable Scale

Henry kept track of how much mail his family received in one week.

He put the data in a table.

MAIL RECEIVED IN A WEEK					
Day	Mon	Tue	Wed	Thu	Fri
Number of Pieces	8	10	6	4	2

He wants to put the data in a line graph. He must select a scale. A **scale** is the set of numbers placed at fixed distances. The difference between one number and the next on the scale is called the **interval**.

The scale must include the numbers 2 through 10. It must include a number less than the least data and a number greater than the greatest data. Look at four ways Henry can display the mail data.

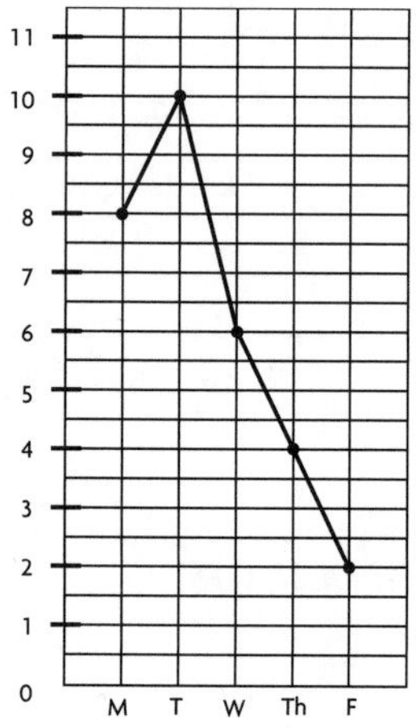

By 1's

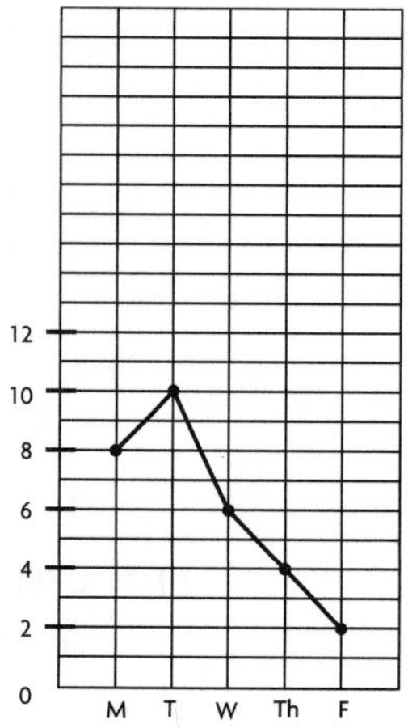

By 2's

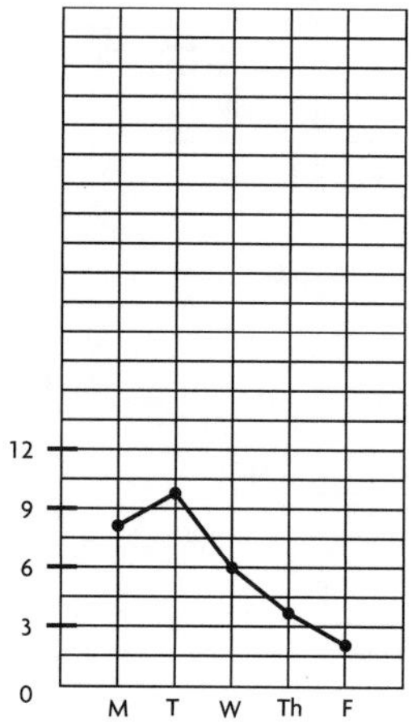

By 3's

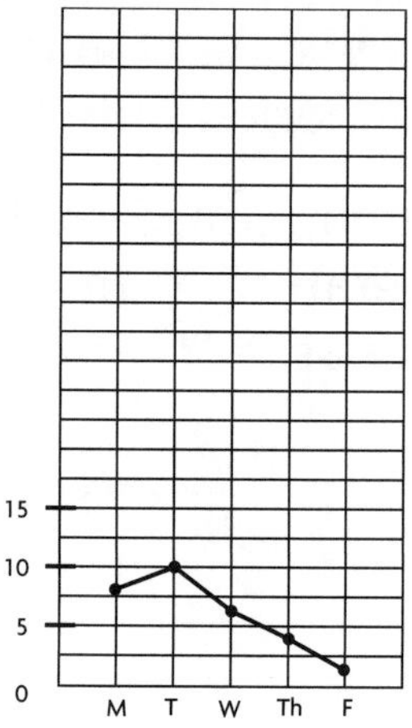

By 5's

Henry selects a scale with intervals of 2.

From the box, choose the most reasonable interval for each set of data. List the numbers needed in the scale.

Interval
a. By 25's
b. By 20's
c. By 10's
d. By 5's

1. 5, 15, 20, 25, 10, 18

____

____

2. 50, 125, 100, 150, 100, 20

____

____

3. 8, 12, 10, 20, 10, 30

____

____

4. 20, 101, 40, 59, 115

____

____

Name ____

Graph Ordered Pairs

Points on a coordinate grid can be given a unique name in the same way each house on a street has a unique number. Houses on a street follow an order so people can tell them apart and points also follow an order.

The order of the numbers in an ordered pair is always expressed the same way. The first number in an ordered pair tells how far to move horizontally from the origin. The second number tells how far to move vertically.

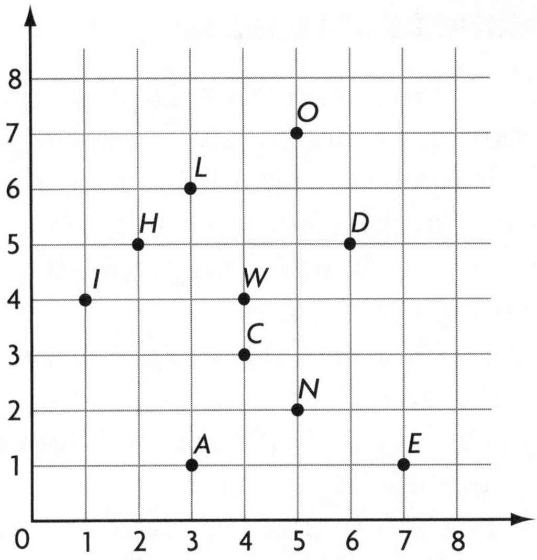

(3, 4)
Move 3 horizontally;
Move 4 vertically

Name the ordered pair for each point.

1. *E* ________ 2. *H* ________

3. *O* ________ 4. *C* ________

5. *A* ________ 6. *D* ________

7. *N* ________ 8. *I* ________

9. *W* ________ 10. *L* ________

Graph and label the following points on a coordinate grid.

11. *M* **(5, 7)** 12. *N* **(0, 5)** 13. *P* **(3, 4)** 14. *R* **(1, 0)**

15. *S* **(6, 2)** 16. *A* **(2, 5)** 17. *V* **(4, 1)** 18. *G* **(3, 7)**

19. *B* **(6, 0)** 20. *H* **(2, 6)** 21. *T* **(1, 7)** 22. *Y* **(6, 3)**

Name ______________________________

Make Line Graphs

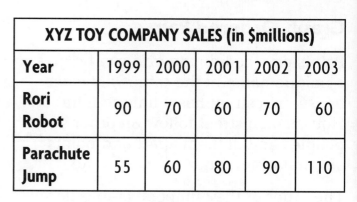

XYZ TOY COMPANY SALES (in $millions)					
Year	1999	2000	2001	2002	2003
Rori Robot	90	70	60	70	60
Parachute Jump	55	60	80	90	110

The table shows XYZ Toy Company sales for five years for their two most popular toys, Rori Robot and Parachute Jump. You can use a double-line graph to display the data.

- The horizontal scale identifies the year.
- The vertical scale shows the sales in millions of dollars.
- The interval is 10. There is a break in the scale from 0 to 50.
- The sales figures for Rori Robot are shown with the dashed line.
- The sales figures for Parachute Jump are shown with the solid line.

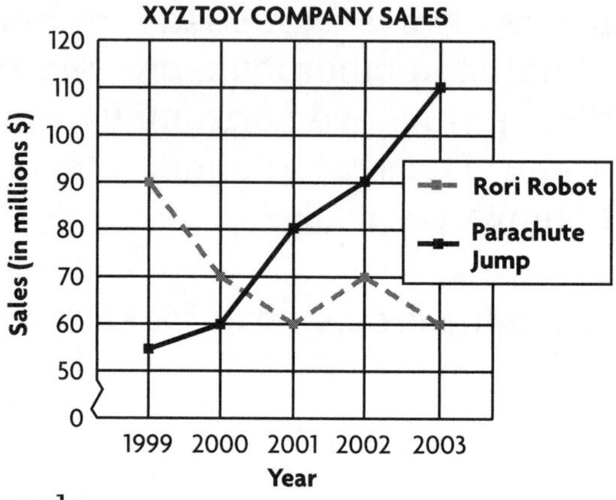

The graph shows that the sales of Parachute Jump have been increasing rapidly while the sales of Rori Robot have been decreasing over the same time period.

Make a line graph or double-line graph for each set of data.

1.

ON-LINE TIME				
Month	Oct	Nov	Dec	Jan
Time (in hours)	30	60	100	125

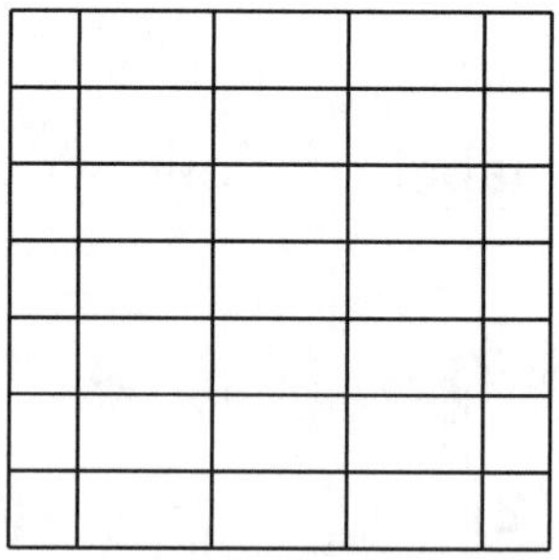

2.

ATTENDANCE AT HOCKEY GAMES					
Game	1	2	3	4	5
Number of Adults	125	135	150	145	130
Number of Children	130	160	180	175	170

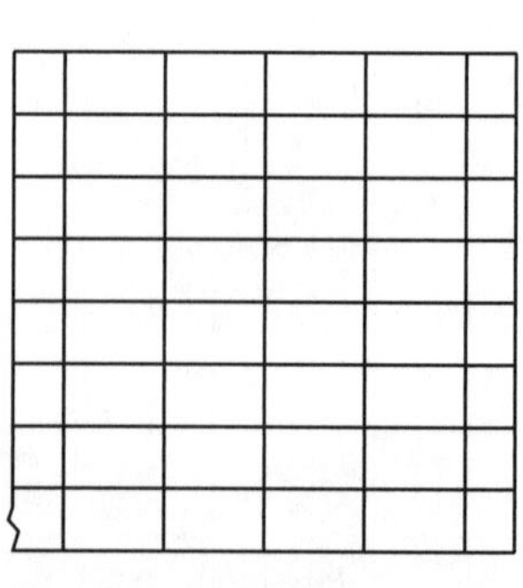

Name ______________________________

Problem Solving Strategy

Draw a Diagram

A dairy conducted a taste test with 3 new ice cream flavors. The results showed that 14 people liked flavor A, 10 liked flavor B, 13 liked flavor C, 3 liked flavors A and B, 5 liked flavors B and C, 7 liked flavors A and C, and 2 people liked all three flavors. How many people participated in the taste test?

You can solve this problem by drawing a Venn diagram. It can be helpful to read the problem backward to draw a Venn diagram.

Step 1 Draw three overlapping ovals. Label each oval with one of the flavors. Since two people liked all three flavors, write 2 in the center part where all 3 ovals overlap.

Step 2 Since 3 people liked flavors A and B, write 1 in the part between A and B. Fill in the other overlapping parts.

Step 3 The numbers in oval A must add to 14. So, write 6 in oval A. Fill in the remaining two parts.

Step 4 Add all the numbers in the diagram to find the number of people who participated in the taste test.
$6 + 5 + 1 + 2 + 4 + 3 + 3 = 24$
So, 24 people participated in the taste test.

Draw a Venn diagram to solve.

1. There are 41 students in the school orchestra and 52 students in the school band. Thirteen students are in both the band and the orchestra. How many students altogether play instruments in the band and orchestra?

   ____

2. In a travel survey, 16 people wanted to visit Italy, 14 wanted to visit England, and 18 wanted to visit France. Nine people wanted to visit both France and Italy, 8 wanted to visit both France and England, 7 wanted to visit both Italy and England, and 6 wanted to visit all three countries. How many people were surveyed?

   ____

Name ______________________________

Histograms

Histograms are a type of bar graph. The bars in a histogram are related and follow an order. They show the number of times the data occur within intervals.

The bars in a bar graph are not related to one another. To decide whether to make a histogram or bar graph, you need to decide whether the data fall within intervals.

Every 30 minutes, the popcorn popper records the number of boxes sold in the movie theater. Here is the information.

5:00	5:30	6:00	6:30	7:00	7:30	8:00	8:30	9:00	9:30	10:00	10:30	11:00
28	26	33	45	56	86	85	57	25	35	48	32	21

Find the range for the set of data.

What interval could you use to make the histogram? Select an interval to divide the data equally.

Make a frequency table with the intervals and record the number of boxes of popcorn sold during these time periods.

Use the frequency table to make the histogram. Label the scale for the number of boxes sold and title the graph. Graph the frequency for each interval.

Remember that the bars in a histogram are side-by-side.

Decide which graph would better represent the data below, a bar graph or histogram. Then make the graph.

MONEY SPENT ON LUNCH	
Amount of Money	**Number of Students**
$1.25	4
$1.75	3
$2.00	5
$2.50	4
$2.75	3
$3.00	1

Name ____________________

LESSON 6.6

Choose the Appropriate Graph

To display data, it is important to select the most appropriate graph or plot.

Two different plots and two different graphs for displaying data are shown.

TEST SCORES					
Test	1	2	3	4	5
Marta	88	75	92	95	98
Phil	83	93	85	80	92

Line Plot

A line plot is used to record data as they are collected.

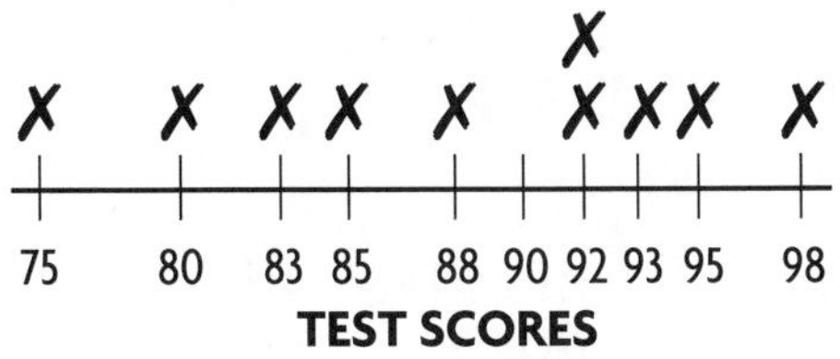

Stem-and-Leaf Plot

A stem-and-leaf plot is used to organize data by place value.

Stem	Leaves
7	5
8	0 3 5 8
9	2 2 3 5 8

Bar Graph

A bar graph is used to compare facts about groups.

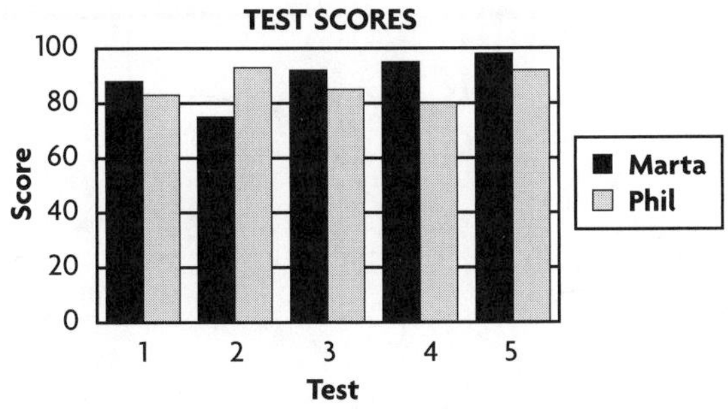

Line Graph

A line graph shows change over time.

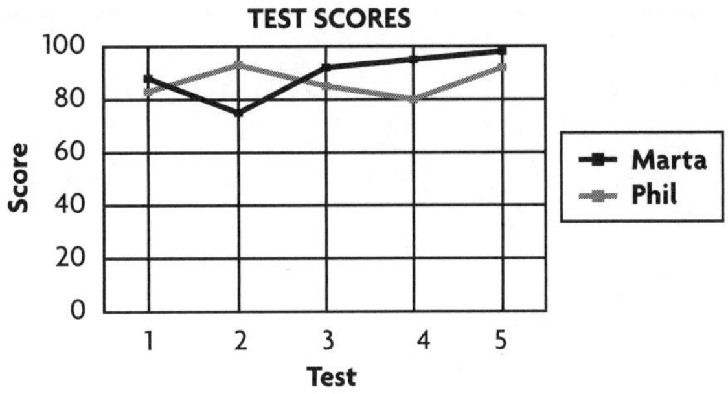

The double-line graph shows how Marta's and Phil's test scores change over time.

Write the best type of graph or plot for the data.

1. Compare the populations of males and females in 6 major cities.

   ____

2. Record the letter grades (A–F) for a class of 30 students.

   ____

3. Display the daily growth of a sunflower in inches.

   ____

4. Record the temperature every hour for 24 hours.

   ____

Name ______________________________

Estimation: Patterns in Multiples

You can round numbers and use basic facts to estimate products. Count the number of zeros in your rounded numbers. They will appear to the right of your basic fact in your estimate.

For 2-digit numbers:

If the ones digit is 0–4, round down.

If the ones digit is 5–9, round up.

For example: Round 40–44 to 40.
Round 45–49 to 50.

$$\begin{array}{r} 45 \\ \times 42 \\ \hline \end{array} \rightarrow \begin{array}{r} 50 \\ \times 40 \\ \hline 2{,}000 \end{array} > \text{2 zeros}$$

For 3-digit numbers:

If the tens digit is 0–4, round down.

If the tens digit is 5–9, round up.

For example: Round 700–749 to 700.
Round 750–799 to 800.

$$\begin{array}{r} 749 \\ \times 44 \\ \hline \end{array} \rightarrow \begin{array}{r} 700 \\ \times 40 \\ \hline 28{,}000 \end{array} > \text{3 zeros}$$

Round each factor and estimate the product.

1. 141 → ____ × 36 → × ____

2. 157 → ____ × 57 → × ____

3. 125 → ____ × 25 → × ____

4. 160 → ____ × 41 → × ____

5. 187 → ____ × 72 → × ____

6. 236 → ____ × 45 → × ____

7. 349 → ____ × 74 → × ____

8. 456 → ____ × 56 → × ____

9. 568 → ____ × 27 → × ____

10. 638 → ____ × 16 → × ____

11. 774 → ____ × 55 → × ____

12. 836 → ____ × 43 → × ____

13. 719 → ____ × 85 → × ____

14. 468 → ____ × 68 → × ____

15. 229 → ____ × 54 → × ____

Name ____

Multiply by 1-Digit Numbers

Multiply the ones.	Multiply the tens.	Multiply the hundreds.
143 × 3 = 9	143 × 3 = 29	143 × 3 = 429

Sometimes you need to regroup.

Step 1 Multiply the ones. 3 × 3 ones = 9 ones

$$\begin{array}{r} 143 \\ \times\ \ 3 \\ \hline 9 \end{array}$$

Step 2 Multiply the tens. 3 × 4 tens = 12 tens
Write the 2. Regroup
the 10 tens as 1 hundred.

$$\begin{array}{r} ^{1}\ \ \ \\ 143 \\ \times\ \ 3 \\ \hline 29 \end{array}$$

Step 3 Multiply the hundreds. 3 × 1 hundred = 3 hundreds
Now add the regrouped hundred.
3 hundreds + 1 hundred = 4 hundreds

$$\begin{array}{r} ^{1}\ \ \ \\ 143 \\ \times\ \ 3 \\ \hline 429 \end{array}$$

So, 3 × 143 = 429.

Tell which place-value positions must be regrouped. Find the product.

1. 451 × 2

____

____

2. 328 × 3

____

____

3. 715 × 5

____

____

4. 1,458 × 6

____

____

5. 2,473 × 2

____

____

6. 6,925 × 4

____

____

7. 3,562 × 7

____

____

8. 20,317 × 4

____

____

9. 13,234 × 3

____

____

Name ______________________________

Multiply by 2-Digit Numbers

You can multiply by two-digit numbers by breaking apart one of the factors.

To find 21 × 14, you can break apart 14 into 1 ten 4 ones.

Step 1 Multiply by the ones.

$$\begin{array}{r} 21 \\ \times\ 4 \\ \hline \end{array}$$

Step 2 Multiply by the tens.

$$\begin{array}{r} 21 \\ \times 10 \\ \hline 210 \end{array}$$

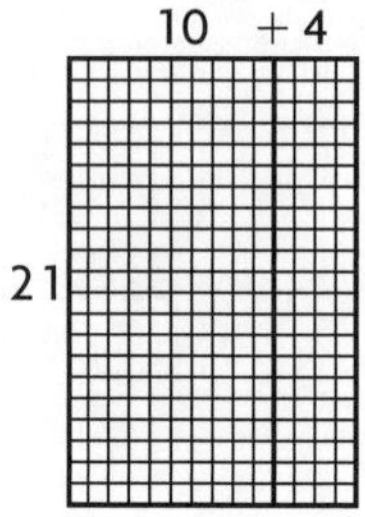

Step 3 Add the products.

$$\begin{array}{rl} 21 & \\ \times\ 14 & \\ \hline 84 & \leftarrow 4 \times 21 \\ +210 & \leftarrow 10 \times 21 \\ \hline 294 & \end{array}$$

So, 21 × 14 = 294.

Complete to find the product.

1. $\begin{array}{r} 13 \\ \times 12 \\ \hline \end{array}$
 ← ____ × ____
+____ ← ____ × ____

2. $\begin{array}{r} 22 \\ \times 15 \\ \hline \end{array}$
 ← ____ × ____
+____ ← ____ × ____

3. $\begin{array}{r} 30 \\ \times 17 \\ \hline \end{array}$
 ← ____ × ____
+____ ← ____ × ____

4. $\begin{array}{r} 28 \\ \times 14 \\ \hline \end{array}$
 ← ____ × ____
+____ ← ____ × ____

5. $\begin{array}{r} 40 \\ \times 19 \\ \hline \end{array}$
 ← ____ × ____
+____ ← ____ × ____

6. $\begin{array}{r} 45 \\ \times 15 \\ \hline \end{array}$
 ← ____ × ____
+____ ← ____ × ____

7. $\begin{array}{r} 37 \\ \times 15 \\ \hline \end{array}$
 ← ____ × ____
+____ ← ____ × ____

8. $\begin{array}{r} 28 \\ \times 16 \\ \hline \end{array}$
 ← ____ × ____
+____ ← ____ × ____

Choose a Method

You can multiply three-digit numbers by breaking apart one of the factors.

To find 312 × 143, break apart 143 into 1 hundred 4 tens 3 ones.

Step 1	**Step 2**	**Step 3**	**Step 4**
Multiply by the ones.	Multiply by the tens.	Multiply by the hundreds.	Add the products.
$\begin{array}{r} 312 \\ \times \quad 3 \\ \hline 936 \end{array}$	$\begin{array}{r} 312 \\ \times \quad 40 \\ \hline 12{,}480 \end{array}$	$\begin{array}{r} 312 \\ \times \quad 100 \\ \hline 31{,}200 \end{array}$	$\begin{array}{rl} 312 & \\ \times \quad 143 & \\ \hline 936 & \leftarrow 3 \times 312 \\ 12{,}480 & \leftarrow 40 \times 312 \\ 31{,}200 & \leftarrow 100 \times 312 \\ \hline 44{,}616 & \end{array}$

So, 312 × 143 = 44,616.

Complete to find the product.

1. $\begin{array}{rl} 423 & \\ \times \quad 146 & \\ \hline & \leftarrow \underline{\quad\quad} \times \underline{\quad\quad} \\ & \leftarrow \underline{\quad\quad} \times \underline{\quad\quad} \\ + \underline{\quad\quad} & \leftarrow \underline{\quad\quad} \times \underline{\quad\quad} \\ \hline & \end{array}$

2. $\begin{array}{rl} 231 & \\ \times \quad 123 & \\ \hline & \leftarrow \underline{\quad\quad} \times \underline{\quad\quad} \\ & \leftarrow \underline{\quad\quad} \times \underline{\quad\quad} \\ + \underline{\quad\quad} & \leftarrow \underline{\quad\quad} \times \underline{\quad\quad} \\ \hline & \end{array}$

3. $\begin{array}{rl} 354 & \\ \times \quad 246 & \\ \hline & \leftarrow \underline{\quad\quad} \times \underline{\quad\quad} \\ & \leftarrow \underline{\quad\quad} \times \underline{\quad\quad} \\ + \underline{\quad\quad} & \leftarrow \underline{\quad\quad} \times \underline{\quad\quad} \\ \hline & \end{array}$

4. $\begin{array}{rl} 438 & \\ \times \quad 253 & \\ \hline & \leftarrow \underline{\quad\quad} \times \underline{\quad\quad} \\ & \leftarrow \underline{\quad\quad} \times \underline{\quad\quad} \\ + \underline{\quad\quad} & \leftarrow \underline{\quad\quad} \times \underline{\quad\quad} \\ \hline & \end{array}$

5. $\begin{array}{rl} 672 & \\ \times \quad 334 & \\ \hline & \leftarrow \underline{\quad\quad} \times \underline{\quad\quad} \\ & \leftarrow \underline{\quad\quad} \times \underline{\quad\quad} \\ + \underline{\quad\quad} & \leftarrow \underline{\quad\quad} \times \underline{\quad\quad} \\ \hline & \end{array}$

6. $\begin{array}{rl} 596 & \\ \times \quad 254 & \\ \hline & \leftarrow \underline{\quad\quad} \times \underline{\quad\quad} \\ & \leftarrow \underline{\quad\quad} \times \underline{\quad\quad} \\ + \underline{\quad\quad} & \leftarrow \underline{\quad\quad} \times \underline{\quad\quad} \\ \hline & \end{array}$

Name ____________________

Problem Solving Skill

Evaluate Answers for Reasonableness

You can use estimation to check if an answer is reasonable. Use your knowledge of patterns in multiples to help you with large numbers.

At the garden center, there were 174 rows of flowers. Each row contained 86 flowers. Estimate first. Then solve the problem and compare it to your estimate to see if it is reasonable.

Estimate

$$\begin{array}{r} 200 \\ \times\ 90 \\ \hline 18{,}000 \end{array} \qquad \begin{array}{r} 174 \\ \times\ 86 \\ \hline 1{,}044 \\ +13{,}920 \\ \hline 14{,}964 \end{array}$$

Your estimate was more than your exact amount because you used greater numbers.

How would your estimate compare to your exact answer if you rounded both factors down?

Choose the most reasonable answer without solving.

1. Joel's dad sold each of his paintings at an art show for $750. He sold 26 at the show. About how much money did he get?

   A $7,000 B $12,000 C $20,000 D $60,000

2. Joel's dad pays $157 for the materials to create each of his paintings. About how much does it cost him to create the 26 paintings he sold?

   F $600 G $1,500 H $5,000 J $60,000

3. A small airport has 21,795 passengers each year. About how many passengers will they have altogether in 8 years?

   A 2,000 B 20,000 C 200,000 D 2,000,000

4. The average length of important rivers in the world is 2,142 miles. If we measured 18 of these rivers, about how many miles would we measure?

   F 4,000 miles G 20,000 miles H 40,000 miles J 400,000 miles

Name ______________________________

Multiply Decimals and Whole Numbers

To multiply a whole number and a decimal, modeling with money can be helpful. To multiply 3 × 0.2, follow these steps.

Step 1
Write 0.2 as 0.20. You can add a zero at the end of a decimal without changing the value. Draw that amount of money.

The 2 dimes equal \$0.20. You could also draw 4 nickels or 20 pennies.

Step 2
Draw 3 groups of coins of \$0.20.

Count the total amount.
\$0.20 + \$0.20 + \$0.20 = \$0.60
So, 3 × 0.2 = 0.60, or 0.6.

Draw the coins that equal the decimal amount. Use the fewest coins possible.

1. 0.28 **2.** 0.30 **3.** 0.16

4. 0.52 **5.** 0.80 **6.** 0.24

Make a money model to find each product.

7. 4 × 0.15 = ________ **8.** 3 × 0.1 = ________ **9.** 2 × 0.21 = ________

10. 4 × 0.01 = ________ **11.** 3 × 0.06 = ________ **12.** 2 × 0.78 = ________

13. 3 × 0.32 = ________ **14.** 4 × 0.12 = ________ **15.** 2 × 0.53 = ________

Name ______________________________

Algebra: Patterns in Decimal Factors and Products

You can use patterns to place the decimal point in a product.

Factors		Product
2 ×	1 =	2
2 ×	0.1 =	0.2
2 ×	0.01 =	0.02

2 × 1 = 2 ← no decimal places in factors

2 × 0.1 = 0.2 ← one decimal place in factors

2 × 0.01 = 0.02 ← two decimal places in factors

The number of decimal places in the factors equals the number of decimal places in the product.

Complete the tables.

1.

2 ×	3 =	
2 ×	0.3 =	
2 ×	0.03 =	

2.

2 ×	4 =	
2 ×	0.4 =	
2 ×	0.04 =	

3.

3 ×	3=	
3 ×	0.3 =	
3 ×	0.03 =	

4.

3 ×	5 =	
3 ×	0.5 =	
3 ×	0.05 =	

5.

3 ×	6 =	
3 ×	0.6 =	
3 ×	0.06 =	

6.

3 ×	7 =	
3 ×	0.7 =	
3 ×	0.07 =	

7.

2 ×	8 =	
2 ×	0.8 =	
2 ×	0.08 =	

8.

4 ×	5 =	
4 ×	0.5 =	
4 ×	0.05 =	

9.

6 ×	7 =	
6 ×	0.7 =	
6 ×	0.07 =	

10.

15 ×	1 =	
15 ×	0.1 =	
15 ×	0.01 =	

11.

28 ×	1 =	
28 ×	0.1 =	
28 ×	0.01 =	

12.

32 ×	1 =	
32 ×	0.1 =	
32 ×	0.01 =	

Name ______________________________

Model Decimal Multiplication

To multiply 0.3 × 0.2, a 10-by-10 model will help.

Step 1: Draw diagonal lines through the bottom 3 rows.

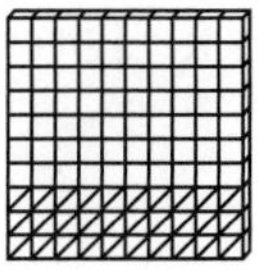

The 3 rows represent 0.3.

Step 2: Draw diagonal lines through 2 columns.

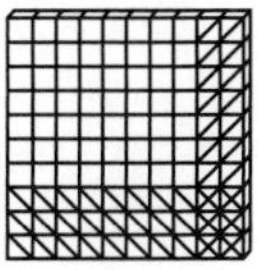

The 2 columns represent 0.2.

Step 3: The overlapping squares that have an x in them show the product of 0.3 × 0.2.

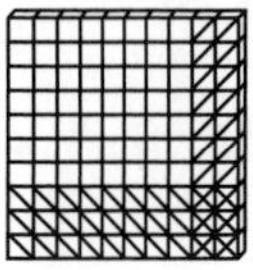

The 6 squares with x's represent 0.06.

The product of 0.3 × 0.2 is 0.06.

Write a number sentence for each drawing.

1. 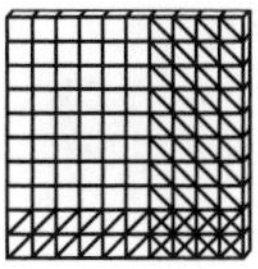 ______________

2. 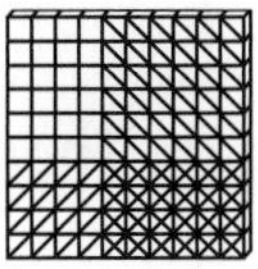 ______________

3. 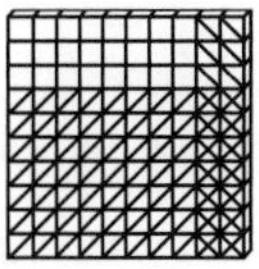 ______________

4. 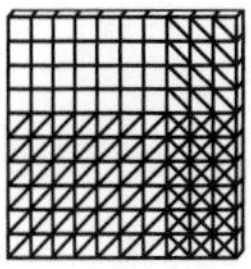 ______________

Make a model. Then find the product.

5. 0.1 × 0.5 = ______________

6. 0.2 × 0.8 = ______________

7. 0.5 × 0.9 = ______________

8. 0.7 × 0.5 = ______________

Name ____________________

Place the Decimal Point

How many decimal places are in the product of 0.21 and 0.03?

Step 1

Add the number of decimal places from each factor.

0.21 × 0.03 = ?

2 places + 2 places = 4 places

$$\begin{array}{r} 0.21 \\ \times\ 0.03 \\ \hline 0.\_\ \_\ \_\ \_ \end{array}$$

Step 2

Multiply the numbers just like whole numbers. To have 4 decimal places, you have to add 2 zeros before the 63.

$$\begin{array}{r} 0.21 \\ \times\ 0.03 \\ \hline 63 \\ +\ 000 \\ \hline 0.\underline{0}\ \underline{0}\ \underline{6}\ \underline{3} \end{array}$$

Write how many decimal places are in each number.

1. 0.105 ____________

2. 0.0006 ____________

3. 0.008 ____________

Write how many decimal places are in each product. Then write the product. The first one has been done for you.

4. 0.3 × 0.5

= **0.** _ _

= **0.15**

5. 0.6 × 0.03

____

____

6. 0.002 × 0.8

____

____

7. 0.24 × 0.01

____

____

8. 0.3 × 0.4

____

____

9. 0.7 × 0.2

____

____

Find each product.

10. 0.5 × 0.03 = ________ **11.** 0.06 × 1.8 = ________ **12.** 7 × 0.08 = ________

Name ______________________________

Zeros in the Product

Be careful when multiplying by decimals to include all of the decimal places in the product.

Example: Find 0.013 × 0.6.

Step 1

Find the number of decimal places the product should have.

0.013 has three decimal places and 0.6 has one decimal place. The product should have 3 + 1 = 4 decimal places.

Step 2

Multiply.

$$\begin{array}{r} 0.013 \\ \times \quad 0.6 \\ \hline 78 \end{array}$$

Step 3

Place the decimal point.

The product should have 4 decimal places. There are two digits, so write 2 zeros in the product and place the decimal point.

$$\begin{array}{r} 0.013 \\ \times \quad 0.6 \\ \hline 0.0078 \end{array}$$

---

1. Find 0.03 × 0.4.

Step 1:
Find the number of decimal places the product should have.

Step 2:
Multiply

$$\begin{array}{r} 0.03 \\ \times \ 0.4 \\ \hline \end{array}$$

Step 3:
Place the decimal point.

$$\begin{array}{r} 0.03 \\ \times \ 0.4 \\ \hline \end{array}$$

2. Find 0.047 × 0.07.

Step 1:

Step 2:

$$\begin{array}{r} 0.047 \\ \times \ 0.07 \\ \hline \end{array}$$

Step 3:

$$\begin{array}{r} 0.047 \\ \times \ 0.07 \\ \hline \end{array}$$

3. Find 0.0732 × 0.8.

Step 1:

Step 2:

Step 3:

4. Find 0.054 × 0.007.

____

5. Find 0.0942 × 0.7.

____

Name ______________________________

Problem Solving Skill

Make Decisions

We make decisions every day. There are often many things to consider. Use the questions below to guide you through making decisions.

Your neighbors have invited you to go with them on Saturday. Julia's family is going to the museum and to a movie. Karl's family is going on a bakery tour and to a football game. You must decide which invitation to accept.

1. If the museum visit will cost $3.00 and the movie will cost $4.75, how much will the trip with Julia's family cost?

____

2. If a football ticket costs $14.50 and the bakery tour is free, how much will the trip with Karl's family cost?

____

3. If you had to make your decision based on total cost, which trip would you choose? Why?

____

____

4. Julia's family will start their trip at 8:30 A.M. Breakfast will take 45 minutes. They plan to stay at the museum for 2 hours. Lunch will take 45 minutes, and the movie will last 2 hours and 30 minutes. When will the trip with Julia's family end?

____

5. The bakery tour will take 1 hour and 30 minutes. Lunch will take 30 minutes. The football game will take 3 hours and 30 minutes, and dinner with Karl's family will take 1 hour. If this trip starts at 11:00 A.M.,when will it end?

____

6. If you had to make your decision based on the total time of the trip, the start time, or the end time of the trip, which invitation would you accept? Why?

____

____

7. If you had to make your decision based on the activities you like better, which invitation would you accept? Why?

____

____

Name ______________________________

Estimate Quotients

Compatible numbers are numbers that are easy to compute mentally. One compatible number divides evenly into the other. Think of number factors to help you find compatible numbers.

What is $8\overline{)554}$?

Step 1

Think: What are the multiples of 8?

8 16 24 32
40 48 **56** 64

Which multiple is closest to 55?
56 is close to 55.
8 and 560 are compatible numbers.

Step 2

Divide.

$560 \div 8 = 70$
A good estimate for $554 \div 8$ is 70.

Follow the steps above to estimate each quotient.

1. $3\overline{)252}$ ______ ______

2. $6\overline{)546}$ ______ ______

3. $4\overline{)154}$ ______ ______

4. $9\overline{)192}$ ______ ______

5. $7\overline{)129}$ ______ ______

6. $4\overline{)265}$ ______ ______

7. $8\overline{)344}$ ______ ______

8. $5\overline{)480}$ ______ ______

9. $2\overline{)497}$ ______ ______

10. $3\overline{)287}$ ______ ______

11. $5\overline{)6,558}$ ______ ______

12. $6\overline{)5,097}$ ______ ______

Name ______________________________

Divide 3-Digit Dividends

Bryan has 522 coins. He divides them among 3 jars. How many coins are in each jar?

Divide. $522 \div 3 = n$

Step 1

Since 5 hundreds can be divided by 3, the first digit is in the hundreds place.
Divide. $3\overline{)5}$
Multiply. 3×1
Subtract. $5 - 3$
Compare. $2 < 3$

$$\begin{array}{r} 1 \\ 3\overline{)522} \\ -3 \\ \hline 2 \end{array}$$

Step 2

Bring down the tens. Divide. $3\overline{)22}$
Multiply. 3×7
Subtract. $22 - 21$
Compare. $1 < 3$

$$\begin{array}{r} 17 \\ 3\overline{)522} \\ -3 \\ \hline 22 \\ -21 \\ \hline 1 \end{array}$$

Step 3

Bring down the ones. Divide. $3\overline{)12}$
Multiply. 3×4
Subtract. $12 - 12$
Compare. $0 < 3$

$$\begin{array}{r} 174 \\ 3\overline{)522} \\ -3 \\ \hline 22 \\ -21 \\ \hline 12 \\ -12 \\ \hline 0 \end{array}$$

Since $n = 174$, each jar contains 174 coins.

Follow the steps above to find each quotient.

1. $3\overline{)928}$ **2.** $7\overline{)149}$ **3.** $5\overline{)845}$ **4.** $4\overline{)892}$

5. $6\overline{)399}$ **6.** $3\overline{)873}$ **7.** $9\overline{)765}$ **8.** $5\overline{)934}$

Name ______________________________

Zeros in Division

There are 618 pencils in the supply room. They are to be divided evenly among 6 classes. How many pencils will each class receive?

You will use division to find the answer. $618 \div 6 = n$

Step 1

Since 6 hundreds can be divided by 6, the first digit will be in the hundreds place. Divide.

$$\begin{array}{r} 1 \\ 6\overline{)618} \\ -6 \\ \hline 0 \end{array}$$

Multiply. $6 \times 1 = 6$
Subtract. $6 - 6 = 0$
Compare. $0 < 6$

Step 2

Bring down the tens. Divide the 1 ten. Since 6 >1, write 0 in the quotient.

$$\begin{array}{r} 10 \\ 6\overline{)618} \\ -6 \\ \hline 01 \\ -0 \\ \hline 1 \end{array}$$

Multiply. $6 \times 0 = 0$
Subtract. $1 - 0 = 1$
Compare. $1 < 6$

Step 3

Bring down the ones. Divide.

$$\begin{array}{r} 103 \\ 6\overline{)618} \\ -6 \\ \hline 01 \\ -0 \\ \hline 18 \\ -18 \\ \hline 0 \end{array}$$

Multiply. $6 \times 3 = 18$
Subtract. $18 - 18 = 0$
Compare. $0 < 6$

So, each class will receive 103 pencils.

Follow the steps above to find each quotient.

1. $3\overline{)927}$ **2.** $8\overline{)872}$ **3.** $5\overline{)542}$ **4.** $6\overline{)608}$

5. $3\overline{)624}$ **6.** $2\overline{)807}$ **7.** $4\overline{)826}$ **8.** $7\overline{)843}$

Name ______________________________

Choose a Method

Divide 42,574 by 7.

Divide 7 into 42 to get 6. Multiply 6 by 7 to get 42.
Subtract 42 from 42 to get 0. Bring down the 5 to get 05.

Divide 7 into 5 to get 0; Multiply 0 by 7 to get 0.
Subtract 0 from 05 to get 5. Bring down the 7 to get 57.

Divide 7 into 57 to get 8. Multiply 8 by 7 to get 56.
Subtract 56 from 57 to get 1. Bring down the 4 to get 14.

Divide 7 into 14 to get 2. Multiply 2 by 7 to get 14.
Subtract 14 from 14 to get 0.

So, 42,574 ÷ 7 = 6,082.

```
   6,082
7)42,574
 - 42↓
    05
   - 0↓
    57
  - 56↓
     14
   - 14
      0
```

Follow the steps above to find each quotient.

1. 9)45,035
2. 5)9,085
3. 4)16,087
4. 5)70,861
5. 6)856,412
6. 5)18,005
7. 4)200,088
8. 5)7,555
9. 5)654,321
10. 5)21,076
11. 3)356,789
12. 3)67,530

Problem Solving Skill

Interpret the Remainder

When there is a remainder in a division problem, you need to look at the question to see what is being asked. You may drop the remainder, or round the quotient to the next greater whole number, or you may use the remainder as a fractional part of your answer.

Andy made punch with 48 ounces of apple juice, 36 ounces of grape juice, and 60 ounces of lemon soda. How many 5-ounce servings did he make?

$48 + 36 + 60 = 144$ oz

$$\begin{array}{r} 28 \text{ r4} \\ 5\overline{)144} \\ -10 \\ \hline 44 \\ -40 \\ \hline 4 \end{array}$$

There are 4 ounces left over. That is not enough for another 5-ounce serving. Drop the remainder.

So, Andy made 28 five-ounce servings.

Solve. Explain how you interpreted the remainder.

1. Mia bought 10 feet of wire for a science project. She divided the wire equally into 3 pieces. How long was each piece of wire?

____

____

2. A total of 325 people will be attending a sports banquet. There will be 8 people seated at each table. How many tables will be needed?

____

____

3. A total of 175 players signed up for a baseball league. There are 9 teams in the league. If the players are divided among the teams, what is the greatest number of players on any team?

____

____

4. Jennie baked 132 cookies. She wants to divide them evenly among her 7 friends. How many cookies will she give to each friend?

____

____

Name ______________________________

Algebra: Patterns in Division

Rick has a 1,313-page book. If he reads 14 pages a day, about how long will it take him to finish reading the book? You divide to find the answer.

$1{,}313 \div 14$

You can estimate to find the number of days it will take Rick to read the book.

Estimate: 1,313 rounds down to 1,000.
14 rounds down to 10.

$1{,}000 \div 10$

There are zeros in the dividend and in the divisor. Cancel out one zero in each.

1,00~~0~~ ÷ 1~~0~~ = 100

So, it will take Rick about 100 days to read the book.

You can check this estimate by multiplying. Multiply the divisor by the quotient.

$10 \times 100 = 1{,}000$

Find each quotient. Cancel out the zeros if appropriate. Write a multiplication sentence to check. The first one is done for you.

1. 1,50~~0~~ ÷ 3~~0~~ = 50
   30 × 50 = 1,500
2. 560 ÷ 70 = ______
   ____
3. 720 ÷ 80 = ______
   ____
4. 2,100 ÷ 70 = ______
   ____
5. 480 ÷ 60 = ______
   ____
6. 2,500 ÷ 50 = ______
   ____
7. 36,000 ÷ 90 = ______
   ____
8. 24,000 ÷ 40 = ______
   ____
9. 5,600 ÷ 80 = ______
   ____

Name ____________________

Estimate Quotients

Compatible numbers are numbers that are close to the actual numbers and are easy to compute mentally. They can help you estimate a quotient.

Estimate. $42\overline{)1{,}574}$

Step 1
Round the divisor.

The number 42 rounds to 40. It can also be rounded to 50.

Step 2
Round the dividend.

The number 1,574 can be rounded up to 1,600 or rounded down to 1,500.

Step 3
Rewrite the division problem with the compatible numbers, and solve.

$$\begin{array}{r} 40 \\ 40\overline{)1{,}600} \end{array} \qquad \begin{array}{r} 30 \\ 50\overline{)1{,}500} \end{array}$$

So, one estimate of the quotient is 40. A second estimate is 30.

Write two pairs of compatible numbers for each. Give two possible estimates.

1. $48\overline{)3{,}367}$

____

____

2. $76\overline{)4{,}117}$

____

____

3. $37\overline{)847}$

____

____

4. $54\overline{)2{,}438}$

____

____

5. $68\overline{)4{,}831}$

____

____

6. $73\overline{)26{,}970}$

____

____

Name ______________________________

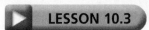

Divide by 2-Digit Divisors

A total of 6,501 people attended the local theater. A movie was shown 20 times during a 5-day period. The same number of people attended each showing except for the first showing. How many people attended each showing?

Step 1

Decide where to place the first digit in the quotient. Are there enough thousands? No, $6 < 20$. Are there enough hundreds? Yes, $65 > 20$. The first digit goes in the hundreds place.

$$20\overline{)6{,}501}$$

$$\begin{array}{r} \square \\ 20\overline{)6{,}501} \end{array}$$

Step 2

Divide the hundreds. $20\overline{)65}$
Write the 3 in the hundreds place.
Multiply. 20×3
Subtract. $65 - 60$
Compare. $5 < 20$

$$\begin{array}{r} 3 \\ 20\overline{)6{,}501} \\ \underline{-6\,0} \\ 5 \end{array}$$

Step 3

Divide the tens. $20\overline{)50}$
Write the 2 in the tens place.
Multiply. 20×2
Subtract. $50 - 40$
Compare. $10 < 20$

$$\begin{array}{r} 32 \\ 20\overline{)6{,}501} \\ \underline{-6\,0} \\ 50 \\ \underline{-40} \\ 10 \end{array}$$

Step 4

Divide the ones. $20\overline{)101}$
Write the 5 in the ones place.
Multiply. 20×5
Subtract. $101 - 100$
Compare. $1 < 20$

$$\begin{array}{r} 325 \text{ r1} \\ 20\overline{)6{,}501} \\ \underline{-6\,0} \\ 50 \\ \underline{-40} \\ 101 \\ \underline{-100} \\ 1 \end{array}$$

So, 325 people attended each showing of the movie, with 1 more person, or 326 people, attending the first showing.

Follow the steps above to find each quotient.

1. $52\overline{)6{,}219}$

2. $81\overline{)9{,}017}$

3. $24\overline{)6{,}008}$

4. $17\overline{)92{,}418}$

5. $32\overline{)6{,}850}$

6. $41\overline{)87{,}409}$

Name ______________________________

Correcting Quotients

Maria collects postcards. She has 389 postcards in her collection. The cards are organized in albums that each hold 48 postcards. How many albums has Maria used?

Divide. 389 ÷ 48

Step 1

Write two pairs of compatible numbers, and estimate the answer.

$$40\overline{)360} = 9 \qquad 50\overline{)400} = 8$$

Step 2

Use one of your estimates.

The divisor, 48, is closer to 50. Use 8 as the first digit in the quotient.

Step 3

Divide.
Since 5 < 48, the estimate is just right.

$$\begin{array}{r} 8 \text{ r}5 \\ 48\overline{)389} \\ -384 \\ \hline 5 \end{array}$$

So, Maria has 8 full albums and 1 album with only 5 postcards in it.

Use the steps above to find each quotient.

1. $19\overline{)67}$ **2.** $31\overline{)97}$ **3.** $48\overline{)235}$ **4.** $74\overline{)975}$

5. $62\overline{)557}$ **6.** $27\overline{)292}$ **7.** $52\overline{)509}$ **8.** $85\overline{)768}$

9. $75\overline{)5{,}387}$ **10.** $49\overline{)8{,}372}$ **11.** $65\overline{)41{,}760}$ **12.** $54\overline{)59{,}534}$

Name ________________________________

Practice Division

Ron's Record Shop received a shipment of 756 tapes. The tapes were packaged in 28 cartons. Each carton held the same number of tapes. How many tapes were in each carton?

Step 1 $756 \div 28$

$$28\overline{)756} \quad \square$$

Decide where to place the first digit.
Are there enough hundreds? No, $7 < 28$.
Place the first digit in the tens place.

Step 2

Divide the 75 tens.
Multiply. 28×2
Subtract. $75 - 56$
Compare. $19 < 28$

$$\begin{array}{r} 2 \\ 28\overline{)756} \\ -56 \\ \hline 19 \end{array}$$

Step 3

Divide the 196 ones.
Multiply. 28×7
Subtract. $196 - 196$

So, each carton held 27 tapes.

$$\begin{array}{r} 27 \\ 28\overline{)756} \\ -56 \\ \hline 196 \\ -196 \\ \hline 0 \end{array}$$

You can use multiplication to check the answer. Multiply the divisor by the quotient. Add any remainder.

$28 \times 27 = 756$ The answer checks.

Follow the steps above to find each quotient. Check by multiplying.

1. $17\overline{)255}$
2. $26\overline{)396}$
3. $33\overline{)458}$
4. $49\overline{)721}$
5. $45\overline{)6{,}004}$
6. $39\overline{)72{,}118}$
7. $15\overline{)497}$
8. $54\overline{)36{,}565}$

Name ______________________________

Problem Solving Strategy

Predict and Test

Rhea has 253 stickers stored in equal groups in containers. She has started a new container with 3 stickers in it. How many containers of stickers does she have? How many stickers are in each container?

Step 1

Subtract the 3 stickers in the new container from the 253 total number of stickers. 253 − 3 = 250
The number 250 can be divided by 5.

Step 2

Use *predict and test* to find the number of equal groups in 250. The number ends with 0, so 250 can be divided by 5.

Step 3

Divide. 250 ÷ 5 = 50

Check.

$$\begin{array}{r} 50 \\ \times\ 5 \\ \hline 250 \end{array} \qquad \begin{array}{r} 250 \\ +\ \ 3 \\ \hline 253 \end{array}$$

✔ The answer checks.

So, Rhea has 5 containers of stickers with 50 stickers in each container. There are 3 stickers in the new container.

Predict and test to solve.

1. James has 467 bookmarks in his collection. He has them stored in equal groups in boxes. He then starts a new box with 5 bookmarks in it. How many boxes of bookmarks does he have? How many bookmarks are in each box?

____

2. Nora baked 156 brownies. She is putting them into packages with an equal number of brownies in each. She eats 2 brownies. How many packages does she make? How many brownies are in each package?

____

Name ______________________________

Algebra: Patterns in Decimal Division

Kara is dividing \$3 equally into 5 boxes. How much money should go into each box?

$\$3 \div 5 = ?$

Look for a pattern in these quotients.

Each time there is one less zero in the dividend, the decimal point in the quotient moves one more place to the left.

$$3{,}000 \div 5 = 600$$
$$300 \div 5 = 60$$
$$30 \div 5 = 6$$
$$3 \div 5 = 0.6$$

So, each box gets 0.6, or \$0.60.

Complete each equation. Look for a pattern.

1. $3{,}000 \div 6 = 500$
   $\_\_\_\_ \div 6 = 50$
   $30 \div 6 = \_\_\_\_$
   $3 \div 6 = \_\_\_\_$

2. $4{,}500 \div 5 = 900$
   $\_\_\_\_ \div 5 = 90$
   $45 \div 5 = \_\_\_\_$
   $4.5 \div 5 = \_\_\_\_$

3. $6{,}400 \div 8 = 800$
   $\_\_\_\_ \div 8 = 80$
   $64 \div 8 = \_\_\_\_$
   $6.4 \div 8 = \_\_\_\_$

4. $2{,}800 \div 7 = 400$
   $280 \div 7 = \_\_\_\_$
   $28 \div 7 = \_\_\_\_$
   $2.8 \div 7 = \_\_\_\_$

Use a pattern to write the quotients.

5. $400 \div 8 = \_\_\_\_$
   $40 \div 8 = \_\_\_\_$
   $4 \div 8 = \_\_\_\_$

6. $600 \div 4 = \_\_\_\_$
   $60 \div 4 = \_\_\_\_$
   $6 \div 4 = \_\_\_\_$

7. $800 \div 5 = \_\_\_\_$
   $80 \div 5 = \_\_\_\_$
   $8 \div 5 = \_\_\_\_$

8. $1{,}400 \div 7 = \_\_\_\_$
   $140 \div 7 = \_\_\_\_$
   $14 \div 7 = \_\_\_\_$
   $1.4 \div 7 = \_\_\_\_$

9. $13{,}000 \div 5 = \_\_\_\_$
   $1{,}300 \div 5 = \_\_\_\_$
   $130 \div 5 = \_\_\_\_$
   $13 \div 5 = \_\_\_\_$

10. $2{,}700 \div 9 = \_\_\_\_$
    $270 \div 9 = \_\_\_\_$
    $27 \div 9 = \_\_\_\_$
    $2.7 \div 9 = \_\_\_\_$

Name ______________________________

LESSON 11.2

Decimal Division

You can use a centimeter ruler to help you divide 1.4 by 2.

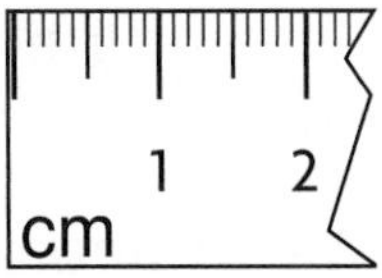

1 stands for 1 centimeter.

Each space stands for $\frac{1}{10}$, or 0.1, cm.

Step 1

Find 1.4 centimeters on the ruler. Count the number of spaces.

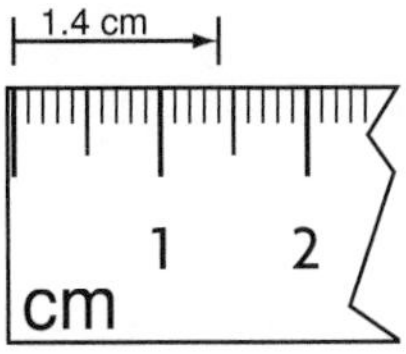

There are 14 spaces.

Step 2

Divide the number of spaces by 2.
$14 \div 2 = 7$

Count over 7 spaces.

The seventh space is 0.7 cm.
So $1.4 \div 2 = 0.7$.

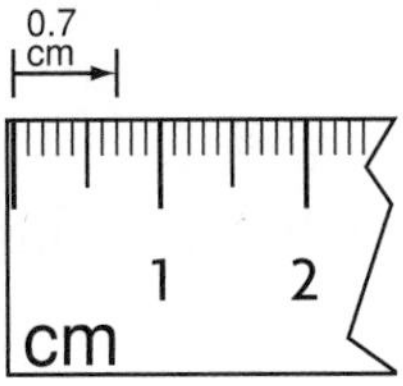

Use the centimeter ruler to find the quotient.

1. $2.4 \div 6 =$ ______

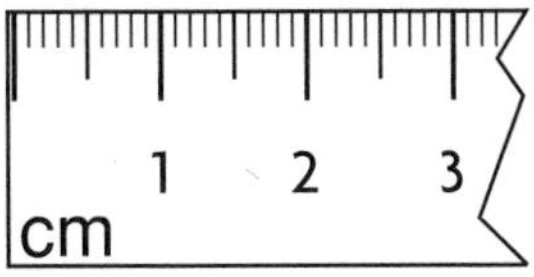

2. $2.5 \div 5 =$ ______

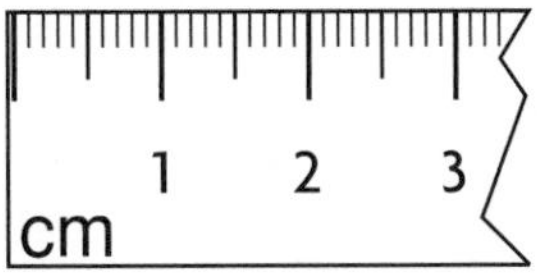

3. $1.8 \div 3 =$ ______

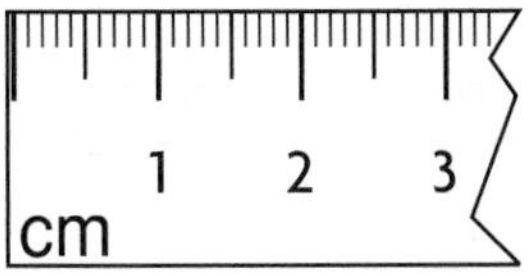

4. $2.4 \div 4 =$ ______

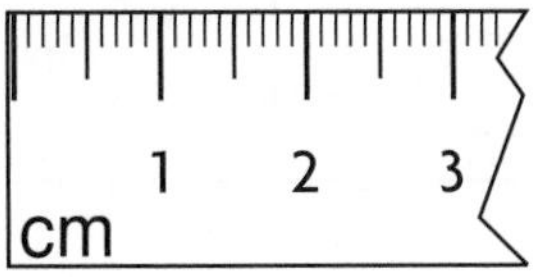

5. $2.1 \div 7 =$ ______

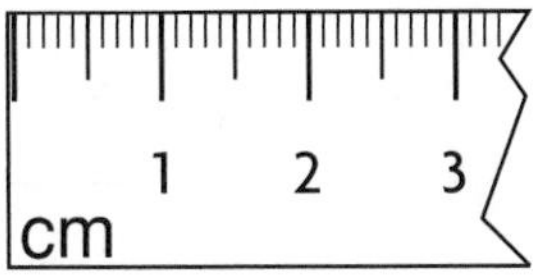

6. $1.6 \div 8 =$ ______

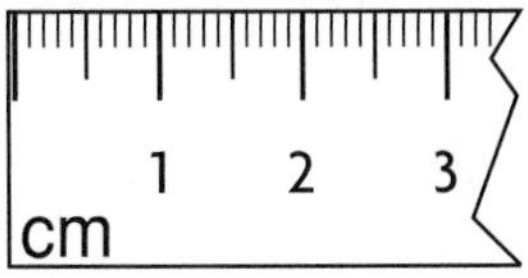

7. $3.9 \div 3 =$ ______

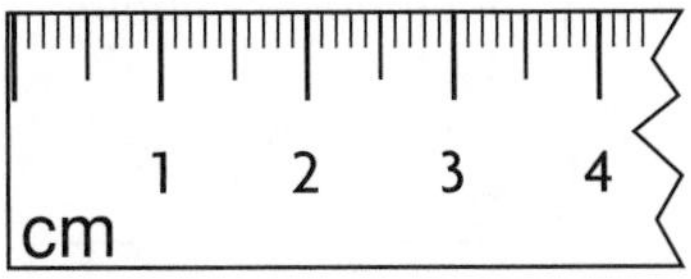

8. $3.3 \div 3 =$ ______

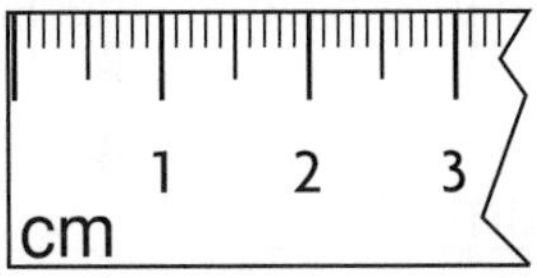

9. $0.8 \div 8 =$ ______

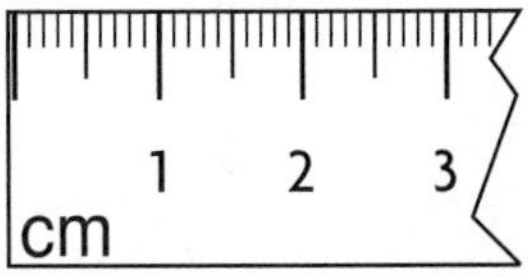

Name ______________________________

Divide Decimals by Whole Numbers

You can use a centimeter ruler to help you divide 3.6 by 2.

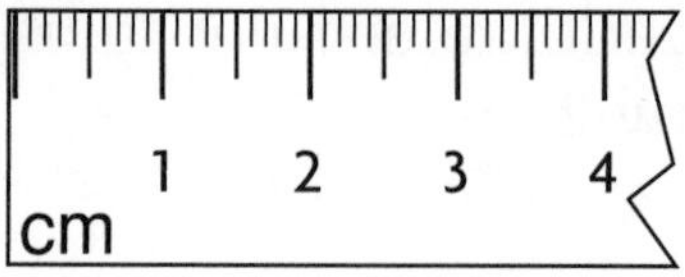

1 stands for 1 centimeter.
Each space stands for $\frac{1}{10}$ or 0.1 cm.

Step 1

Find 3.6 centimeters on the ruler.

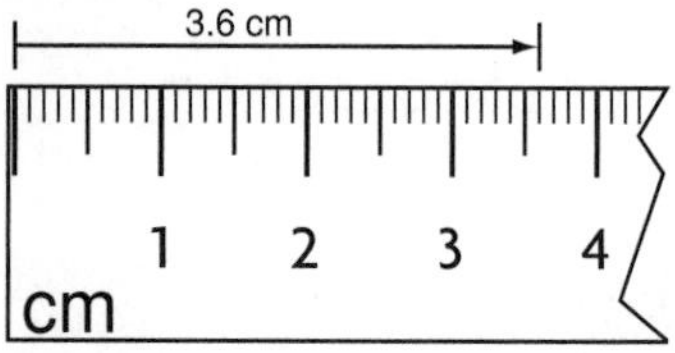

Step 2

There are 3 whole centimeters. Divide them into 2 equal groups. There is 1 centimeter in each group with 1.6 centimeters left over.

$$\begin{array}{r} 1 \\ 2\overline{)3.6} \\ -\ 2.0 \\ \hline 1.6 \end{array}$$

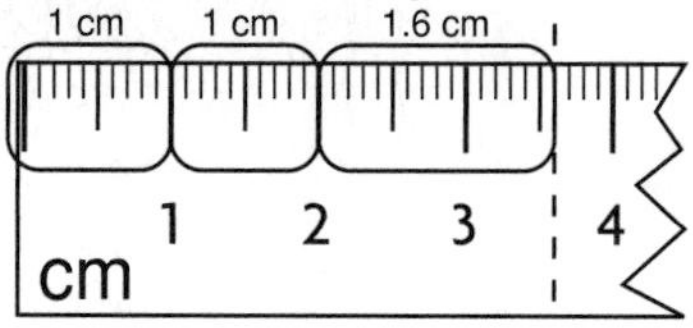

Step 3

Count the spaces for the remaining 1.6 cm. There are 16 spaces. Divide them into 2 groups. There are 2 groups of 8 spaces. Each group is 0.8 centimeter.

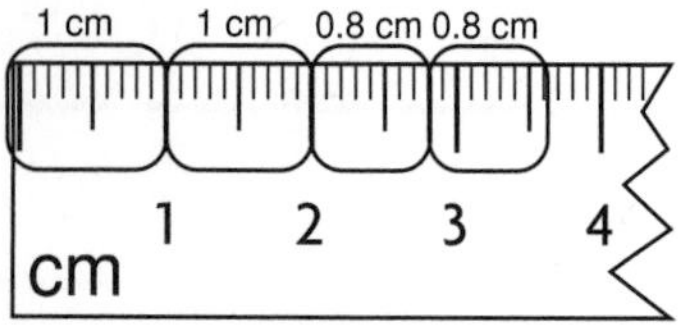

Step 4

There are 2 equal groups of 1.8 centimeters.

So, 3.6 ÷ 2 = 1.8

$$\begin{array}{r} 1.8 \\ 2\overline{)3.6} \\ -\ 2.0 \\ \hline 1.6 \\ -\ 1.6 \\ \hline 0 \end{array}$$

Use the ruler to find the quotient.

1. $3\overline{)3.6}$

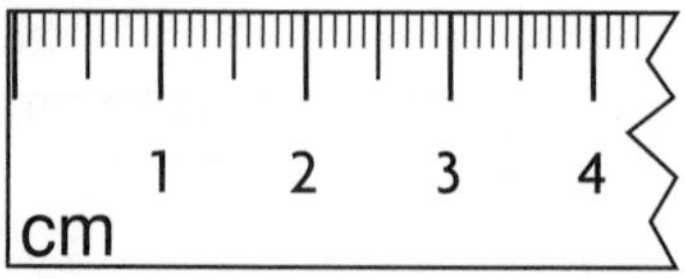

2. $2\overline{)2.8}$

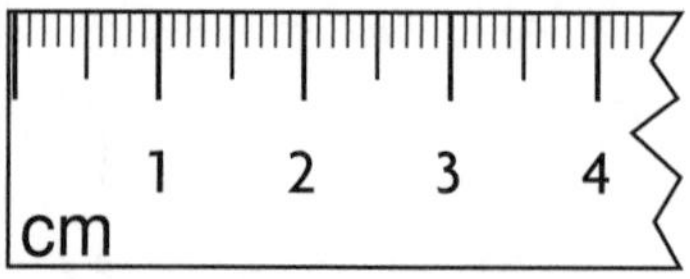

3. $2\overline{)3.2}$

4. $4\overline{)4.0}$

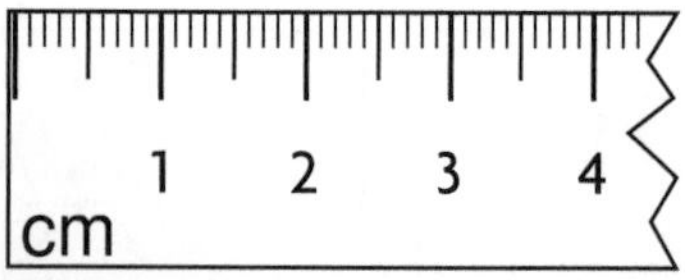

5. $2\overline{)1.2}$

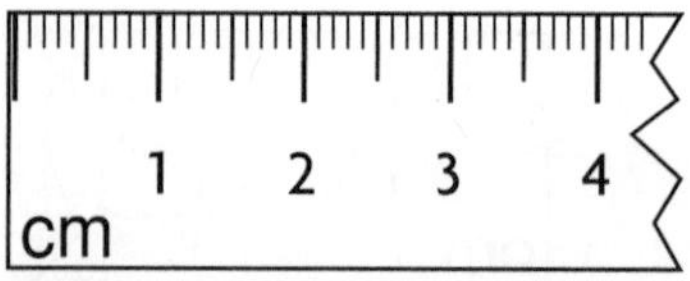

6. $4\overline{)3.6}$

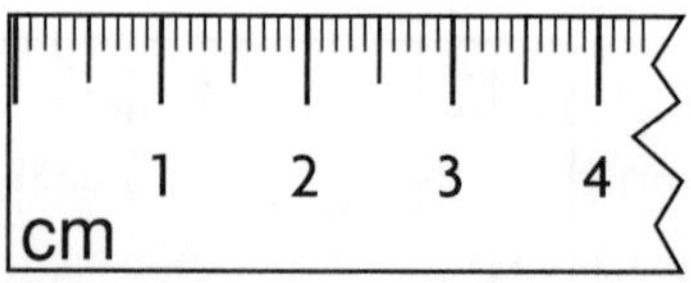

Name ______________________________

Problem Solving Skill

Choose the Operation

Ricardo and his two friends raise small animals. Ricardo buys rabbits, hamsters, mice, and gerbils. If Ricardo and his friends each take an equal number of animals, how many animals will each person get?

Type of Animal	Number
Rabbits	15
Hamsters	27
Mice	36
Gerbils	9

There are 15 rabbits for 3 people.

Should you multiply? or Should you divide?

$15 \times 3 = 45$ $15 \div 3 = 5$

Which answer makes more sense? Since they bought only 15 rabbits, 5 rabbits each makes the most sense. You should divide.

For Problems 1–6, use the table to solve each problem. Name the operation you used.

Type of Food	Amount (in pounds)
Rabbit Food	186.3
Hamster Food	53.1
Mouse Food	26.9
Gerbil Food	12.6

1. Ricardo and his two friends purchase animal food. They share what they buy equally. What is Ricardo's share of the rabbit food?

   ____

2. Ricardo buys the same amount of gerbil food each month for 5 months. How much gerbil food does Ricardo buy?

   ____

3. Ricardo pays $1.25 per pound for a month's worth of gerbil food. How much does the gerbil food cost in all?

   ____

4. Ricardo spent $37.17 buying hamster food. What was the cost per pound for the hamster food?

   ____

5. How much animal food do Ricardo and his friends buy in all?

   ____

6. What is Ricardo's share of the hamster food?

   ____

Name ______________________

Divide to Change a Fraction to a Decimal

Fractions can be written as decimals by dividing the numerator by the denominator.

$\frac{\text{numerator}}{\text{denominator}} \rightarrow \text{denominator}\overline{)\text{numerator}}$

To write $\frac{3}{5}$ as a decimal, divide 3 by 5.

$$\frac{3}{5} = 5\overline{)3.0} \leftarrow \text{numerator}$$

Quotient: 0.6

denominator ↑ (points to 5)

$$\begin{array}{r} 0.6 \\ 5\overline{)3.0} \\ \underline{3.0} \\ 0 \end{array}$$

Write as a decimal.

1. $\frac{3}{50}$ ______
2. $\frac{4}{10}$ ______
3. $\frac{16}{100}$ ______
4. $\frac{3}{4}$ ______
5. $\frac{20}{40}$ ______
6. $\frac{8}{10}$ ______
7. $\frac{15}{20}$ ______
8. $\frac{4}{5}$ ______
9. $\frac{42}{50}$ ______
10. $\frac{10}{25}$ ______
11. $\frac{63}{100}$ ______
12. $\frac{1}{8}$ ______
13. $\frac{1}{4}$ ______
14. $\frac{4}{8}$ ______
15. $\frac{6}{25}$ ______
16. $\frac{3}{8}$ ______
17. $\frac{3}{15}$ ______
18. $\frac{721}{1,000}$ ______
19. $\frac{4}{100}$ ______
20. $\frac{5}{8}$ ______
21. $\frac{14}{25}$ ______
22. $\frac{47}{50}$ ______
23. $\frac{8}{1,000}$ ______
24. $\frac{7}{8}$ ______
25. $\frac{30}{1,000}$ ______

Name ______________________

Expressions and Equations

An **expression** combines numbers or variables with operations.

Problem: six times a number **Expression:** $6 \times n$

The **value** of the expression depends on n. If n is 3, the value is **18**. If n is 6, the **value** is 36.

An **equation** is a number sentence that uses an equal sign to show that two amounts are equal.

Problem: six times a number is forty-eight. **Equation:** $6 \times n = 48$

To solve the equation, think: 6 times what number equals 48?

You can predict and test to solve.

Predict: 7 Test: $6 \times 7 = 42$; too low. Predict: 8 Test: $6 \times 8 = 48$; correct

---

Evaluate the expression for *n*.

1. $48 \div n$
   $n = 2, 6, 12$
   ____
2. $n \times 10$
   $n = 6, 7, 10$
   ____
3. $n \div 12$
   $n = 12, 36, 72$
   ____
4. $9 \times n$
   $n = 2, 6, 18$
   ____

Determine which value is the solution for the given equation.

5. $7 \times n = 49$
   $n = 5, 6,$ or 7
   ____
6. $65 \times n = 195$
   $n = 2, 3,$ or 4
   ____
7. $n \div 6 = 8$
   $n = 36, 42,$ or 48
   ____
8. $n \div 5 = 50$
   $n = 200, 250,$ or 300
   ____
9. $n \times 50 = 350$
   $n = 5, 6,$ or 7
   ____
10. $200 \div n = 5$
    $n = 30, 40,$ or 50
    ____
11. $n \div 6 = 12$
    $n = 72, 76,$ or 78
    ____
12. $n \times 6 = 84$
    $n = 12, 13,$ or 14
    ____

Solve each equation. Then, check the solution.

13. $45 \div n = 5$ ______________
14. $100 \div n = 10$ ______________
15. $n \times 6 = 36$ ______________
16. $12 \times n = 108$ ______________
17. $13 \times n = 65$ ______________
18. $n \times 30 = 120$ ______________
19. $n \div 3 = 31$ ______________
20. $n \div 4 = 21$ ______________

Name ______________________________

Order of Operations

When an expression has more than one operation, you evaluate it using the order of operations. The order of operations is a set of rules that tells you which operation to do first.

Evaluate $18 + (4 \times 6) \div 2$.

Step 1 Operate inside parentheses.

Step 2 Multiply and divide from left to right.

Step 3 Add and subtract from left to right.

$18 + (4 \times 6) \div 2$

$4 \times 6 = 24$

$18 + 24 \div 2$

$24 \div 2 = 12$

$18 + 12$

$18 + 12 = 30$

30

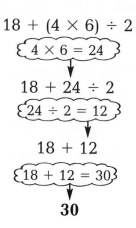

So, $18 + (4 \times 6) \div 2 = 30$

Complete to evaluate the expression.

1. $10 + (7 \times 4) - 8$

$10 +$ ________ $- 8$

________ $- 8$

____

2. $15 \div 5 \times 9 - 4$

________ $\times 9 - 4$

________ $- 4$

____

Evaluate the expression.

3. $14 - (5 + 2) \times 2$ ________

4. $2 \times 8 + (16 \div 4)$ ________

5. $5 \times 7 - 24 \div 8$ ________

6. $4 + (55 \div 11) \times 6$ ________

7. $29 - (6 \times 3) \div 2$ ________

8. $(27 \div 9) \times 8 + 7$ ________

9. $8 \times 6 - 7 \times 2$ ________

10. $30 - (10 \div 10) + 13$ ________

11. $6 \times 7 - 4 \times 5$ ________

12. $19 - 7 \times (12 \div 6)$ ________

13. $7 + 48 \div (7 + 5)$ ________

14. $27 \div 3 - (1 \times 5)$ ________

Name ______________________________

Number Patterns

The numbers 3, 7, 11, 15, 19, and 23 form a pattern. How can you find the next two numbers in the pattern? Look for a relationship between numbers that are next to each other.

3, 7, 11, 15, 19, 23, _____, _____

Look at each number in the pattern.
The numbers are increasing.

$3 + \mathbf{4} = 7$, $7 + \mathbf{4} = 11$, $11 + \mathbf{4} = 15$, $15 + \mathbf{4} = 19$, $19 + \mathbf{4} = 23$

Adding 4 to each number gives you the next number.
Continue the pattern to find the next two numbers.

$23 + 4 = \mathbf{27}$, $27 + 4 = \mathbf{31}$

So, the pattern is 3, 7, 11, 15, 19, 23, 27, 31.

Sometimes a pattern involves more than one relationship.

8, 40, 20, 100, _____, 250, 125

Look at the first number in the pattern.

- If the next number is greater, try adding or multiplying.
- If the next number is less, try subtracting or dividing.

Look at the first and second numbers; 8 is less than 40.
Look at the second and third numbers: 40 is greater than 20.

The relationship appears to be multiply by 5 and then divide by 2.
Check to see if it works for all the numbers in the pattern.

$8 \times \mathbf{5} = 40$, $40 \div \mathbf{2} = 20$, $20 \times \mathbf{5} = 100$, $100 \div \mathbf{2} = 50$, $50 \times \mathbf{5} = 250$, $250 \div \mathbf{2} = 125$

The pattern is 8, 40, 20, 100, 50, 250, 125. So, the missing number is 50.

Write a rule for each pattern. Then find the missing number(s).

1. 30, 27, 24, 21, _____, _____

____

2. 5, 10, 20, 40, _____, _____

____

3. 1, 9, 17, _____, 33, 41

____

4. 96, 48, 24, _____, 6, 3

____

5. 2, 7, 14, 19, 38, _____, 86

____

6. 243, 81, 72, 24, _____, 5

____

Name ______________________________

Functions

When one quantity depends on another quantity, the relationship between the quantities is called a function.

Paintbrushes cost $4 each. How much will 5 paintbrushes cost?

You can write an equation to represent the function.

Number of dollars	=	4	×	the number of paintbrushes
d	=	4	×	p
d	=	4	×	5
d	=	20		

You can also use a function table to show the number of dollars different numbers of paintbrushes cost.

paintbrushes, p	1	2	3	4	5
dollars, d	4	8	12	16	20

So, 5 paint brushes will cost $20.

Complete the function table.

1. $b = 9c$

c	2	4	6	8	10
b					

2. $s = 7t$

t	6	7	8	9	10
s					

3. $h = 6j + 4$

j	8	6	4	2	0
h					

4. $f = 6 + 5g$

g	0	5	10	15	20
f					

5. $d = 3a - 2$

a	12	10	8	6	4
d					

6. $n = 15 + 2m - 4$

m	3	5	7	9	11
n					

Use the function. Find the output, y for each input, x.

7. $y = 8x - 7$ for $x = 3, 4, 5$

____

8. $y = 100 - 4x$ for $x = 5, 10, 20$

____

9. $y = 6x + 15$ for $x = 6, 7, 8$

____

10. $y = 49 - 3x$ for $x = 8, 9, 10$

____

Name ____________________

Problem Solving Strategy

Compare Strategies

Problem Since the school year began, Jill has grown 0.75 inches. Now she measures 58.5 inches. What did she measure when the year began?

What strategy can you use?

Work backward: What information can you use to find out how tall Jill was when the year began? You can start by using the information at the end. Now she is 58.5 inches. Then use the fact that she grew 0.75 inch. Work backward to find out how tall she was at the beginnning of the year.

58.5 = current height

0.75 = height she grew $58.5 - 0.75 = 57.75$

57.75 inches = height at beginning of school year.

Work backward

You can also use *predict and test.*

Predict: She was 57 inches. Test: $57 + 0.75 = 57.75$; too low

Predict again, using a higher number.

Predict: She was 57.75 inches.

Test: $57.75 + 0.75 = 58.5$ inches ✓

Predict and Test

Solve and write the problem solving strategy you used: *work backward* or *predict and test.*

1. Anthony started with his favorite number. Then he subtracted 7 from it. He multiplied this difference by 3 and then added 5. Finally he divided this number by 11. His end result was 1. What was Anthony's favorite number?

   ____

2. Forty-seven baseball players need a ride to the play-off game. Each car has seat belts for 4 players and can make 2 trips. How many cars will be needed?

   ____

3. The sum of 2 numbers is 40 and their difference is 2. What are the two numbers?

   ____

4. The school spent \$438.75 to buy art supplies and gym supplies. The total cost of the art supplies was \$230.60. How much was spent on the gym supplies?

   ____

Name ______________________________

Use Multiplication Properties

You can use mental math and the **properties of multiplication** to solve problems.

Property of Multiplication	Example	Explanation
Commutative Property	$4 \times 2 = n \times 4$ $4 \times 2 = 2 \times 4$ $n = 2$	You can multiply numbers in any order. The product is always the same.
Associative Property	$(3 \times n) \times 5 = 3 \times (4 \times 5)$ $(3 \times 4) \times 5 = 3 \times (4 \times 5)$ $n = 4$	You can group factors differently. The product is always the same.
Property of One	$n \times 1 = 5$ $5 \times 1 = 5$ $n = 5$	When one of the factors is 1, the product equals the other number.
Zero Property	$4 \times n = 0$ $4 \times 0 = 0$ $n = 0$	When one factor is 0, the product is 0.

Solve the equation. Identify the property used.

1. $n \times 3 = 0$

____

____

2. $n \times 3 = 3 \times 2$

____

____

3. $4 \times (2 \times 5) = (n \times 2) \times 5$

____

____

4. $1 \times n = 8$

____

____

5. $(n \times 3) \times 2 = 5 \times (3 \times 2)$

____

____

6. $6 \times 7 = 7 \times n$

____

____

7. $(7 \times 3) \times n = 7 \times (3 \times 2)$

____

____

8. $8 \times 2 = n \times 8$

____

____

9. $3 \times n = 3$

____

____

Name ____________________

The Distributive Property

You can use the **Distributive Property** to break apart numbers to make them easier to multiply.

To find 20×13, you can break apart 13.

$20 \times 13 = 20 \times (10 + 3)$ ← Break apart.

$= (20 \times 10) + (20 \times 3)$ ← Multiply.

$= (200) + (60)$ ← Add.

$= 260$

Use the Distributive Property to restate each expression. Find the product.

1. 20×12

Break apart. $20 \times$ (____ + ____)

Multiply. $20 \times$ ____ = ____

$20 \times$ ____ = ____

Add. $200 +$ ____ = ____

____

2. 20×18

Break apart. $20 \times$ (____ + ____)

Multiply. $20 \times$ ____ = ____

$20 \times$ ____ = ____

Add. ____ + ____ = ____

____

3. 30×16

Break apart. $30 \times$ (____ + ____)

Multiply. $30 \times$ ____ = ____

$30 \times$ ____ = ____

Add. ____ + ____ = ____

____

4. 12×45

Break apart. $12 \times$ (____ + ____)

Multiply. $12 \times$ ____ = ____

$12 \times$ ____ = ____

Add. ____ + ____ = ____

____

5. 30×26

Break apart. $30 \times$ (____ + ____)

Multiply. $30 \times$ ____ = ____

$30 \times$ ____ = ____

Add. ____ + ____ = ____

____

6. 25×17

Break apart. $25 \times$ (____ + ____)

Multiply. $25 \times$ ____ = ____

$25 \times$ ____ = ____

Add. ____ + ____ = ____

____

Name ______________________________

Divisibility

The rules for divisibility by 3 and 9 are special. They depend on finding the sum of the digits.

- A number is divisible by 3 if the sum of the digits of the number is divisible by 3.
- A number is divisible by 9 if the sum of the digits of the number is divisible by 9.

---

1. Decide if 615 is divisible by 3.

a. What is the sum of the digits 6, 1, and 5? ____________

b. Is 12 divisible by 3? ____________

c. Is 615 divisible by 3? ____________

2. Decide if 615 is divisible by 9.

a. What is the sum of the digits 6, 1, and 5? ____________

b. Is 12 divisible by 9? ____________

c. Is 615 divisible by 9? ____________

Tell if each number is divisible by 3 or 9. Write 3, 9, or neither.

3. 90 ____________

4. 315 ____________

5. 390 ____________

6. 405 ____________

7. 75 ____________

8. 4,770 ____________

9. 320 ____________

10. 3,705 ____________

11. 801 ____________

12. 408 ____________

13. 117 ____________

14. 490 ____________

15. 81 ____________

16. 906 ____________

17. 432 ____________

18. 235 ____________

19. 123 ____________

20. 684 ____________

21. 963 ____________

22. 91 ____________

Name ____________________

Greatest Common Factor

You can find the **greatest common factor** of two numbers. It is the greatest factor that the two numbers have in common.

Find the greatest common factor of 9 and 15.

Step 1

List all the factors of each number.

9: 1, 3, 9

15: 1, 3, 5, 15

Step 2

Note the common factors.

The common factors of 9 and 15 are 1 and 3.

Step 3

Which factor is greater?

3 is greater than 1.

So, the greatest common factor of 9 and 15 is 3.

Use the factors given to find the greatest common factor (GCF) for each pair of numbers.

1. 10: 1, 2, 5, 10

25: 1, 5, 25

GCF ____________

2. 18: 1, 2, 3, 6, 9, 18

21: 1, 3, 7, 21

GCF ____________

3. 28: 1, 2, 4, 7, 14, 28

35: 1, 5, 7, 35

GCF ____________

4. 21: 1, 3, 7, 21

49: 1, 7, 49

GCF ____________

List the factors of each number. Write the greatest common factor (GCF) for each pair of numbers. The first one is done for you.

5. 8 1, 2, 4, 8

12 1, 2, 3, 4, 6, 12

GCF 4

6. 6 ____________

24 ____________

GCF ____________

7. 9 ____________

27 ____________

GCF ____________

8. 4 ____________

14 ____________

GCF ____________

Name ____________________

Multiples and the Least Common Multiple

Sam and Mary love to count. Sam counts by 3's and Mary counts by 4's.

Sam | Mary

3, 6, 9, (12), 15, 18, 21, (24), 27, 30, 33, . . . 4, 8, (12), 16, 20, (24), 28, 32, 36, 40, . . .

Sam and Mary both say the numbers 12 and 24. These numbers are called the **common multiples** of 3 and 4. The first common multiple is 12, so it is called the **least common multiple** of 3 and 4.

List the first 6 multiples of the number.

1. 2 ____________________
2. 5 ____________________
3. 6 ____________________
4. 7 ____________________
5. 8 ____________________
6. 9 ____________________
7. 10 ____________________
8. 11 ____________________
9. 12 ____________________

Find the first 2 common multiples of each pair of numbers.

10. 2 and 5 ____________
11. 4 and 8 ____________
12. 6 and 8 ____________
13. 4 and 12 ____________

Find the least common multiple of each pair of numbers.

14. 3 and 8 ____________
15. 6 and 9 ____________
16. 5 and 8 ____________
17. 3 and 7 ____________

Name ______________________________

Problem Solving Skill

Identify Relationships

Identifying relationships can help you solve some word problems.

There is a relationship between the product of two numbers and the product of their least common multiple (LCM) and greatest common factor (GCF).

Example:

- Find the relationship between the product of 6 and 9, and the product of their LCM and GCF.

  The LCM of 6 and 9 is 18.
  The GCF of 6 and 9 is 3.

  $6 \times 9 = \mathbf{54}$ $\text{LCM} \times \text{GCF} = 18 \times 3 = \mathbf{54}$

So, the product of two numbers is equal to the product of their LCM and GCF.

Use the relationship between the given numbers to complete the table.

First Number	Second Number	Product of Numbers	Product of LCM and GCF
6	15	90	______
8	4	______	32
______	8	56	______
12	______	______	36

Use the relationships between the given numbers to solve.

1. The product of the LCM and GCF of 4 and another number is 36. What is the other number?

   ____

2. The product of two numbers is 98. The GCF of the two numbers is 7. What is their LCM?

   ____

3. The product of the LCM and GCF of two numbers is 55, and neither of the numbers is 1. What are the two numbers?

   ____

4. The product of two numbers is 320. The GCF of the two numbers is 4, and one of the numbers is 16. What is the other number?

   ____

Name ______________________________

Introduction to Exponents

You can represent numbers using exponents.

$10 \times 10 = 10^2 = 100$
10^2 = the second power of ten, or ten squared

$3 \times 3 \times 3 \times 3 = 3^4 = 81$

3^4 = the fourth power of three

Show the third power of five in three different ways.

Exponent Form	Expanded Form	Standard Form
5^3	$5 \times 5 \times 5$	125

Write in exponent form. Then find the value.

1. the third power of three

____

2. the sixth power of two

____

3. the seventh power of ten

____

4. the second power of twelve

____

5. $20 \times 20 \times 20$

____

6. $4 \times 4 \times 4 \times 4$

____

Write as a multiplication problem. Then find the value.

7. 3^5

____

8. 6^2

____

9. 1^6

____

10. 2^3

____

11. 10^4

____

12. 5^4

____

Name ______________________

Exponents and Expanded Form

The table shows powers of 10. Notice that the exponent shows the number of zeros in the standard form of the number.

Power of 10	Meaning	Standard Form
10^4	$10 \times 10 \times 10 \times 10$	10,000
10^3	$10 \times 10 \times 10$	1,000
10^2	10×10	100
10^1	10	10
10^0	1	1

Any number raised to the first power equals that number.	Any number raised to the zero power equals 1.
$10^1 = 10$ $4^1 = 4$ $8^1 = 8$	$10^0 = 1$ $3^0 = 1$ $7^0 = 1$

Write 45,139 in expanded form.

Step 1 To express a number in expanded form, use place value to write the value of each digit.

$45{,}139 = 40{,}000 + 5{,}000 + 100 + 30 + 9$

$= (4 \times 10{,}000) + (5 \times 1{,}000) + (1 \times 100) + (3 \times 10) + (9 \times 1)$

Step 2 Now write the powers of 10 for each multiple of 10 in standard form.

$45{,}139 = (4 \times 10^4) + (5 \times 10^3) + (1 \times 10^2) + (3 \times 10^1) + (9 \times 10^0)$

Find the value.

1. 5^0 ______ **2.** 10^3 ______ **3.** 12^1 ______ **4.** 14^0 ______ **5.** 6^1 ______

Write in expanded form with exponents.

6. 67,135 ______________________

7. 209,854 ______________________

Write in standard form.

8. $(9 \times 10^3) + (2 \times 10^2) + (3 \times 10^1) + (6 \times 10^0)$ ______________

9. $(2 \times 10^6) + (5 \times 10^4) + (7 \times 10^2) + (3 \times 10^0)$ ______________

Name ____________________

Prime and Composite Numbers

You can use squares to see if a number is prime or composite.

A **prime number** has exactly two factors, 1 and the number itself.

Is the number 5 prime or composite?

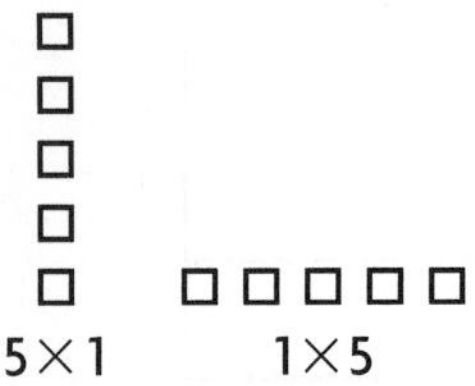

Only 2 arrangements of squares are possible (5 × 1, 1 × 5). The number 5 has exactly two factors, so it is a prime number.

A **composite number** has more than two factors.

Is the number 8 prime or composite?

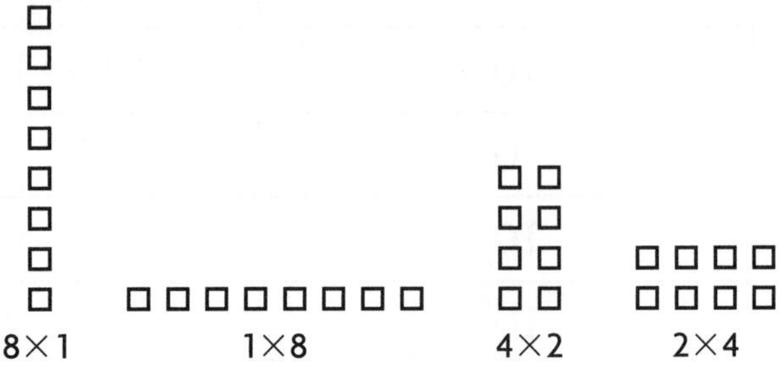

More than 2 arrangements of squares are possible (8 × 1, 1 × 8, 4 × 2, 2 × 4). The number 8 has more than two factors, so it is a composite number.

Draw squares to see if each number is prime or composite. Write *prime* or *composite.*

1. 7 ____________________

2. 6 ____________________

Write the possible arrangements of squares for each number. Then write *prime* or *composite*. The first one is done for you.

3. 4 1 × 4, 4 × 1, 2 × 2; composite

4. 9 ____________________

5. 10 ____________________

6. 11 ____________________

7. 12 ____________________

8. 13 ____________________

Name ____________________

Prime Factors and Exponents

You can think about prime factorization as a series of division problems.

Begin with the number you need to factor: **48**

What is the least possible prime number that divides 48? **2**

Keep dividing by prime divisors until you get 1 as a quotient.

Divide 2 into 48.

1. Is the quotient 1? No. $2\overline{)48}$ = 24

Repeat the process.

2. Is the quotient 1? No. $2\overline{)24}$ = 12

Repeat the process.

3. Is the quotient 1? No. $2\overline{)12}$ = 6

Repeat the process.

4. Is the quotient 1? No. $2\overline{)6}$ = 3

Repeat the process.

5. Is the quotient 1? Yes. $3\overline{)3}$ = 1

Stop.

Write the prime divisors as factors of 48.

$48 = 2 \times 2 \times 2 \times 2 \times 3$

Use what you know about exponents to write the factors.

$48 = 2^4 \times 3$

Write the prime factorization of the number. Use exponents when possible.

1. 12 ______

2. 24 ______

3. 28 ______

4. 45 ______

5. 36 ______

6. 125 ______

7. 256 ______

8. 81 ______

Name ____

Problem Solving Strategy

Make a Table

Andrew ran one lap around the track in Week 1. Each week he plans to run twice as many laps as he ran the previous week until he is up to 32 laps. How many weeks will it take him to reach his goal of 32 laps?

Making a table can help you solve a problem.

- Decide on a title and row labels.
- Fill in the table.
- Use the table to answer the question.

LAPS							
Week	1	2	3	4	5	6	7
Number of Laps	1	2	4	8	16	32	64

So, it will take Andrew **6** weeks to reach his goal.

Rachel did 10 pushups on Monday and continued to do 1 more pushup each day than she did the previous day. Complete the table.

1.

PUSHUPS										
Day	1	2	3	4						
Number of Pushups	10	11	12							

2. What is the total number of pushups Rachel did in 10 days?

____

3. On which day will Rachel be doing 20 pushups?

____

Leora makes jewelry with beads. She pays $6 for each pack of 25 beads. Complete the table.

4.

BEAD COST									
Beads	25	50	75						
Cost ($)	6	12							

5. How much will it cost Leora to buy 175 beads?

____

6. Leora uses 25 beads to make a bracelet. She spent $54 on beads. How many bracelets did she make?

____

Name ______________________________

Equivalent Fractions

You can use different fractions to name the same amount.

Fractions that name the same amount are called **equivalent fractions**.

You can find equivalent fractions in three ways.

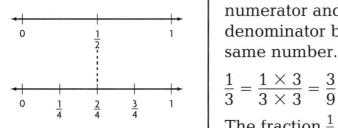

Use a number line.

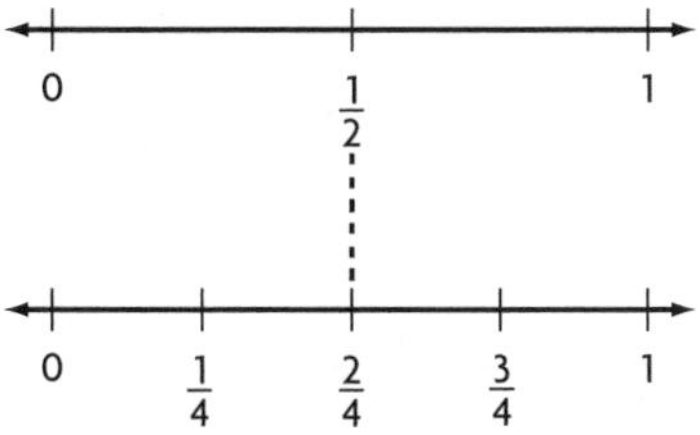

You can see that $\frac{1}{2} = \frac{2}{4}$, so they are equivalent fractions.

Multiply both the numerator and the denominator by the same number.

$$\frac{1}{3} = \frac{1 \times 3}{3 \times 3} = \frac{3}{9}$$

The fraction $\frac{1}{3}$ names the same amount as $\frac{3}{9}$, so they are equivalent fractions.

Divide both the numerator and the denominator by the same number.

$$\frac{6}{8} = \frac{6 \div 2}{8 \div 2} = \frac{3}{4}$$

The fractions $\frac{6}{8}$ and $\frac{3}{4}$ are equal, so they are equivalent fractions.

Use the number lines to find out if the fractions are equivalent. Write *yes* or *no*.

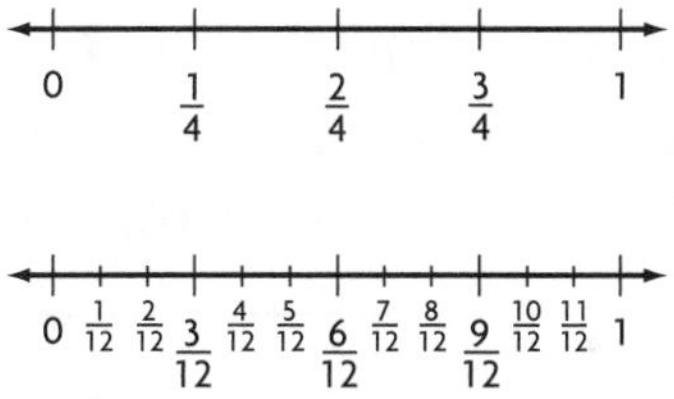

1. $\frac{1}{4} = \frac{3}{12}$ ______

2. $\frac{8}{12} = \frac{3}{4}$ ______

Multiply both the numerator and the denominator by the same number to name an equivalent fraction.

3. $\frac{3}{8} = \frac{3 \times 2}{8 \times 2} = \frac{\square}{\square}$

4. $\frac{2}{3} = \frac{2 \times 5}{3 \times 5} = \frac{\square}{\square}$

5. $\frac{1}{7} = \frac{1 \times 4}{7 \times 4} = \frac{\square}{\square}$

6. $\frac{4}{5} = \frac{4 \times 3}{5 \times 3} = \frac{\square}{\square}$

Divide both the numerator and the denominator by the same number to name an equivalent fraction.

7. $\frac{12}{16} = \frac{12 \div 4}{16 \div 4} = \frac{\square}{\square}$

8. $\frac{7}{28} = \frac{7 \div 7}{28 \div 7} = \frac{\square}{\square}$

9. $\frac{10}{15} = \frac{10 \div 5}{15 \div 5} = \frac{\square}{\square}$

10. $\frac{16}{24} = \frac{16 \div 8}{24 \div 8} = \frac{\square}{\square}$

Name ____

Simplest Form

You can use fraction bars to find the simplest form of a fraction.

Find the simplest form for $\frac{3}{12}$.

Step 1 Model $\frac{3}{12}$ with fraction bars.

Step 2 Line up other fraction bars to find all the equivalent fractions for $\frac{3}{12}$. You can see that $\frac{2}{8}$ and $\frac{1}{4}$ are equivalent fractions for $\frac{3}{12}$.

Step 3 The equivalent fraction that has the largest fraction bar possible is in the simplest form.

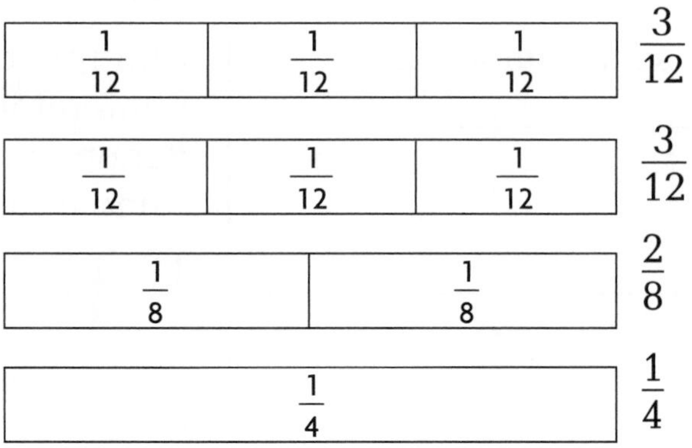

So, $\frac{1}{4}$ is the simplest form of $\frac{3}{12}$.

Use the fraction bar outlines below to model each fraction and equivalent fractions. Divide the outline into equal parts or keep it whole. Write the fraction in its simplest form.

1. $\frac{9}{12}$

______

______ Simplest form ______

______

2. $\frac{4}{12}$

______

______ Simplest form ______

______

Name ______________________________________

Understand Mixed Numbers

John drank $2\frac{3}{4}$ cartons of milk with his lunch.

The number $2\frac{3}{4}$ is a mixed number. A **mixed number** is made up of a whole number and a fraction.

In the mixed number $2\frac{3}{4}$, the whole number 2 represents two whole cartons of milk.

In the mixed number $2\frac{3}{4}$, the fraction $\frac{3}{4}$ represents a part of another carton.

You can divide all three cartons into 4 equal parts to show how many fourths John drank.

There are 11 shaded parts. Each part is $\frac{1}{4}$ carton.

So, John drank $\frac{11}{4}$, or $2\frac{3}{4}$, cartons of milk.

$2\frac{3}{4}$

↗ ↖

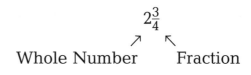

Whole Number Fraction

2 cartons

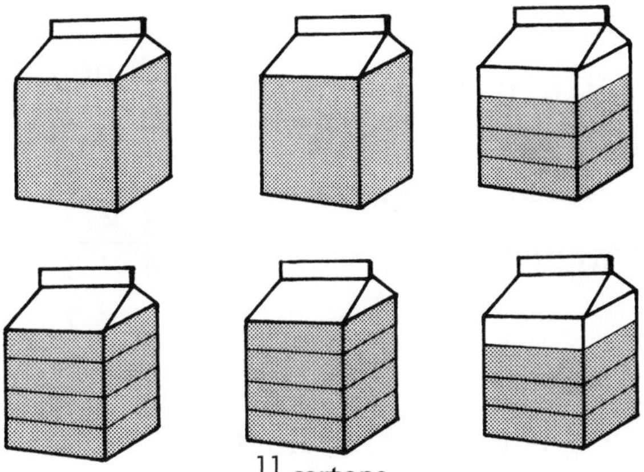

$\frac{11}{4}$ cartons

Write both a fraction and a mixed number for each figure.

1. 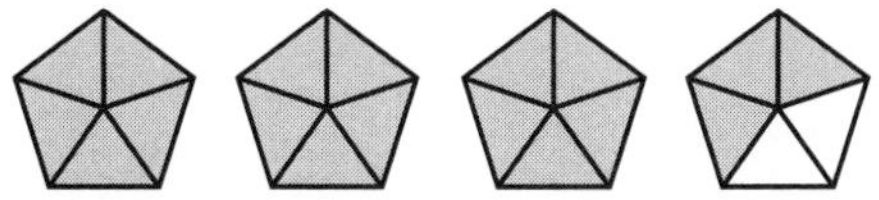

____

2. 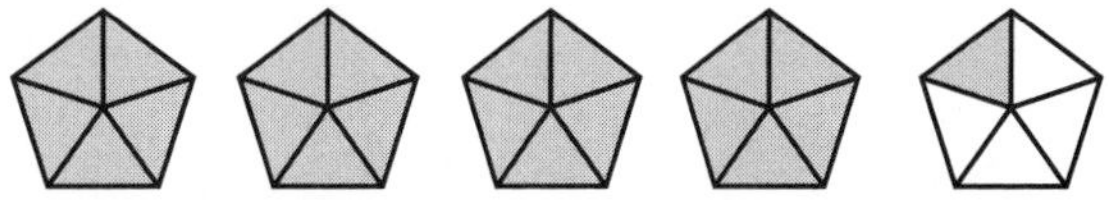

____

3. 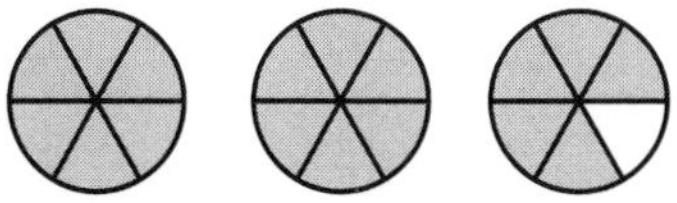

____

4. 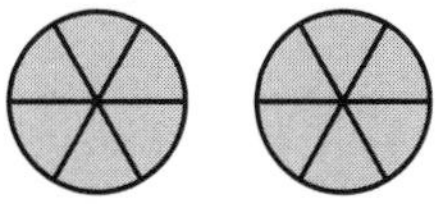

____

5. 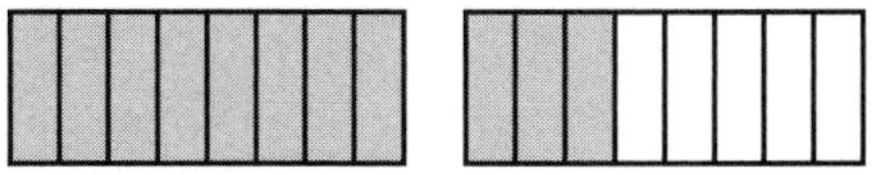

____

6. 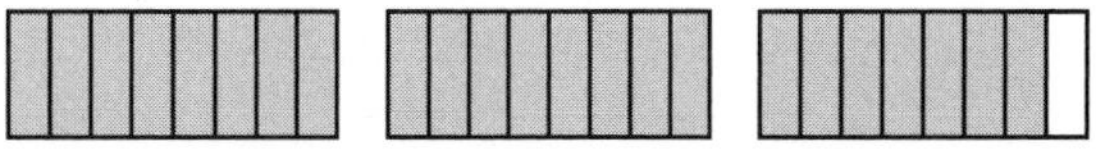

____

Name ______________________________

Compare and Order Fractions and Mixed Numbers

The three fractions $\frac{2}{3}$, $\frac{3}{4}$, and $\frac{2}{6}$ are arguing about who is the greatest. You can settle the argument by finding the least common multiple (LCM) for the denominators.

Step 1

Find the LCM of 3, 4, and 6.

3: 3, 6, 9, **12**, 15, 18
4: 4, 8, **12**, 16, 20
6: 6, **12**, 18, 24

The LCM is 12.

Step 2

Rename each fraction so that 12 is the denominator.

$$\frac{2 \times 4}{3 \times 4} = \frac{8}{12}$$

$$\frac{3 \times 3}{4 \times 3} = \frac{9}{12}$$

$$\frac{2 \times 2}{6 \times 2} = \frac{4}{12}$$

Step 3

Compare the numerators. Put them in order from least to greatest.

$$\frac{4}{12} < \frac{8}{12} < \frac{9}{12}$$

$$\downarrow \quad \downarrow \quad \downarrow$$

$$\frac{2}{6} < \frac{2}{3} < \frac{3}{4}$$

So, $\frac{3}{4}$ is the largest fraction.

To compare mixed numbers, first compare the whole number part. $5\frac{1}{4} > 3\frac{7}{8}$ because $5 > 3$. If the whole number parts are the same, then compare the fractions.

Compare. Write <, >, or = in each ◯.

1. $\frac{1}{5}$ ◯ $\frac{1}{4}$
2. $\frac{3}{10}$ ◯ $\frac{2}{5}$
3. $\frac{2}{6}$ ◯ $\frac{1}{9}$
4. $\frac{3}{8}$ ◯ $\frac{1}{6}$
5. $4\frac{2}{3}$ ◯ $4\frac{5}{6}$
6. $1\frac{3}{5}$ ◯ $1\frac{1}{2}$
7. $3\frac{2}{7}$ ◯ $3\frac{5}{14}$
8. $8\frac{1}{3}$ ◯ $8\frac{5}{12}$

Write in order from least to greatest.

9. $\frac{2}{5}, \frac{3}{4}, \frac{5}{7}$ ______________
10. $4\frac{2}{9}, 4\frac{1}{3}, 4\frac{1}{2}$ ______________
11. $\frac{1}{2}, \frac{1}{5}, 1\frac{1}{8}$ ______________
12. $\frac{1}{2}, \frac{2}{5}, \frac{2}{3}$ ______________
13. $1\frac{1}{4}, 1\frac{1}{6}, \frac{7}{8}$ ______________
14. $3\frac{3}{4}, 3\frac{7}{8}, 3\frac{2}{3}$ ______________

Name ____________________

Problem Solving Strategy

Make a Model

Trisha spent $\frac{3}{4}$ hour on math homework, $\frac{3}{8}$ hour on science, and $\frac{1}{2}$ hour on language arts. Which homework did she spend the most time on?

You can *make a model* to solve this problem.

Step 1 For each fraction, draw a box. Shade the box to show the fraction.

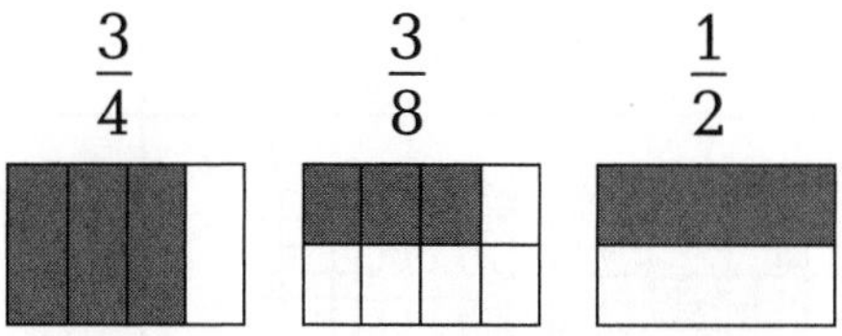

Step 2 Find the LCD, and divide each box into that many equal parts.

The LCD is 8.

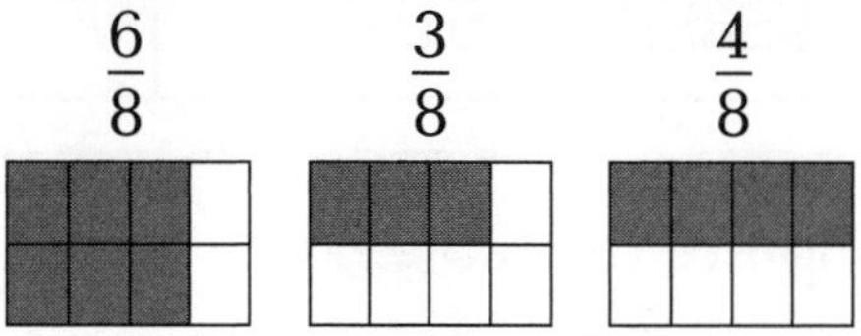

Step 3 Compare the numerators. $\frac{6}{8}$ is the greatest fraction.

So, Trisha spent the most time on math homework.

Make a model to solve.

1. Joe loves to cook. Last weekend he used flour in three different recipes. The amounts were $\frac{3}{4}$ cup, $\frac{2}{4}$ cup, and $\frac{1}{4}$ cup. What was the least amount called for?

   ____

2. Karen walked $\frac{5}{6}$ of a mile from her house to a friend's house. Joe walked $\frac{7}{12}$ of a mile to his friend's house. Who walked a greater distance?

   ____

3. Nick bought $\frac{2}{3}$ pound ground beef, $\frac{11}{12}$ pound ground turkey, and $\frac{3}{4}$ pound ground veal. Which meat did he buy the most of?

   ____

4. In the store display, $\frac{2}{5}$ of the T-shirts were yellow and $\frac{1}{4}$ were blue. Were there more yellow or blue T-shirts?

   ____

Name ____________________

LESSON 15.6

Relate Fractions and Decimals

You can write a fraction or a decimal to tell what part is shaded.

Model	Fraction	Decimal		
		O	T	H
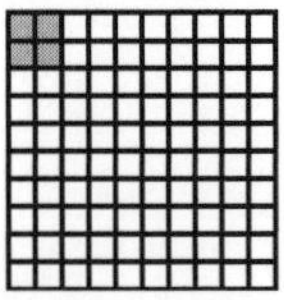	$\frac{\text{4 shaded parts}}{\text{100 parts}} = \frac{4}{100} = \frac{1}{25}$	0 •	0	4
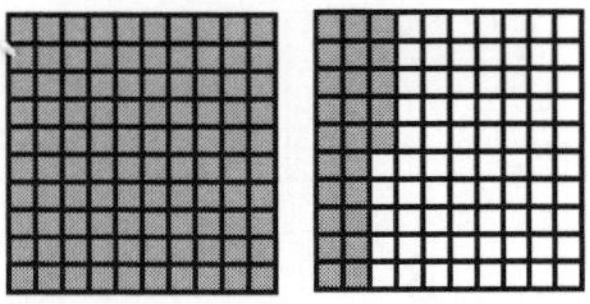	$1 \text{ whole} + \frac{\text{25 shaded parts}}{\text{100 parts}}$ $= 1 + \frac{25}{100} = 1\frac{25}{100} = 1\frac{1}{4}$	1 •	2	5

Complete the table.

Model	Fraction	Decimal		
		O	T	H
1. 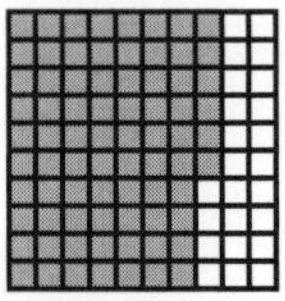		•		
2. 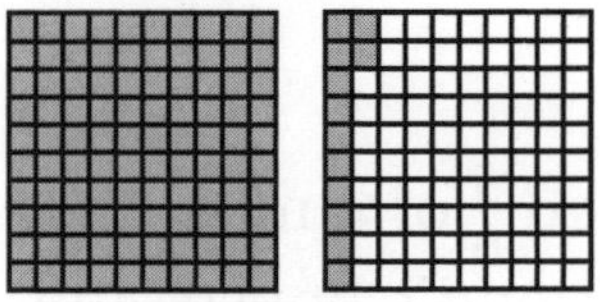		•		
3. 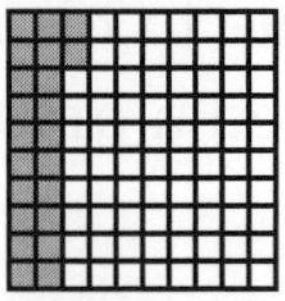		•		
4. 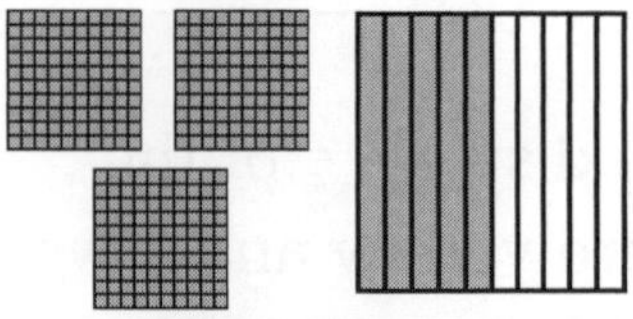		•		
5. 		•		

Name ______________________________

Add and Subtract Like Fractions

The denominators must be the same when adding or subtracting fractions.

Add $\frac{2}{6} + \frac{1}{6}$.

Step 1

Are the denominators the same? Yes.

$$\begin{array}{r} \frac{2}{6} \\ +\frac{1}{6} \\ \hline \end{array}$$

Step 2

Add the numerators. The denominator stays the same.

$$\begin{array}{rll} \frac{2}{6} & \leftarrow & 2 \text{ sixths} \\ +\frac{1}{6} & \leftarrow + & 1 \text{ sixth} \\ \hline & & 3 \text{ sixths} \end{array}$$

Step 3

Write the sum over the denominator. Write it in simplest form.

$$\begin{array}{r} \frac{2}{6} \\ +\frac{1}{6} \\ \hline \frac{3}{6} = \frac{1}{2} \end{array}$$

So, $\frac{2}{6} + \frac{1}{6} = \frac{1}{2}$.

To subtract like fractions, subtract the numerators. Remember, the denominator stays the same. Then write the difference over the denominator.

Find the sum or difference. Write it in simplest form.

1. $\frac{1}{5} + \frac{2}{5}$ ____________

2. $\frac{3}{7} + \frac{2}{7}$ ____________

3. $\frac{4}{9} + \frac{2}{9}$ ____________

4. $\frac{8}{9} - \frac{7}{9}$ ____________

5. $\frac{7}{8} - \frac{1}{8}$ ____________

6. $\frac{9}{12} - \frac{5}{12}$ ____________

7. $\frac{2}{6} + \frac{3}{6}$ ____________

8. $\frac{1}{8} + \frac{3}{8}$ ____________

9. $\frac{6}{10} + \frac{3}{10}$ ____________

10. $\frac{6}{8} - \frac{1}{8}$ ____________

11. $\frac{4}{6} - \frac{1}{6}$ ____________

12. $\frac{7}{14} - \frac{4}{14}$ ____________

Add and Subtract Unlike Fractions

You can use fraction circles to help you add or subtract fractions with unlike denominators. To do this, you trade fraction-circle pieces for the fractions with unlike denominators for equivalent pieces for fractions with like denominators.

Example 1: Add. $\frac{1}{6} + \frac{2}{3}$

Step 1 Take a $\frac{1}{6}$ piece and two $\frac{1}{3}$ pieces to model the fractions with unlike denominators.

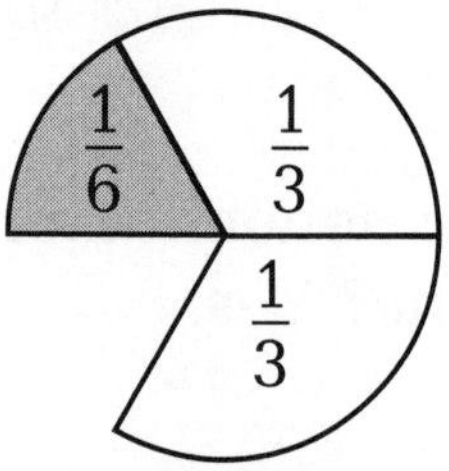

Step 2 Trade each $\frac{1}{3}$ piece for two $\frac{1}{6}$ pieces.

$\frac{1}{6} + \frac{2}{3} = \frac{1}{6} + \frac{4}{6}$

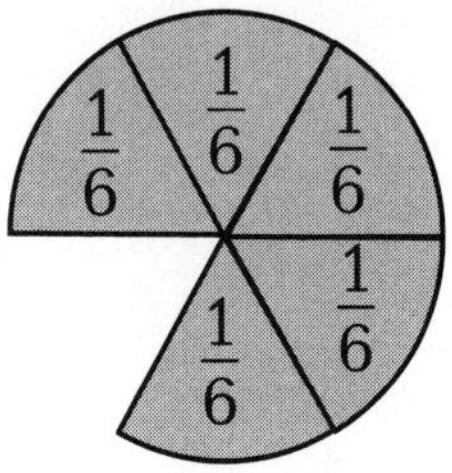

Step 3 Add the fractions with like denominators.

$\frac{1}{6} + \frac{4}{6} = \frac{5}{6}$ So, $\frac{1}{6} + \frac{2}{3} = \frac{5}{6}$

Example 2: Subtract. $\frac{1}{2} - \frac{1}{6}$

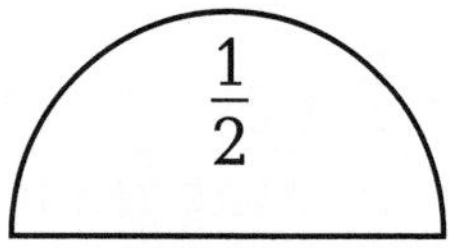

Step 1 Take a $\frac{1}{2}$ piece to model the first fraction.

Step 2 Trade the $\frac{1}{2}$ piece for three $\frac{1}{6}$ pieces.

$\frac{1}{2} - \frac{1}{6} = \frac{3}{6} - \frac{1}{6}$

Step 3 Subtract the fractions with like denominators.

$\frac{3}{6} - \frac{1}{6} = \frac{2}{6}$ So, $\frac{1}{2} - \frac{1}{6} = \frac{2}{6}$, or $\frac{1}{3}$

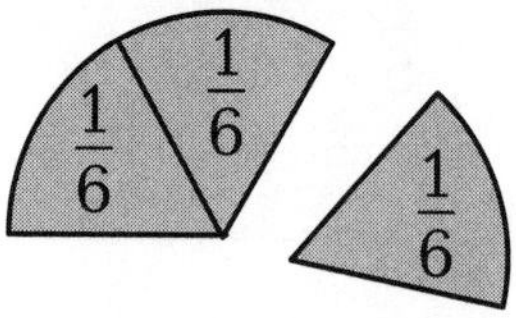

Use fraction pieces to find the sum or difference.

1. $\frac{1}{2} + \frac{1}{8}$ ________

2. $\frac{1}{3} + \frac{1}{6}$ ________

3. $\frac{1}{4} + \frac{5}{8}$ ________

4. $\frac{3}{8} + \frac{1}{2}$ ________

5. $\frac{3}{4} - \frac{1}{2}$ ________

6. $\frac{7}{8} - \frac{3}{4}$ ________

7. $\frac{5}{6} - \frac{1}{3}$ ________

8. $\frac{2}{3} - \frac{1}{6}$ ________

Name ______________________________

Estimate Sums and Differences

You can round fractions to 0, to $\frac{1}{2}$, or to 1 to estimate sums and differences.

Estimate the sum $\frac{3}{5} + \frac{8}{9}$.

Step 1 Find $\frac{3}{5}$ on the number line.
Is it closest to 0, $\frac{1}{2}$, or 1?
The fraction $\frac{3}{5}$ is closest to $\frac{1}{2}$.

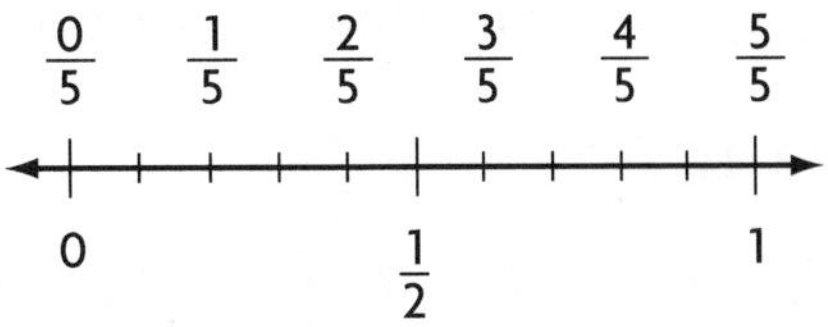

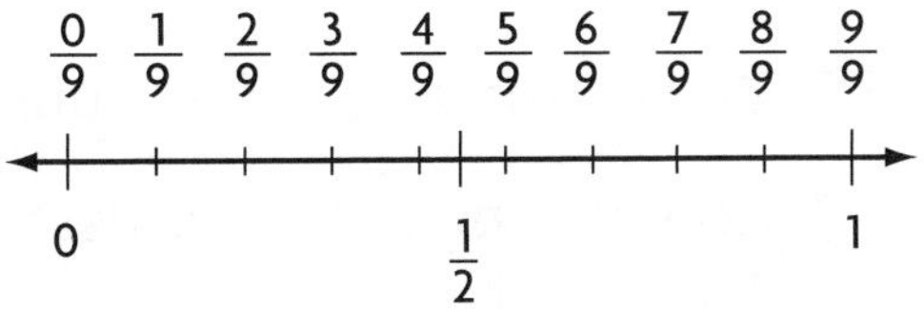

Step 2 Find $\frac{8}{9}$ on the number line.
Is it closest to 0, $\frac{1}{2}$, or 1?
The fraction $\frac{8}{9}$ is closest to 1.

Step 3 To estimate the sum $\frac{3}{5} + \frac{8}{9}$, add the two rounded numbers.

$\frac{1}{2} + 1 = 1\frac{1}{2}$

So, $\frac{3}{5} + \frac{8}{9}$ is about $1\frac{1}{2}$.

Use the number lines to estimate whether each fraction is closest to 0, to $\frac{1}{2}$, or to 1. Then find the sum or difference. The first one is done for you.

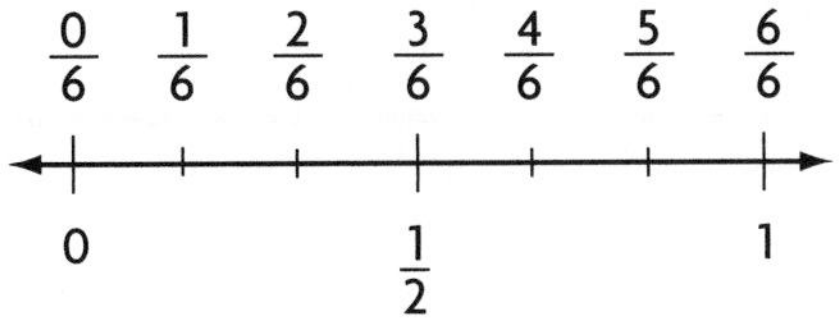

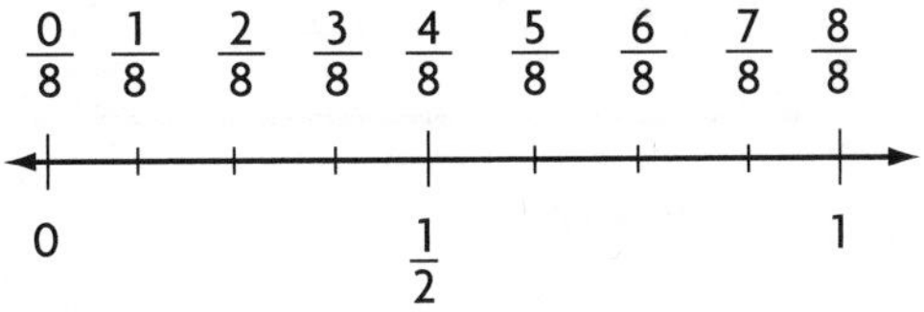

1. $\frac{4}{6} + \frac{1}{8}$

$\boxed{\frac{1}{2}} + \boxed{0}$

$\frac{1}{2}$

2. $\frac{2}{6} + \frac{7}{8}$

$\square + \square$

______

3. $\frac{5}{6} - \frac{3}{8}$

$\square - \square$

______

4. $\frac{4}{6} + \frac{3}{8}$

$\square + \square$

______

5. $\frac{7}{8} - \frac{5}{6}$

$\square - \square$

______

6. $\frac{1}{6} + \frac{7}{8}$

$\square + \square$

______

Name ________________________________

Use Common Denominators

To add or subtract unlike fractions, you need to rename them as like fractions. You can do this by making a list of equivalent fractions. When you find two fractions with the same denominator, they are like fractions.

Example 1: Add. $\frac{1}{4} + \frac{2}{5}$

Step 1 Write equivalent fractions for $\frac{1}{4}$. $\frac{1}{4}, \frac{2}{8}, \frac{3}{12}, \frac{4}{16}, \mathbf{\frac{5}{20}}, \frac{6}{24}$

Step 2 Write equivalent fractions for $\frac{2}{5}$. $\frac{2}{5}, \frac{4}{10}, \frac{6}{15}, \mathbf{\frac{8}{20}}$

Stop when you find 2 fractions with like denominators.

Step 3 Rewrite the problem using the equivalent fractions. Then add.

$$\frac{1}{4} + \frac{2}{5} = \frac{5}{20} + \frac{8}{20} = \frac{13}{20}$$

Example 2: Subtract. $\frac{7}{9} - \frac{1}{6}$

Step 1 Write equivalent fractions for $\frac{7}{9}$. $\frac{7}{9}, \mathbf{\frac{14}{18}}, \frac{21}{27}, \frac{28}{36}$

Step 2 Write equivalent fractions for $\frac{1}{6}$. $\frac{1}{6}, \frac{2}{12}, \mathbf{\frac{3}{18}}$

Stop when you find 2 fractions with like denominators.

Step 3 Rewrite the problem using the equivalent fractions. Then subtract.

$$\frac{7}{9} - \frac{1}{6} = \frac{14}{18} - \frac{3}{18} = \frac{11}{18}$$

Find the sum or difference.

1. $\frac{3}{5} + \frac{1}{3}$ ________

2. $\frac{1}{2} + \frac{2}{5}$ ________

3. $\frac{1}{4} + \frac{1}{6}$ ________

4. $\frac{1}{5} + \frac{3}{4}$ ________

5. $\frac{7}{8} - \frac{1}{4}$ ________

6. $\frac{3}{4} - \frac{2}{3}$ ________

7. $\frac{9}{10} - \frac{4}{5}$ ________

8. $\frac{8}{9} - \frac{5}{6}$ ________

Name ______________________________

Use the Least Common Denominator

When you add or subtract two fractions with unlike denominators, you need to make the denominators the same. Find the least common denominator (LCD), and change the fractions to like fractions.

Add. $\frac{2}{3} + \frac{1}{4} = n$

Step 1

Find the multiples of both denominators to determine the LCM.

$3 = 3, 6, 9, 12, \ldots$

$4 = 4, 8, 12, 16, \ldots$

The LCM of 3 and 4 is 12. So, the LCD of $\frac{2}{3}$ and $\frac{1}{4}$ is 12.

Step 2

Use the LCD to make like fractions. Multiply the numerator and denominator by the same number.

$$\frac{2}{3} = \frac{2 \times 4}{3 \times 4} = \frac{8}{12}$$

$$+\frac{1}{4} = \frac{1 \times 3}{4 \times 3} = \frac{3}{12}$$

Step 3

Add the fractions.

$$\frac{8}{12} + \frac{3}{12} = \frac{11}{12}$$

So, $n = \frac{11}{12}$.

So, the sum of $\frac{2}{3} + \frac{1}{4} = \frac{11}{12}$. This answer is in simplest form.

To subtract fractions with unlike denominators, follow these 3 steps. However, in Step 3, subtract the fractions and write the answer in simplest form.

Write like fractions. Then find the sum or difference. Write the answer in simplest form.

1. $\frac{1}{3} = \frac{1 \times \square}{3 \times \square} = \frac{\square}{\square}$

$+\frac{4}{9} = \frac{\square}{\square}$

$\frac{\square}{\square}$

Simplest form: ________

2. $\frac{1}{2} = \frac{1 \times \square}{2 \times \square} = \frac{\square}{\square}$

$-\frac{2}{5} = \frac{2 \times \square}{5 \times \square} = \frac{\square}{\square}$

$\frac{\square}{\square}$

Simplest form: ________

3. $\frac{3}{9} = \frac{3 \times \square}{9 \times \square} = \frac{\square}{\square}$

$+\frac{1}{6} = \frac{1 \times \square}{6 \times \square} = \frac{\square}{\square}$

$\frac{\square}{\square}$

Simplest form: ________

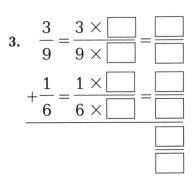

Name ______________________

Problem Solving Strategy

Work Backward

The students in Jason's class started measuring their heights at the beginning of January. By March 1, Jason had grown $\frac{3}{4}$ inch. In February, Jason grew $\frac{3}{8}$ inch. How much did he grow in January?

You can solve the problem by working backward.

Start with the amount he had grown by March 1, and subtract the amount he grew in February.

Find $\frac{3}{4} - \frac{3}{8}$ by using the LCD method.

The LCD of 4 and 8 is 8. Change each fraction into eighths, and subtract the numerators.

$\frac{3}{4} \times \boxed{\frac{2}{2}} = \frac{6}{8}$ $\frac{3}{8} \times \boxed{\frac{1}{1}} = \frac{3}{8}$ $\frac{6}{8} - \frac{3}{8} = \frac{3}{8}$

So, Jason grew $\frac{3}{8}$ inch in January.

Work backward to solve.

1. Paula is in Jason's class. By March 1, she had grown $\frac{7}{8}$ inch. In February, she grew $\frac{1}{4}$ inch. How much did she grow in January?

____

2. Sid is in Jason's class. By April 1, he had grown $\frac{15}{16}$ inch. In March, he grew $\frac{1}{8}$ inch, and in February, he grew $\frac{3}{8}$ inch. How much did he grow in January?

____

3. Harry started the day by trading 5 of his comic books for 7 of Jenny's. Next, he bought 8 at the store. Then he gave Tom 9 comic books. Harry came home with 12 comic books. How many did Harry start the day with?

____

4. Wesley started with his favorite number. Then he subtracted 7 from it. He multiplied this difference by 3 and then added 5. Finally, he divided this number by 11. His end result was 1. What is Wesley's favorite number?

____

Name ____________________

Add Mixed Numbers

Fred and Gregg are going to put up a tent. They need two pieces of rope to secure the tent. One has to be $3\frac{1}{4}$ feet long and the other $2\frac{1}{2}$ feet long. How much rope do they need?

To find the answer, you must add $3\frac{1}{4} + 2\frac{1}{2}$.

You can add mixed numbers by following these steps.

Step 1

Add the whole numbers. $3 + 2 = 5$

Step 2

Find the LCD. Write equivalent fractions. Add the fractions.

multiples of 4: (4,) 8, 12

multiples of 2: 2, (4,) 6

$\frac{1 \times 1}{4 \times 1} = \frac{1}{4}$ $\frac{1 \times 2}{2 \times 2} = \frac{2}{4}$

$\frac{1}{4} + \frac{1}{2} =$

$\frac{1}{4} + \frac{2}{4} = \frac{3}{4}$

Step 3

Add the sum of the whole numbers to the sum of the fractions. Write the answer in simplest form if needed.

$5 + \frac{3}{4} = 5\frac{3}{4}$

So, $3\frac{1}{4} + 2\frac{1}{2} = 5\frac{3}{4}$.

Find the sum in simplest form.

1. $3\frac{5}{8} + 2\frac{1}{8}$

2. $6\frac{1}{3} + 2\frac{1}{12}$

3. $4\frac{1}{4} + 2\frac{1}{4}$

4. $5\frac{3}{7} + 1\frac{3}{7}$

5. $7\frac{1}{2} + 2\frac{1}{3}$

6. $4\frac{3}{5} + 2\frac{1}{10}$

7. $4\frac{1}{2} + 3\frac{3}{8}$

8. $3\frac{3}{4} + 2\frac{1}{8}$

Name ______________________________

Subtract Mixed Numbers

Sonia cut out a pattern for a new skirt from $3\frac{1}{2}$ yards of fabric. The pattern used $2\frac{1}{3}$ yards. How much material was left?

You can answer the question by subtracting, $3\frac{1}{2} - 2\frac{1}{3}$.

To subtract mixed numbers, follow these steps.

Step 1

Find the LCD of the fractions by listing the multiples of each number.

Multiples of 2: 2, 4, (6,) 8, 10

Multiples of 3: 3, (6,) 9, 12, 15

Since 6 is the first common multiple, it is the least common multiple.

Step 2

Change the fractions into like fractions with 6 as the denominator.

$$\frac{1 \times 3}{2 \times 3} = \frac{3}{6} \qquad \frac{1 \times 2}{3 \times 2} = \frac{2}{6}$$

Step 3

Subtract the fractions.

$$\begin{array}{rcr} 3\frac{1}{2} & = & 3\frac{3}{6} \\ -2\frac{1}{3} & = & -2\frac{2}{6} \\ \hline & & \frac{1}{6} \end{array}$$

Step 4

Subtract the whole numbers.

$$\begin{array}{rcr} 3\frac{1}{2} & = & 3\frac{3}{6} \\ -2\frac{1}{3} & = & -2\frac{2}{6} \\ \hline & & 1\frac{1}{6} \end{array}$$

So, Sonia has $1\frac{1}{6}$ yards left.

Find the difference in simplest form.

1. $$\begin{array}{rcr} 4\frac{4}{5} & = & 4\frac{8}{10} \\ -1\frac{1}{10} & = & -1\frac{1}{10} \\ \hline \end{array}$$

2. $$\begin{array}{rcr} 6\frac{2}{3} & = & 6\frac{4}{6} \\ -4\frac{1}{6} & = & -4\frac{1}{6} \\ \hline \end{array}$$

3. $$\begin{array}{rcr} 7\frac{3}{4} & = & 7\frac{9}{12} \\ -4\frac{5}{12} & = & -4\frac{5}{12} \\ \hline \end{array}$$

4. $$\begin{array}{rcr} 8\frac{1}{3} & = & 8\frac{4}{12} \\ -1\frac{1}{4} & = & -1\frac{3}{12} \\ \hline \end{array}$$

5. $$\begin{array}{rcr} 2\frac{7}{8} & = & 2\frac{7}{8} \\ -1\frac{1}{2} & = & -1\frac{4}{8} \\ \hline \end{array}$$

6. $$\begin{array}{rcr} 6\frac{7}{9} & = & 6\frac{7}{9} \\ -4\frac{2}{3} & = & -4\frac{6}{9} \\ \hline \end{array}$$

Name ____ LESSON 17.3

Subtraction with Renaming

Wayne had $4\frac{1}{4}$ feet of rope. He gave $2\frac{2}{3}$ feet to his friend. How much rope did he have left?

You can answer the question by subtracting, $4\frac{1}{4} - 2\frac{2}{3}$.

To subtract mixed numbers, follow these steps.

Step 1

Find the LCD.

Multiples of 4: 4, 8, (12,) 16

Multiples of 3: 3, 6, 9, (12)

So, 12 is the LCD.

Step 2

Change each fraction into a fraction with the denominator 12.

$$\frac{1 \times 3}{4 \times 3} = \frac{3}{12}$$

$$\frac{2 \times 4}{3 \times 4} = \frac{8}{12}$$

Step 3

Replace the unlike fractions with the like fractions.

$$\begin{array}{rcr} 4\frac{1}{4} & = & 4\frac{3}{12} \\ -2\frac{2}{3} & = & -2\frac{8}{12} \\ \hline \end{array}$$

Step 4

Rename 1 whole from 4 to subtract the fractions. Rename the 1 as $\frac{12}{12}$.

$$\begin{array}{rcr} 4\frac{3}{12} & = & 3\frac{15}{12} \\ -2\frac{8}{12} & = & -2\frac{8}{12} \\ \hline \end{array} \qquad \frac{12}{12} + \frac{3}{12} = \frac{15}{12}$$

Step 5

Subtract the fractions.

$$\begin{array}{rcr} 4\frac{3}{12} & = & 3\frac{15}{12} \\ -2\frac{8}{12} & = & -2\frac{8}{12} \\ \hline & & \frac{7}{12} \end{array}$$

Step 6

Subtract the whole numbers.

$$\begin{array}{rcr} 4\frac{3}{12} & = & 3\frac{15}{12} \\ -2\frac{8}{12} & = & -2\frac{8}{12} \\ \hline & & 1\frac{7}{12} \end{array}$$

So, Wayne has $1\frac{7}{12}$ feet left.

Find the difference in simplest form.

1. $\begin{array}{r} 5\frac{1}{4} \\ -\ \frac{1}{2} \\ \hline \end{array}$

2. $\begin{array}{r} 6\frac{1}{8} \\ -2\frac{1}{4} \\ \hline \end{array}$

3. $\begin{array}{r} 5\frac{3}{10} \\ -1\ \frac{3}{5} \\ \hline \end{array}$

4. $\begin{array}{r} 4\frac{1}{6} \\ -2\frac{2}{3} \\ \hline \end{array}$

Name ______________________________

Practice with Mixed Numbers

Larry made $2\frac{5}{6}$ pounds of baked ziti. He and his brother ate $1\frac{1}{3}$ pounds. How much was left over? Use fraction bars to find the answer.

Subtract. $2\frac{5}{6} - 1\frac{1}{3}$ Estimate: about $1\frac{1}{2}$ pounds

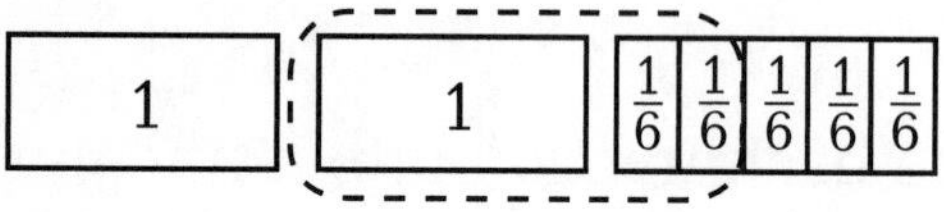

$2\frac{5}{6} - 1\frac{1}{3} = 1\frac{3}{6}$, or $1\frac{1}{2}$ pounds

---

Add or subtract. Write the answer in simplest form. Estimate to check.

1. $3\frac{13}{15} + 2\frac{1}{5}$

2. $1\frac{5}{12} + 2\frac{1}{6}$

3. $5\frac{3}{4} - 3\frac{7}{8}$

4. $6\frac{2}{3} - 1\frac{10}{12}$

5. $2\frac{3}{8} + 4\frac{7}{8}$

6. $9\frac{4}{5} - 2\frac{2}{3}$

7. $7\frac{1}{12} - 2\frac{1}{6}$

8. $4\frac{2}{5} + 1\frac{1}{3}$

Algebra Find the value of *n*.

9. $3\frac{1}{2} + n = 5$ ______________

10. $n - 4\frac{1}{8} = 6\frac{1}{2}$ ______________

11. $4\frac{6}{7} - n = 2\frac{1}{7}$ ______________

12. $n + 11\frac{1}{6} = 15\frac{1}{3}$ ______________

Name ______________________________

Problem Solving Skill

Multistep Problems

Hank bought a piece of wood that was 8 feet long. He used $1\frac{1}{4}$ feet for a shelf in his room and $2\frac{1}{4}$ feet for a shelf in his sister's room. Then he made a box using another $3\frac{1}{4}$ feet. How much of the wood does he have left?

You can solve the problem by doing more than one operation. First add the $1\frac{1}{4}$ feet for his shelf, the $2\frac{1}{4}$ feet for his sister's shelf, and the $3\frac{1}{4}$ feet for his box.

$$\begin{array}{r} 1\frac{1}{4} \\ 2\frac{1}{4} \\ +3\frac{1}{4} \\ \hline 6\frac{3}{4} \end{array}$$

Then subtract the total amount of $6\frac{3}{4}$ feet from the 8 feet he bought. $8 - 6\frac{3}{4} = 1\frac{1}{4}$

So, Hank has $1\frac{1}{4}$ feet of wood left.

Solve.

1. Ralph bought 12 feet of wood. He made four projects. The first one used $3\frac{1}{2}$ feet, the second one used $2\frac{1}{4}$ feet, the third one used $2\frac{3}{4}$ feet, and the fourth one used $1\frac{1}{4}$ feet. How much wood did he have left?

   ____

2. Nancy read every day for five days. She read 8 pages on Monday, 12 pages on Tuesday, 25 pages on Thursday, and 40 pages on Friday. If she read a total of 156 pages, how many pages did she read on Wednesday?

   ____

3. On Monday Charley drove 32 miles, on Tuesday 58 miles, on Wednesday 88 miles, and on Thursday 94 miles. His total for five days was 335 miles. How far did he drive on Friday?

   ____

4. Lacy was serving pizza at a party. She gave the first person $\frac{1}{8}$ of the pizza, the second person $\frac{3}{8}$, and the third person $\frac{1}{4}$ of the pizza. How much of the pizza was left?

   ____

Name ______________________________

Multiply a Fraction by a Fraction

Multiply. $\frac{3}{4} \times \frac{3}{5}$

To multiply fractions you can use a rectangle model. Follow these guidelines:

- Draw a rectangle, and divide the rectangle into 5 equal columns. This is for the denominator of $\frac{3}{5}$.
- Shade 3 of the columns. This is for the numerator of $\frac{3}{5}$.

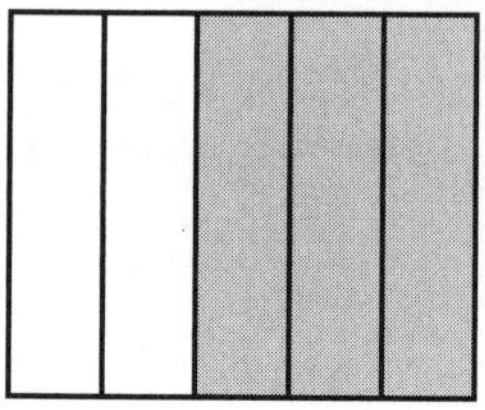

- Divide the rectangle into 4 equal rows. This is for the denominator of $\frac{3}{4}$.
- Shade 3 of the rows with diagonal lines. This is for the numerator of $\frac{3}{4}$.

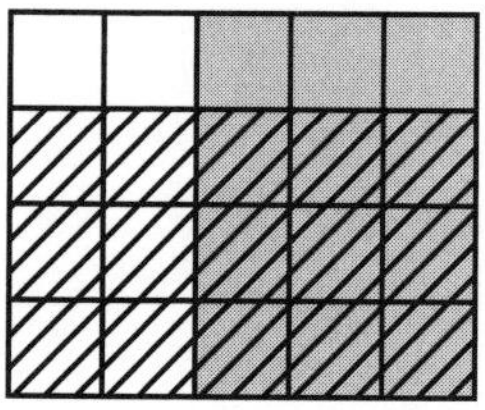

- Count how many pieces the rectangle is divided into. There are 20 pieces. This is the new denominator.
- Count how many pieces have overlapping lines and shading. There are 9. This is the new numerator.

So, $\frac{3}{4} \times \frac{3}{5} = \frac{9}{20}$.

Divide and shade a rectangle model to find the product.

1. $\frac{1}{3} \times \frac{5}{6} =$ ______

2. $\frac{5}{8} \times \frac{3}{4} =$ ______

3. $\frac{1}{4} \times \frac{3}{8} =$ ______

4. $\frac{2}{5} \times \frac{1}{3} =$ ______

5. $\frac{1}{2} \times \frac{7}{8} =$ ______

6. $\frac{5}{6} \times \frac{3}{4} =$ ______

7. $\frac{1}{4} \times \frac{5}{6} =$ ______

8. $\frac{2}{3} \times \frac{1}{4} =$ ______

9. $\frac{2}{7} \times \frac{3}{4} =$ ______

10. $\frac{3}{5} \times \frac{3}{5} =$ ______

11. $\frac{4}{5} \times \frac{1}{2} =$ ______

12. $\frac{5}{9} \times \frac{1}{2} =$ ______

Name ____

Multiply Fractions and Whole Numbers

Hector had 12 baseball cards. He gave $\frac{2}{3}$ of them to his friend Ned. How many baseball cards did he give to Ned?

You can answer the question by multiplying $\frac{2}{3} \times 12$. To multiply a fraction and a whole number you can use a model:

Step 1 Draw 12 rectangles to show the cards.

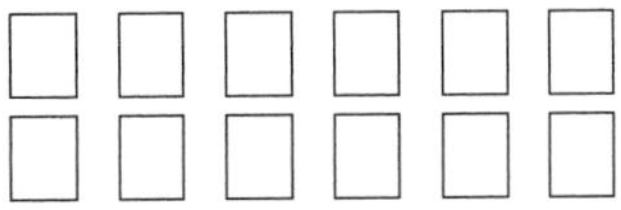

Step 2 The denominator of the fraction $\frac{2}{3}$ is 3. This means there are 3 equal parts, so divide the rectangles into 3 equal groups.

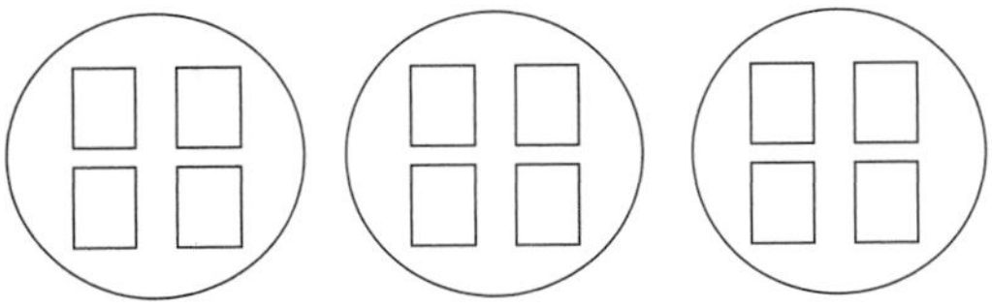

Step 3 The numerator of the fraction $\frac{2}{3}$ is 2. This means there are 2 parts given, so shade 2 of the groups.

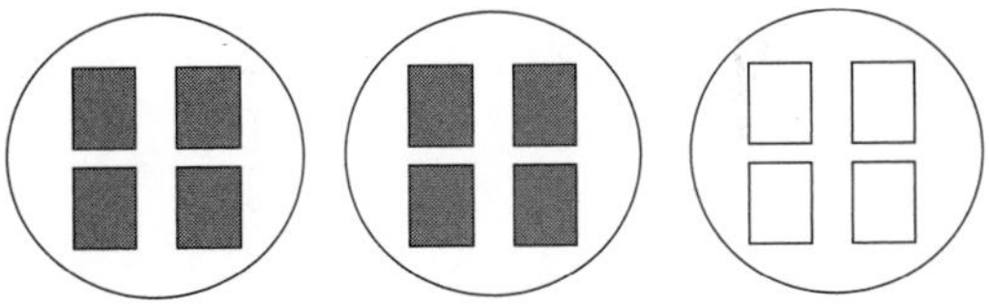

Step 4 Count the shaded rectangles, or cards. There are 8 cards.

So, $\frac{2}{3} \times 12 = 8$.

Write the number sentence each model represents.

1. 

____

2. 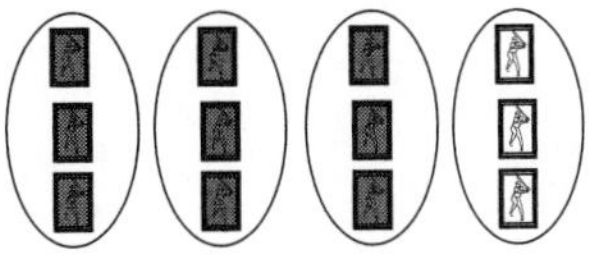

____

3. 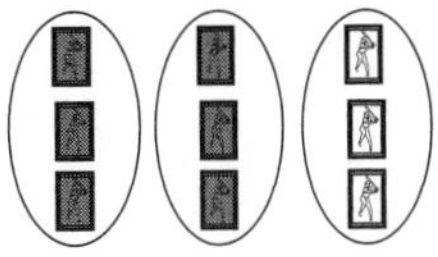

____

Draw a picture to help you multiply. Find the product.

4. $\frac{4}{9} \times 27 =$ ________

5. $\frac{1}{6} \times 12 =$ ________

6. $\frac{3}{5} \times 20 =$ ________

Name ___________________________

Multiply Fractions and Mixed Numbers

Multiply. $\frac{2}{3} \times 2\frac{1}{4}$

You can find the product by using the Distributive Property. The Distributive Property allows you to break apart numbers to multiply.

To multiply a fraction and a mixed number, break apart the mixed number.

$$\frac{2}{3} \times 2\frac{1}{4} = \frac{2}{3} \times \left(2 + \frac{1}{4}\right) \quad \longleftarrow \text{Break apart the mixed number.}$$

$$= \left(\frac{2}{3} \times 2\right) + \left(\frac{2}{3} \times \frac{1}{4}\right) \quad \longleftarrow \text{Multiply each part.}$$

$$= \frac{4}{3} + \frac{2}{12}$$

$$= \frac{16}{12} + \frac{2}{12} \quad \longleftarrow \text{Find the LCD and rename the fractions.}$$

$$= \frac{18}{12} = 1\frac{1}{2} \quad \longleftarrow \text{Add the products. Simplify the sum.}$$

So, $\frac{2}{3} \times 2\frac{1}{4} = 1\frac{1}{2}$.

Multiply. Write the answer in simplest form.

1. $\frac{1}{3} \times 3\frac{1}{5} =$ ____________

2. $\frac{1}{2} \times 2\frac{3}{4} =$ ____________

3. $\frac{1}{6} \times 3\frac{2}{3} =$ ____________

4. $\frac{1}{4} \times 2\frac{5}{6} =$ ____________

5. $\frac{1}{3} \times 3\frac{1}{2} =$ ____________

6. $\frac{1}{8} \times 4\frac{1}{4} =$ ____________

7. $\frac{3}{8} \times 1\frac{1}{4} =$ ____________

8. $\frac{4}{5} \times 2\frac{1}{2} =$ ____________

Name ____________________

Multiply with Mixed Numbers

Multiply. $1\frac{2}{3} \times 1\frac{1}{2}$

To multiply two mixed numbers, follow the same steps you use to multiply a fraction and a mixed number.

Step 1

Write each mixed number as a fraction.

$$1\frac{2}{3} = \frac{(3 \times 1) + 2}{3} = \frac{5}{3}$$

$$1\frac{1}{2} = \frac{(2 \times 1) + 1}{2} = \frac{3}{2}$$

Step 2

Multiply the fractions,

$$\frac{5 \times 3}{3 \times 2} = \frac{15}{6}$$

or cancel the 3 in the numerator and denominator.

$$\frac{5 \times \overset{1}{\cancel{3}}}{\underset{1}{\cancel{3}} \times 2} = \frac{5}{2}$$

Step 3

Write the product as a mixed number in simplest form.

$$\frac{15}{6} = 2\frac{3}{6} = 2\frac{1}{2}$$

or

$$\frac{5}{2} = 2\frac{1}{2}$$

Multiply. Write the answer in simplest form.

1. $2\frac{1}{2} \times 1\frac{1}{5} =$ ____________

2. $1\frac{1}{3} \times 1\frac{1}{2} =$ ____________

3. $1\frac{1}{2} \times 1\frac{1}{4} =$ ____________

4. $1\frac{3}{4} \times 3\frac{1}{2} =$ ____________

5. $6\frac{1}{2} \times 1\frac{3}{5} =$ ____________

6. $1\frac{2}{3} \times 1\frac{2}{3} =$ ____________

7. $1\frac{1}{5} \times 1\frac{1}{2} =$ ____________

8. $2\frac{1}{2} \times 1\frac{3}{5} =$ ____________

Problem Solving Skill

Sequence and Prioritize Information

The Perez family planned an evening event that includes a snack, dinner, dessert, and game time.

There are 6 hours planned for the evening. $\frac{1}{3}$ of the evening's time will be devoted to dinner. $\frac{1}{6}$ of the time will be spent on having a snack. How many hours will be spent on playing games and dessert?

Sequencing the information may help you solve this problem. Start with events for which you have some information.

Event	Time
Dinner	6 hours total $\times \frac{1}{3} =$ 2 hours for dinner
Snack	6 hours total $\times \frac{1}{6} =$ 1 hour for snacks

Now subtract the snack and dinner time to find how much time can be devoted to games and dessert.

Event	Time
Games and Dessert	Total time spent on dinner and snacks $=$ 3 hours 6 hours total $-$ 3 hours for dinner and snacks $=$ 3 hours left for games and dessert

---

Sequence the information by starting with the information you know. Then solve the problem.

1. John drives a total of 350 miles a day. He makes 3 stops. He drives 150 miles to his first stop. From the second stop to the third stop, he drives 75 miles. How many miles does he drive from the first stop to the second stop?

   ____

2. Mary spent $45.00 altogether at the store. She bought some food for $32.75 and some school supplies. How much did she spend on school supplies?

   ____

Name ____________________

Explore Division of Fractions

You can use pictures to model division of fractions.

$$5 \div \frac{1}{3}$$

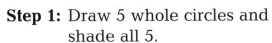

Step 1: Draw 5 whole circles and shade all 5.

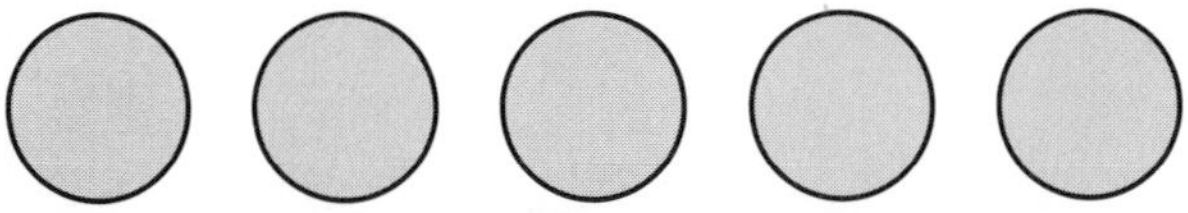

Step 2: Divide each circle into **thirds.**

Step 3: Count the number of shaded thirds.

There are 15 thirds in 5. So, $5 \div \frac{1}{3} = 15$.

$$\frac{4}{5} \div \frac{1}{10}$$

Step 1: Draw one whole rectangle and shade four fifths of it.

Step 2: Divide the rectangle into **tenths.**

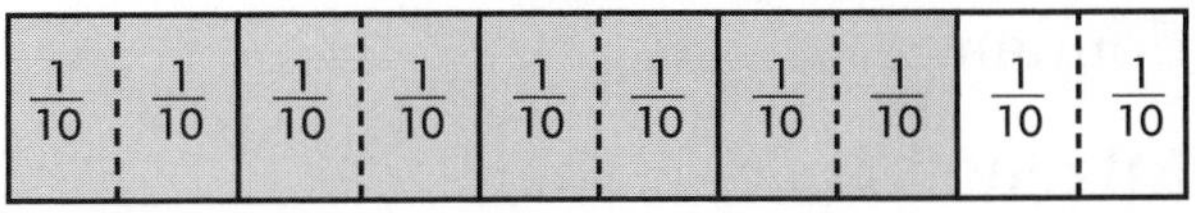

Step 3: Count the number of shaded tenths.

There are 8 tenths in $\frac{4}{5}$. So, $\frac{4}{5} \div \frac{1}{10} = 8$.

Draw a model for the division problem and find the quotient.

1. $\frac{2}{3} \div \frac{1}{9} =$ ________

2. $2 \div \frac{1}{5} =$ ________

3. $\frac{3}{4} \div \frac{1}{8} =$ ________

4. $3 \div \frac{1}{4} =$ ________

5. $\frac{1}{2} \div \frac{1}{8} =$ ________

6. $\frac{1}{3} \div \frac{1}{6} =$ ________

Name ____

Reciprocals

Reciprocals are two fractions that have a product of 1.

Fractions:

To find the reciprocal of a fraction, switch the numerator and denominator.

The reciprocal of $\frac{3}{8}$ is $\frac{8}{3}$.

$\frac{3}{8} \times \frac{8}{3} = \frac{24}{24} = 1$

Whole Numbers:

To find the reciprocal of a whole number, first write it as a fraction. Then switch the numerator and denominator.

$7 = \frac{7}{1}$.

The reciprocal of $\frac{7}{1}$ is $\frac{1}{7}$.

Mixed Numbers:

To find the reciprocal of a mixed number, first write it as a fraction. Then switch the numerator and denominator.

$5\frac{2}{3} = \frac{17}{3}$

The reciprocal of $\frac{17}{3}$ is $\frac{3}{17}$.

Are the two numbers reciprocals? Write *yes* or *no*.

1. $\frac{1}{9}$ and 19 ________

2. $\frac{3}{10}$ and $\frac{10}{3}$ ________

3. $1\frac{3}{5}$ and $\frac{8}{5}$ ________

4. 5 and $\frac{1}{5}$ ________

5. $\frac{5}{13}$ and $2\frac{3}{5}$ ________

6. $\frac{1}{10}$ and $\frac{1}{10}$ ________

7. $2\frac{1}{4}$ and $\frac{4}{9}$ ________

8. $\frac{7}{12}$ and $\frac{12}{7}$ ________

Write the reciprocal of each number.

9. $\frac{1}{7}$ ________

10. $\frac{5}{12}$ ________

11. 6 ________

12. $3\frac{5}{9}$ ________

13. $\frac{6}{5}$ ________

14. $\frac{2}{11}$ ________

15. 11 ________

16. $1\frac{3}{8}$ ________

17. $\frac{1}{2}$ ________

18. 100 ________

Name ________________________________

Divide Whole Numbers by Fractions

Beth is working on a science project. She needs pieces of wire that are $\frac{2}{3}$ yd long for the project. She bought a piece of wire that is 6 yd long at the hardware store.

How many $\frac{2}{3}$ pieces can she cut from this 6-yd piece?

Step 1: Write a division sentence to find this amount. $\frac{6}{1} \div \frac{2}{3}$ **Think:** Write 6 as $\frac{6}{1}$.

Step 2: Use the reciprocal of the divisor to write a multiplication problem. $\frac{6}{1} \times \frac{3}{2}$ **Think:** The reciprocal of $\frac{2}{3}$ is $\frac{3}{2}$.

Step 3: Multiply. $\frac{6}{1} \times \frac{3}{2} = \frac{18}{2} = 9$

So, Beth can cut 9 pieces of wire.

Use the reciprocal to write a multiplication problem. Solve the problem. Write the answer in simplest form.

1. $3 \div \frac{1}{8}$

$\frac{3}{1} \times \frac{8}{1} = 24$

2. $5 \div \frac{1}{2}$ ____________

3. $10 \div \frac{2}{3}$ ____________

4. $27 \div \frac{3}{5}$ ____________

5. $12 \div \frac{4}{5}$ ____________

6. $8 \div \frac{3}{4}$ ____________

7. $18 \div \frac{3}{8}$ ____________

8. $7 \div \frac{4}{5}$ ____________

9. $6 \div \frac{3}{4}$ ____________

10. $16 \div \frac{4}{5}$ ____________

11. $9 \div \frac{6}{7}$ ____________

12. $2 \div \frac{3}{10}$ ____________

13. $9 \div \frac{3}{8}$ ____________

14. $9 \div \frac{1}{5}$ ____________

15. $6 \div \frac{3}{20}$ ____________

16. $20 \div \frac{4}{5}$ ____________

Name ______________________________

Divide Fractions

Connie is working on a craft project. She needs $\frac{3}{8}$-yd pieces of ribbon for the project. She bought a $\frac{3}{4}$-yd piece of ribbon at the craft store.

How many $\frac{3}{8}$-yd pieces can she cut from $\frac{3}{4}$-yd piece?

Step 1: Write a division sentence to find this amount. $\frac{3}{4} \div \frac{3}{8}$

Step 2: Use the reciprocal of the divisor to write a multiplication problem. $\frac{3}{4} \times \frac{8}{3}$ **Think:** The reciprocal of $\frac{3}{8}$ is $\frac{8}{3}$.

Step 3: Multiply. $\frac{3}{4} \times \frac{8}{3} = \frac{24}{12} = 2$

So, Connie can cut 2 pieces of ribbon.

Use the reciprocal to write a multiplication problem. Solve the problem. Write the answer in simplest form.

1. $\frac{3}{8} \div 24$ ____________

2. $\frac{5}{9} \div \frac{2}{3}$ ____________

3. $\frac{4}{5} \div \frac{2}{3}$ ____________

4. $\frac{5}{12} \div \frac{5}{8}$ ____________

5. $\frac{5}{6} \div \frac{1}{3}$ ____________

6. $\frac{5}{8} \div \frac{3}{4}$ ____________

7. $\frac{4}{5} \div 6$ ____________

8. $1\frac{1}{15} \div 7$ ____________

9. $2\frac{1}{4} \div \frac{1}{3}$ ____________

10. $1\frac{1}{4} \div 2\frac{1}{3}$ ____________

11. $\frac{1}{3} \div \frac{1}{2}$ ____________

12. $1\frac{1}{3} \div 1\frac{1}{2}$ ____________

13. $\frac{1}{2} \div \frac{1}{4}$ ____________

14. $\frac{3}{4} \div 1\frac{1}{4}$ ____________

15. $\frac{5}{6} \div \frac{1}{3}$ ____________

16. $1\frac{2}{3} \div \frac{1}{3}$ ____________

Name ____

Problem Solving Strategy

Solve a Simpler Problem

The bank gave Jim a loan of \$4,000. This is $\frac{1}{8}$ of the amount they gave him last year. How much did the bank loan Jim last year?

You can solve a more difficult problem by first solving a simpler one.

Step 1: If you can, change the numbers so that they are easier to work with.

Let 4 represent 4,000.

Step 2: Write the problem, using the new number.

$4 \div \frac{1}{8} = \frac{4}{1} \times \frac{8}{1}$ **Think:** The reciprocal of $\frac{1}{8}$ is $\frac{8}{1}$.

Step 3: Solve the problem, using the new number.

$\frac{4}{1} \times \frac{8}{1} = 32$

Step 4: Adjust the answer, using the original number.

Multiply the answer by 1,000 to adjust.

So, $32 \times 1{,}000 = 32{,}000$.

So, the bank loaned Jim \$32,000 last year.

Use a simpler problem to solve. Then adjust your answer.

1. Charles spent \$600 on a new bike. This was $\frac{2}{3}$ of his savings. How much money was in his savings?

   ____

2. The distance from Barbara's house to Raymond's house is 3,200 miles. You can travel $\frac{3}{4}$ of the distance by highway. How many miles cannot be traveled by highway?

   ____

Lines and Angles

In geometry, objects have special names.

You can make lines by connecting any two points. Lines go on forever. You show this by putting arrows at the ends of the line.

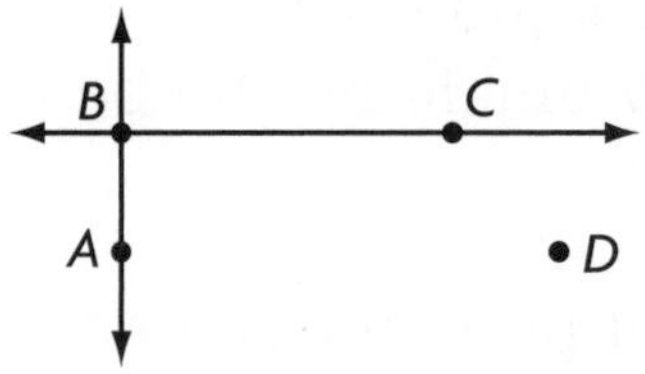

line *AB*, or $\overleftrightarrow{AB}$, and line *BC*, or $\overleftrightarrow{BC}$

A **line** is a straight path in a plane. It has no ends. It can be named by any two points on the line.

You can make line segments by joining two points. Line segments do not go on forever. They do not have arrows at the ends.

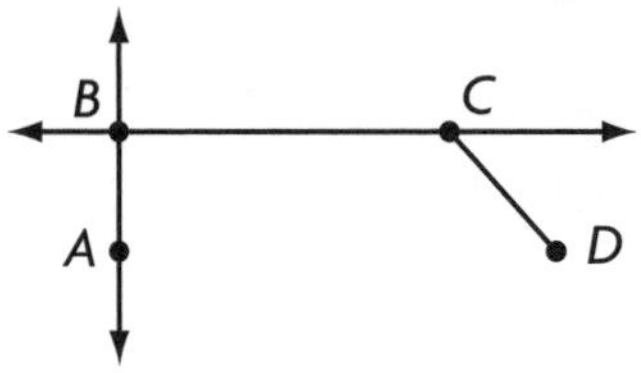

line segment *CD*, or $\overline{CD}$

A **line segment** is part of a line. It is the shortest distance between two points on a line.

$\overleftrightarrow{CD}$ and $\overleftrightarrow{AD}$ cross each other at point *D*.

$\overleftrightarrow{AB}$ and $\overleftrightarrow{AD}$ intersect to form right angles.

$\overleftrightarrow{BC}$ and $\overleftrightarrow{AD}$ go on forever, and they will never cross.

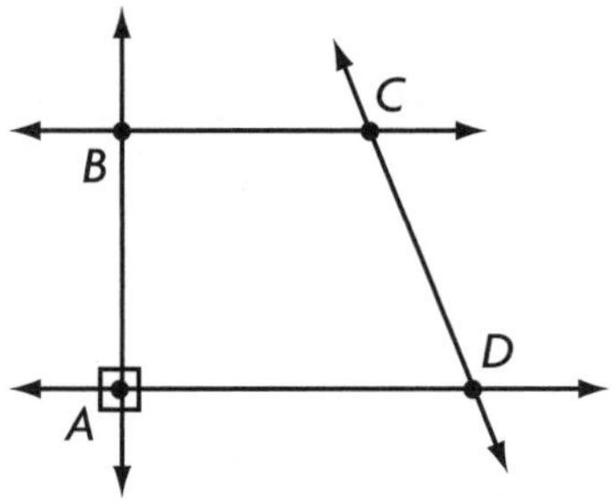

Lines that cross at one point are **intersecting**.

Lines that intersect to form four right angles are **perpendicular**.

Lines in a plane that never intersect and are the same distance from each other are **parallel**.

Draw and label each object.

1. lines *AB* and *CD* parallel to each other
2. line segment *KL*
3. line *FG*
4. lines *EF* and *GH* intersecting at point *A*
5. lines *NO* and *QR* perpendicular to each other
6. lines *HI* and *JK* parallel to each other

Name ______________________________

Measure and Draw Angles

You can use a protractor to measure the angle at the right. A protractor is a tool for measuring the size of the opening of an angle. The unit used to measure an angle is a degree.

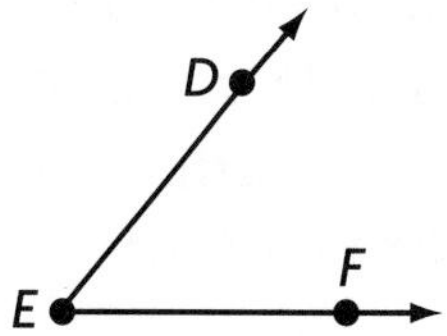

A protractor has a center point at the bottom where two lines form right angles. To the right of this is the 0° mark. To the left is the 180° mark.

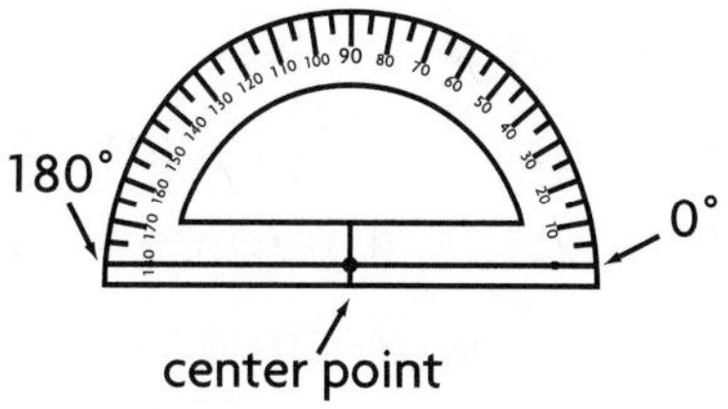

Step 1

Place the protractor on the angle so that the center point lines up with the vertex and the horizontal line on the protractor lines up with ray *EF*.

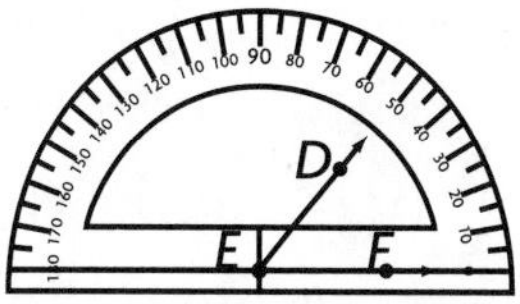

Step 2

To measure the angle, place a pencil on top of the other ray of the angle.

Read the number of degrees the pencil is pointing to.

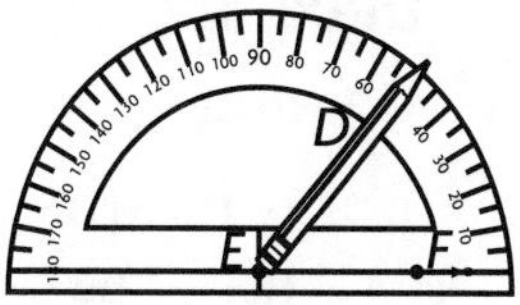

So, the measure of $\angle DEF$ is 50°.

Use a protractor to measure and classify the angle.

1.

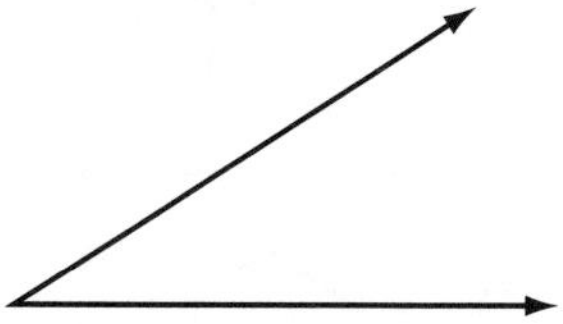

____

2.

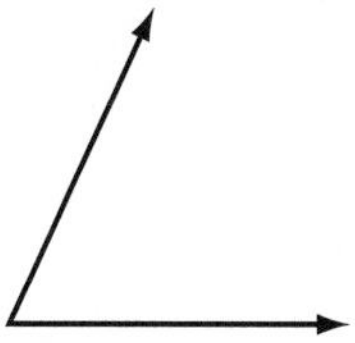

____

3.

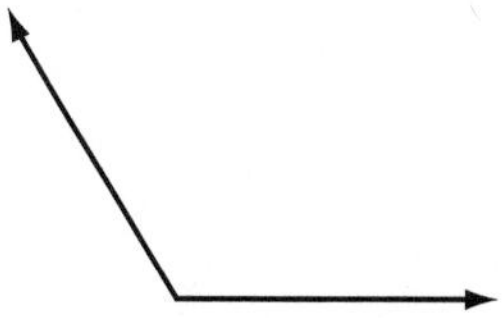

____

4.

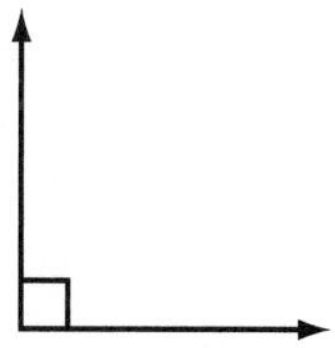

____

5.

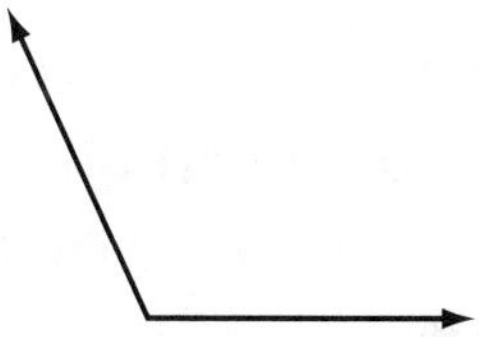

____

6.

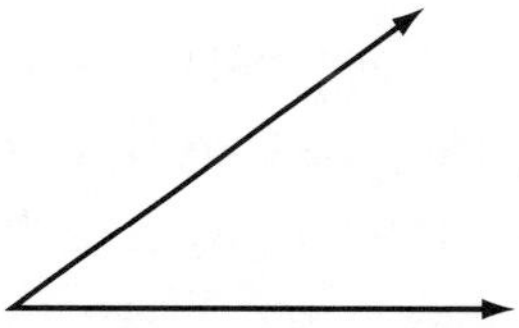

____

Name ______________________________

Angles and Polygons

How can you remember polygons and their angles? One way is to learn the meanings of the words that describe each shape. Remembering other words that use the same roots can also help you remember the figures.

triangle *tri-* means 3

tricycle — a 3-wheeled bicycle

quadrilateral *quad-* means 4

quadruplets — 4 babies born at once to the same mother

pentagon *pent-* means 5

the Pentagon — a 5-sided building in Washington, D.C.

hexagon *hex-* means 6

hex sign — Pennsylvania Dutch art that uses 6-sided figures drawn inside a circle

octagon *oct-* means 8

octopus — an animal with 8 legs

October — used to be the 8th month on the calendar

decagon *deca-* means 10

decade — 10 years

polygon *poly-* means many

polyhedra — a term used for the many-sided shapes of crystals

---

Name each polygon.

1. 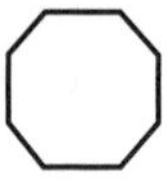 ____________

2. 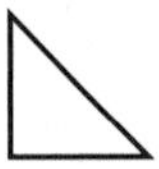 ____________

3. 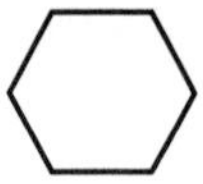 ____________

4. 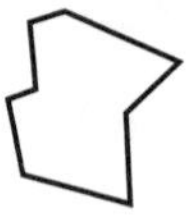 ____________

5. 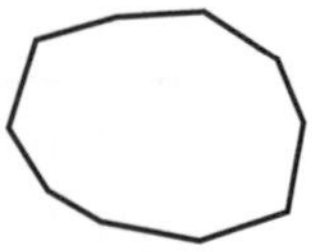 ____________

6.  ____________

7.  ____________

8.  ____________

Many root words for quadrilateral shapes have their own meanings as well. Look in the dictionary and find these meanings. Find another word that can help you remember the meaning. Then draw the shape.

9. trapezoid **10.** parallelogram **11.** rectangle **12.** rhombus

Name ____________________

Circles

You need a centimeter ruler and a compass to construct a circle with a radius of 2 cm.

A **radius** is a line segment with one endpoint at the center of a circle and the other endpoint on the circle.

A **diameter** is a line segment that passes through the center of a circle and has its endpoints on the circle.

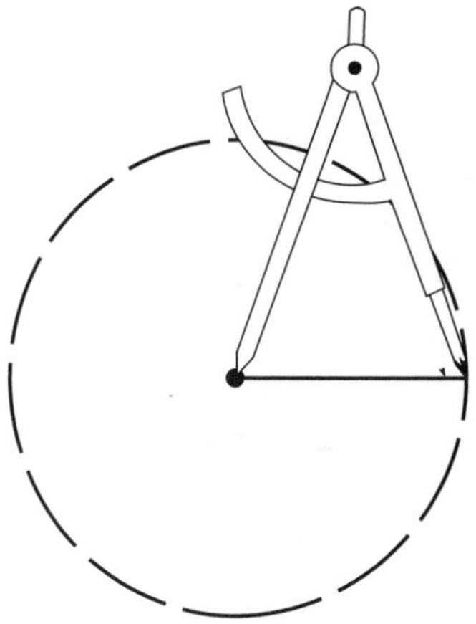

- Draw a point at the center of the circle.
- Start at the point. Use a centimeter ruler to draw a line segment 2 cm long. This is the radius.
- Place the point of the compass on the center point. Place the pencil point on the other end of the radius.
- Hold the compass point still. Turn the compass around on the point to make a complete circle.

Use a centimeter ruler and a compass to construct each circle.

1. radius = 1 cm

2. radius = 1.5 cm

3. radius = 2 cm

4. diameter = 1.0 cm

5. diameter = 2.4 cm

6. diameter = 5.0 cm

Name ____

Congruent and Similar Figures

Two figures are similar if they have the same shape. They do not have to be the same size.

Two figures are congruent if their corresponding sides and angles are equal.

To determine if triangles *ABC* and *DEF* are congruent:

- Measure the sizes of the corresponding angles to see if they are equal.
- Measure the lengths of the corresponding sides to see if they are equal.

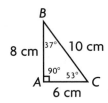

Lengths of Sides
$\overline{AB} = \overline{DE}$, $\overline{BC} = \overline{EF}$, and $\overline{AC} = \overline{DF}$

Angles
$\angle A = \angle D$, $\angle B = \angle E$, and $\angle C = \angle F$

The corresponding sides are equal, and the corresponding angles are equal. So, the two triangles are congruent.

For 1–2, use figures A–H.

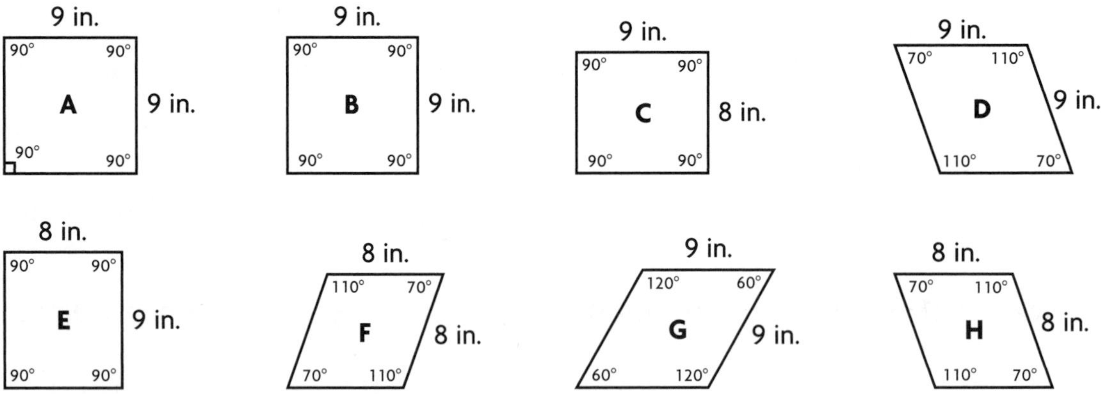

1. Find one pair of figures that is similar but not congruent.

____

2. Find four pairs of figures that are congruent.

____

Name ____

Symmetric Figures

A figure has line symmetry when it can be folded on a line so that its two parts match exactly. The two halves of the pentagon match exactly.

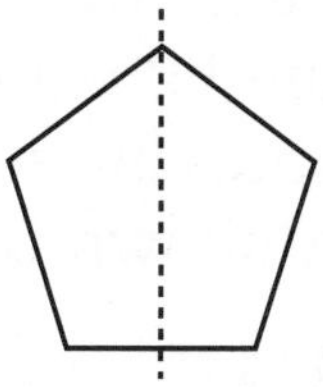

Trace the pentagon. Fold it in half along the dotted line. The left half is congruent to the right half. A figure can have more than one line of symmetry. Find all the lines of symmetry for the pentagon.

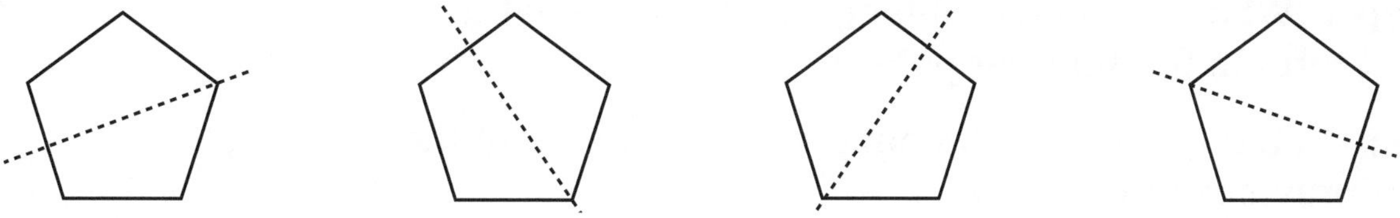

The pentagon has five lines of symmetry in all.

Draw the lines of symmetry. How many lines of symmetry does each figure have?

1.

____

2.

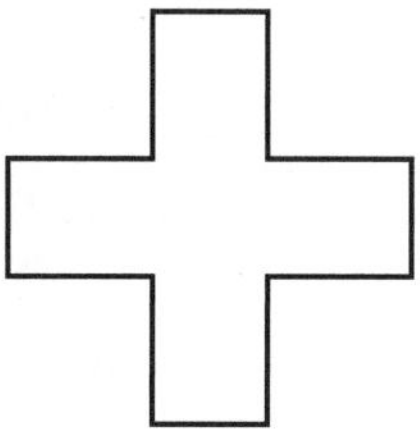

____

3.

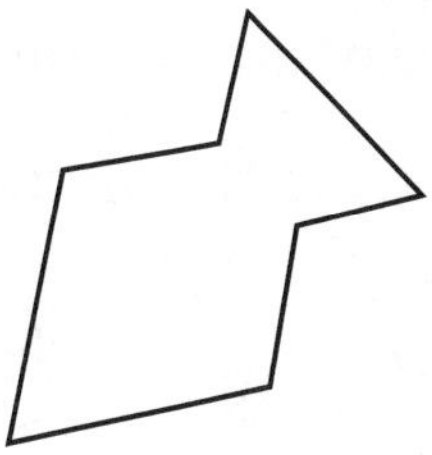

____

4.

____

5.

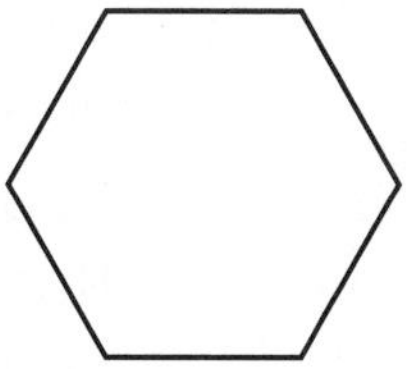

____

6.

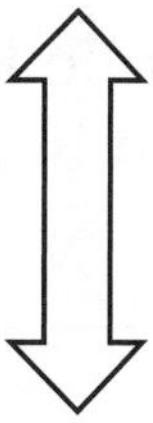

____

Name ______________________________ **LESSON 20.7**

Problem Solving Strategy

Find a Pattern

Leonardo Fibonacci was one of the most talented mathematicians of the Middle Ages. One of his hobbies was studying number patterns. One of his most famous patterns is shown below. What is the next term in the pattern?

1, 1, 2, 3, 5, 8

Step 1 What does the problem ask? It asks what the next term in the number pattern is.

Step 2 Find a pattern. The next term is the sum of the two previous terms.

$1 + 1 = 2$, $1 + 2 = 3$, $2 + 3 = 5$, $3 + 5 = 8$

Step 3 Use this information to solve the problem.

$5 + 8 = 13$. 13 is the next term in the pattern.

Find a pattern to solve.

1. What is the next shape in this pattern?

____

2. When Fred's number is 1, Ann's number is 3. When Fred's number is 2, Ann's number is 5. If Fred's is 6, what is Ann's number?

____

____

3. Write a rule for the pattern described in Problem 2.

____

____

____

4. Alex read 45 pages on Sunday, 90 pages on Monday and 135 pages on Tuesday. If he continues this pattern, how many pages will he read on Friday?

____

Name ______________________________

Triangles

Triangles are polygons with 3 sides and 3 angles. One method of classifying triangles is by the lengths of their sides.

To classify a triangle using this method, you need to know the lengths of its sides.

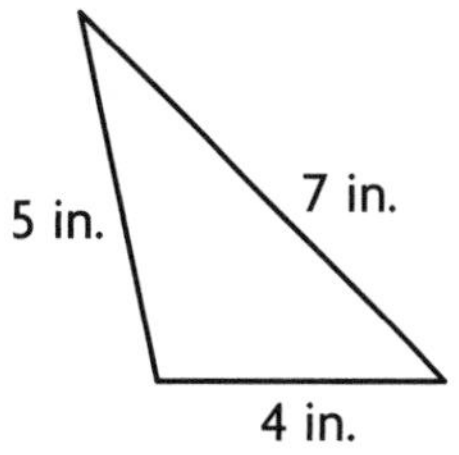

3 congruent sides = **equilateral** triangle

2 congruent sides = **isosceles** triangle

0 congruent sides = **scalene** triangle

Each side is a different length, so this is a scalene triangle.

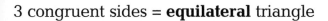

List the number of congruent sides. Then name each triangle. Write *isosceles*, *scalene*, or *equilateral*.

1.

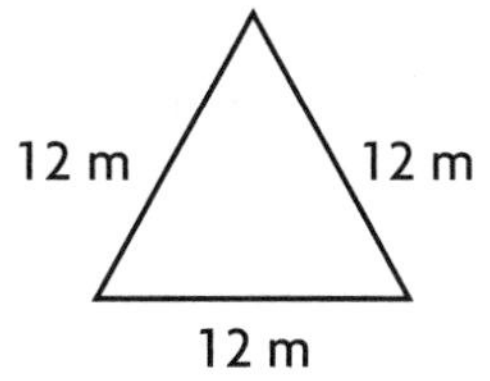

2.

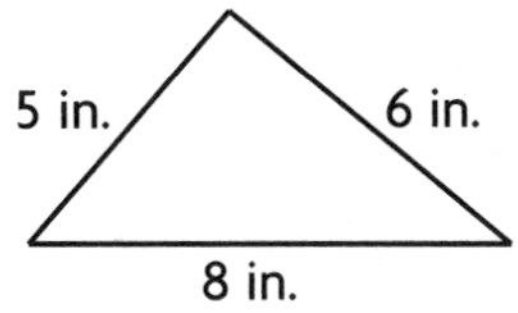

3.

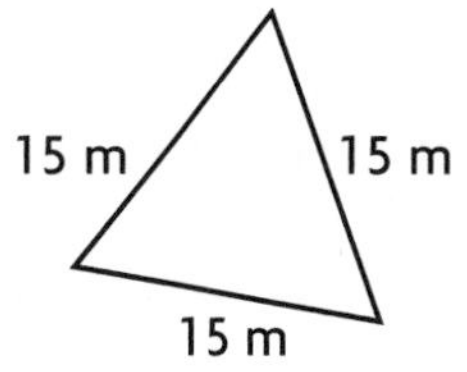

4.

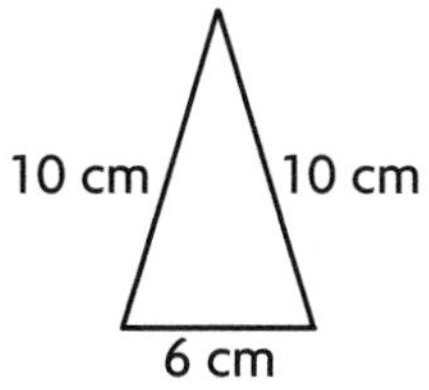

5.

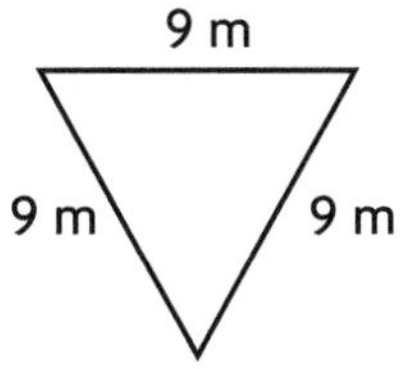

6.

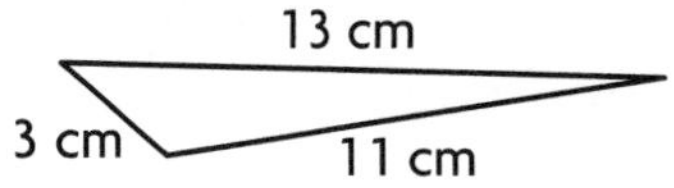

7.

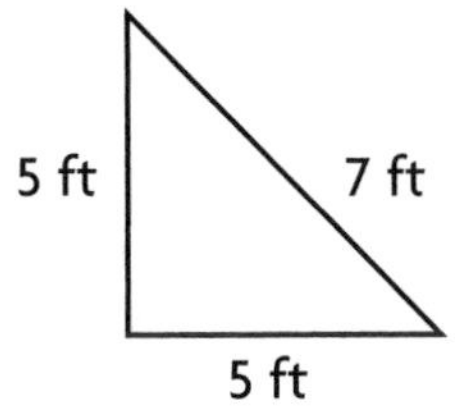

8.

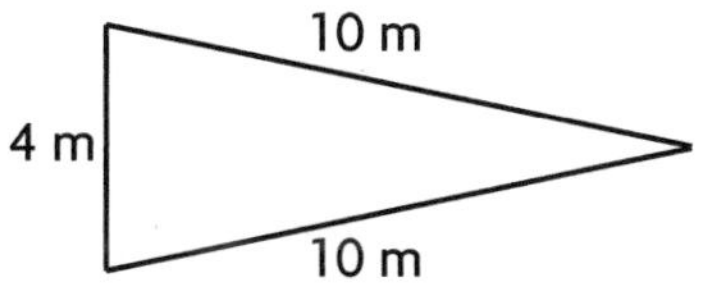

9.

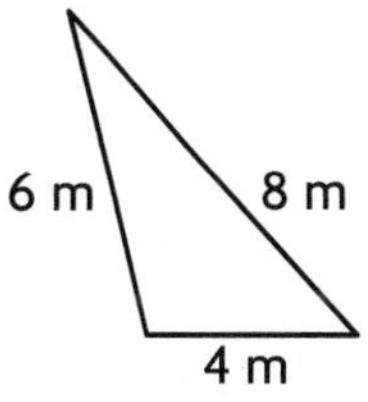

Name ______________________________

Quadrilaterals

Polygons that have 4 sides and 4 angles are **quadrilaterals**. Quadrilaterals can be classified by looking at the number of parallel sides, the lengths of their sides, and the measures of their angles.

	Trapezoid	Parallelogram	Rectangle	Rhombus	Square
Number of parallel sides	1 pair	2 pairs	2 pairs	2 pairs	2 pairs
Number of congruent sides	0 pair	2 pairs	2 pairs	all 4 sides	all 4 sides
Number of congruent angles	0 pair	2 pairs	all 4 angles	2 pairs	all 4 angles
Examples	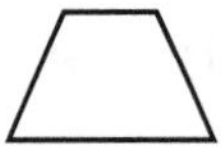	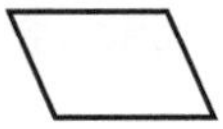			

To classify the quadrilateral at the right, identify the following characteristics.

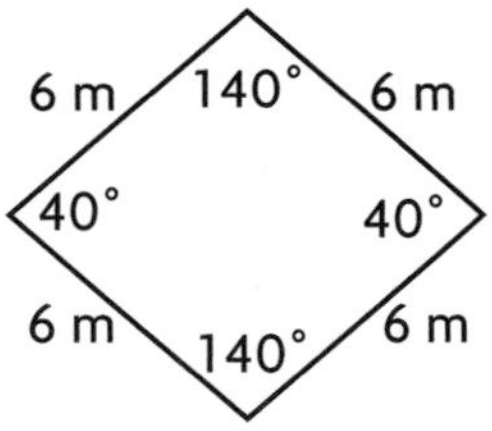

Number of parallel sides: 2 pairs

Number of congruent sides: all 4 sides

Number of congruent angles: 2 pairs

So, the figure is a rhombus.

Classify each quadrilateral. Write *quadrilateral, trapezoid, parallelogram, rectangle, rhombus,* or *square.*

1.

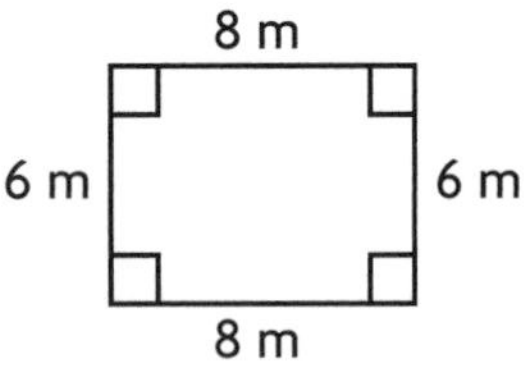

____

2.

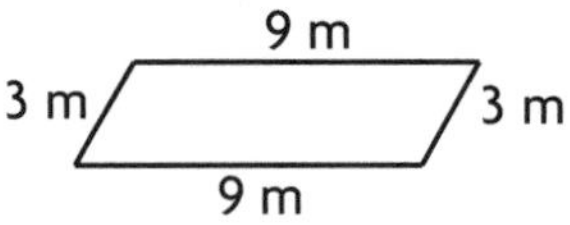

____

3.

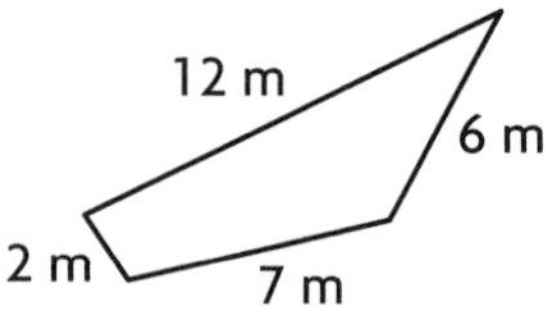

____

4.

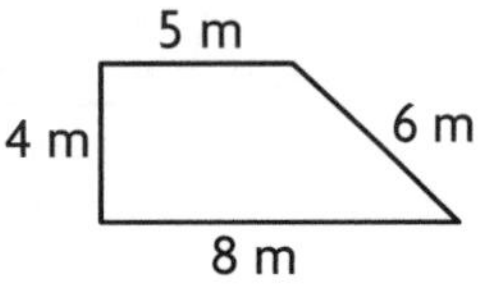

____

5.

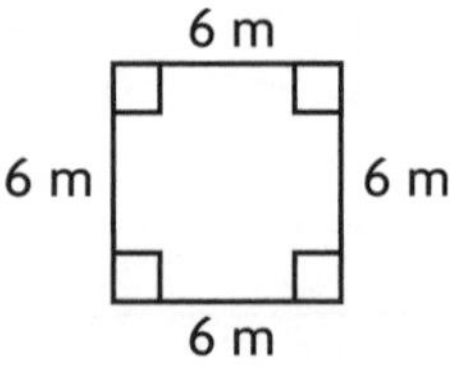

____

6.

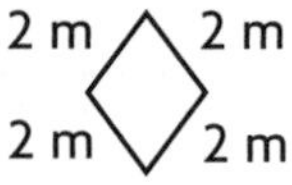

____

Name ____________________

Transformations and Tessellations

A **translation** slides a figure to a new position along a straight line.

A **rotation** turns the figure clockwise or counterclockwise around a point.

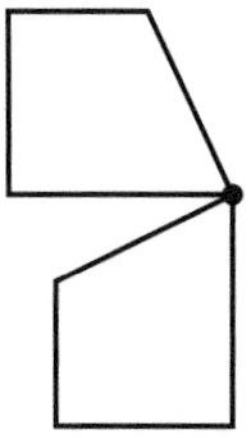

A **reflection** shows the mirror image of the figure.

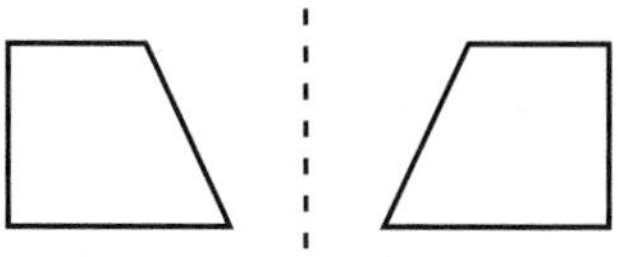

A **tessellation** covers a surface with no gaps or overlaps.

These figures form a tessellation. There are no gaps or overlaps.

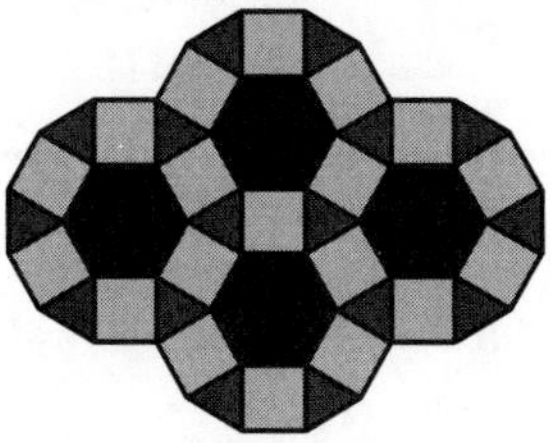

These figures do not form a tessellation. There are gaps.

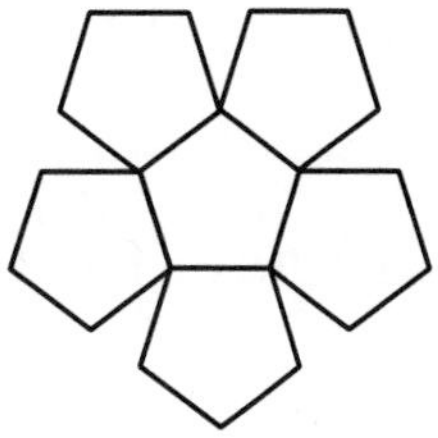

Tell how each figure was moved. Write *translation*, *reflection*, or *rotation*.

1. 

____

2. 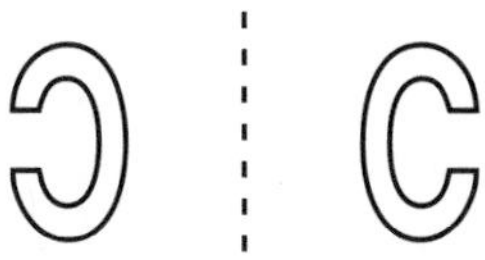

____

3. 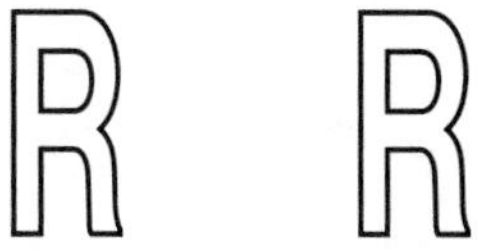

____

Trace and cut out several of each figure. Tell if the figure or pair of figures will tessellate. Write *yes* or *no*.

4. 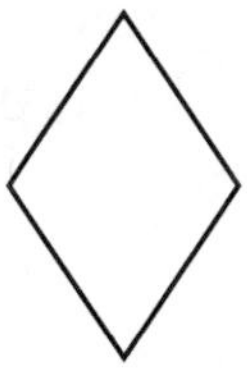

____

5. 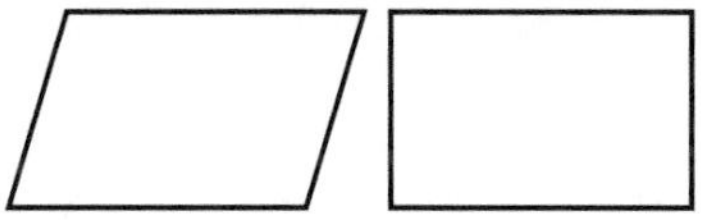

____

6. 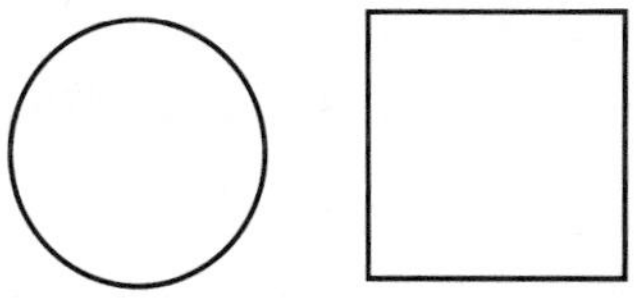

____

Name ______________________________

Solid Figures

A **prism** is a solid figure that has two congruent faces called **bases.** A prism is named by the polygons that form its bases.

The prism at the right is a hexagonal prism.

- The faces of this solid figure are rectangles.
- The bases of this solid figure are hexagons.

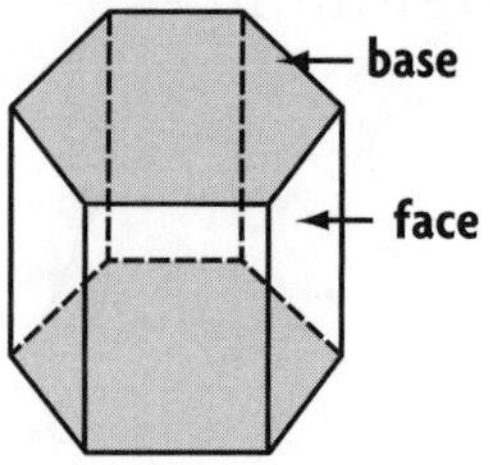

A **pyramid** is a solid figure with one base that is a polygon and three or more faces that are triangles with a common vertex. A pyramid is named by the polygon that forms its base.

This is a hexagonal pyramid.

- The faces of this solid figure are triangles.
- The base of this solid figure is a hexagon.

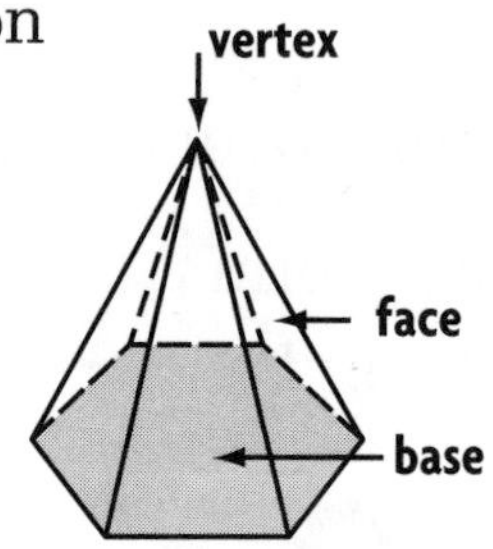

Classify the solid figure. Then write the number of faces, vertices, and edges.

1.

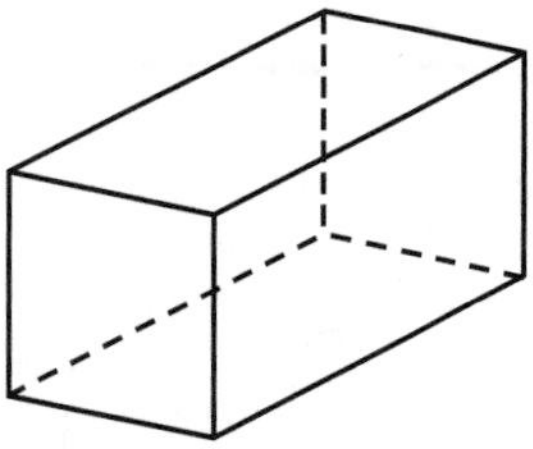

____

____

2.

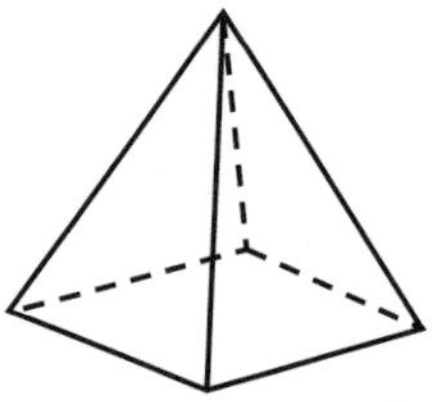

____

____

3.

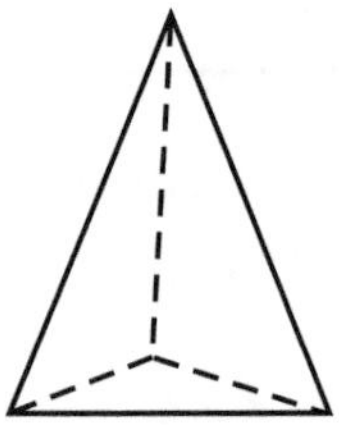

____

____

Write the name of the solid figure.

4. I have a base with 5 equal sides. My faces are 5 triangles.

____

____

5. All 6 of my faces are squares.

____

____

6. I have 2 congruent pentagons for bases. I have 5 rectangular faces.

____

____

Name ____________________

Draw Solid Figures from Different Views

A solid figure looks different when it is viewed from different positions.

Look at the solid figure at the right.

- There are 2 cubes in the top layer.
- There are 4 cubes in the middle layer.
- There are 6 cubes in the bottom layer.

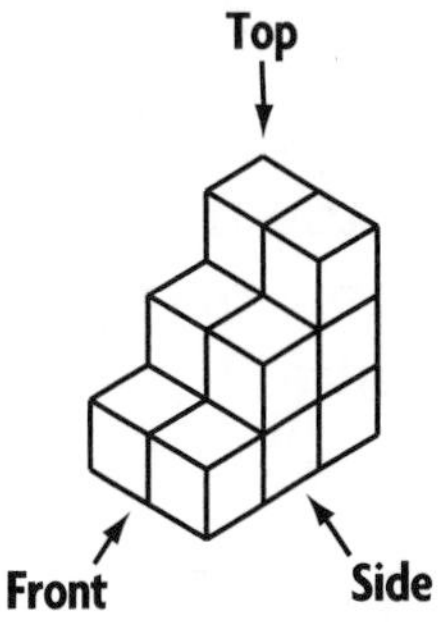

This is a drawing of the figure viewed from the top.

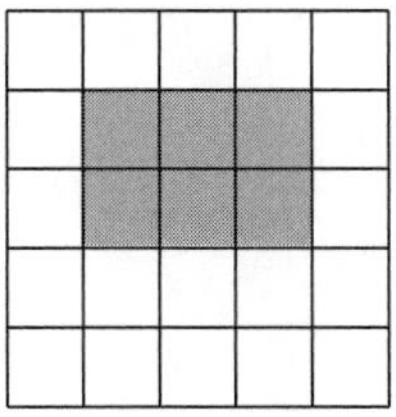

This is a drawing of the figure viewed from the side.

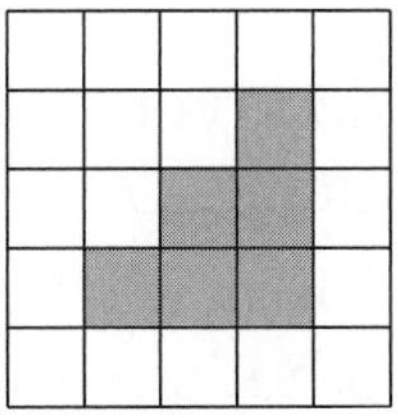

This is a drawing of the figure viewed from the front.

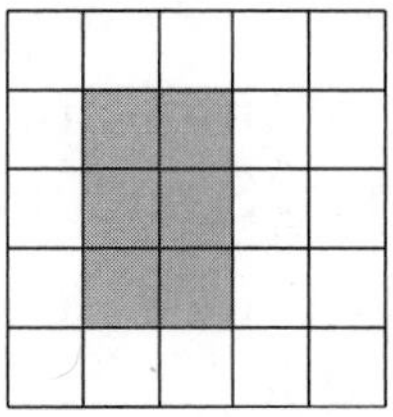

For 1–6, use the figure on the right.
Tell how many cubes are in each row.

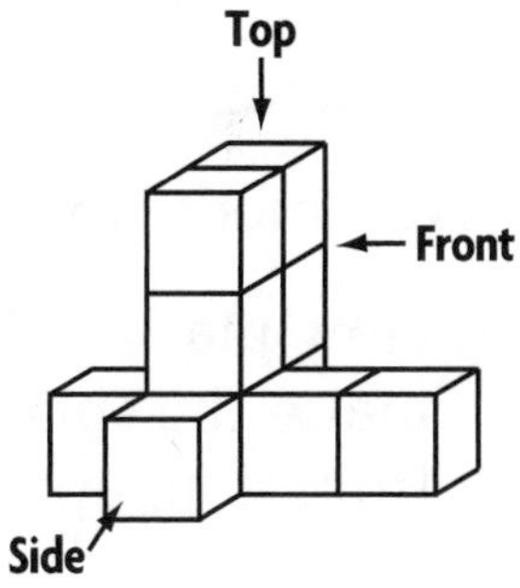

1. top layer ____________________

2. middle layer ____________________

3. bottom layer ____________________

Draw the figure from different views.

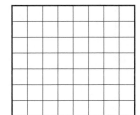

4. top view

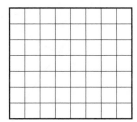

5. side view

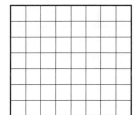

6. front view

Name ___________________________

Problem Solving Strategy

Make a Model

Tracey wants to build a solid figure with cubes. The figure will have the front, top, and side views shown. How can she find out how many cubes to put in each layer and where to put the cubes?

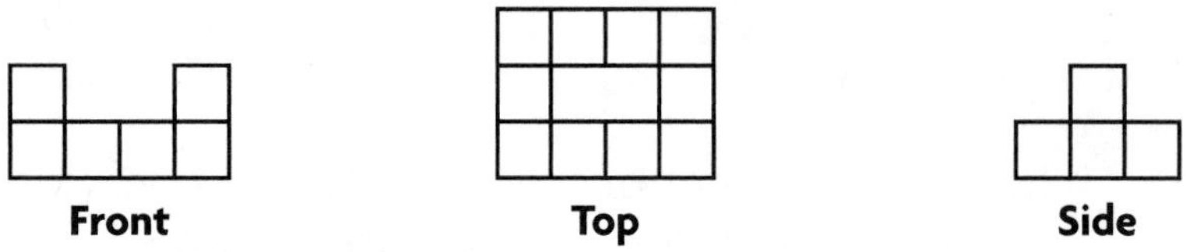

- Look at the top view. It has has 10 squares. So, the bottom layer will have 10 cubes.
- Look at the front view. The second layer has at least 2 cubes. Some may be behind others.
- Look at the side view. You can only see 1 square in the second layer in the middle. The other square must be behind it. So there are 2 cubes in the second layer.

Tracey needs 12 cubes.
The solid figure will look like this.

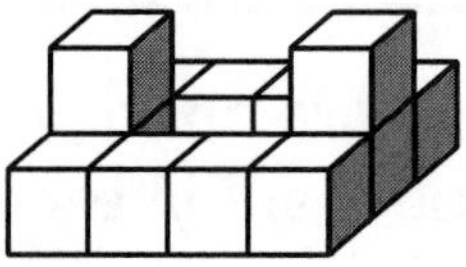

Make a model to solve.

1. How many cubes are needed to make the solid figure that has the front, top, and side views shown?

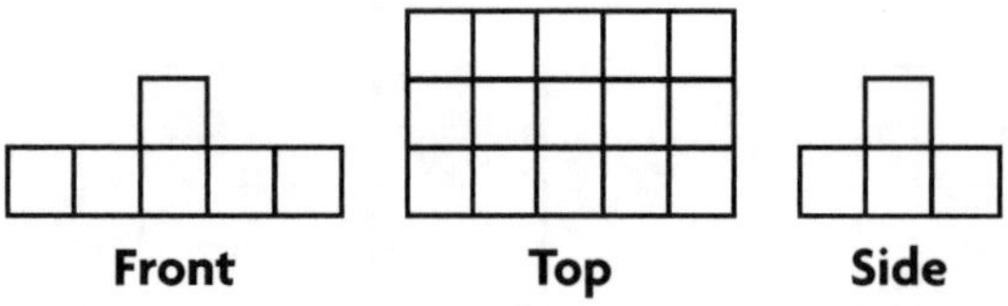

____

2. Three line segments can be drawn using 3 points. Six line segments can be drawn using 4 points. How many line segments can be drawn using 6 points?

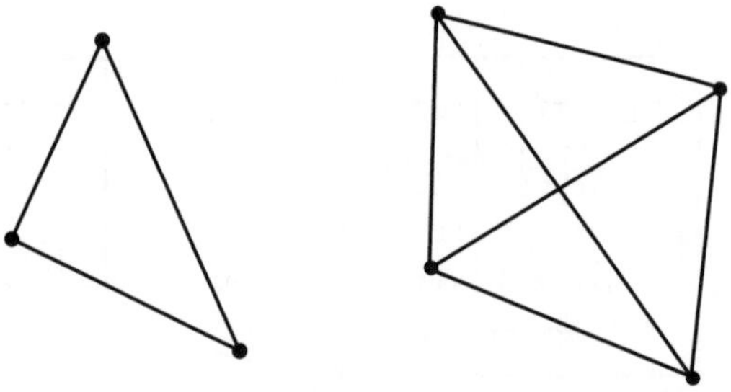

____

Name ______________________________

Understand Integers

Integers are whole numbers and their opposites.

The positive integers are to the right of 0. The negative integers are to the left of 0. 0 is neither positive nor negative.

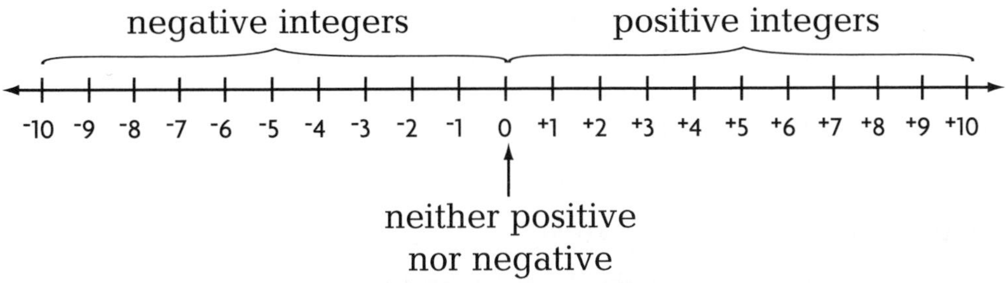

How far from 0 is $^{+}5$ and in what direction? ______________________

How far from 0 is $^{-}5$ and in what direction? ______________________

$^{+}5$ and $^{-}5$ are **opposites.** They are the same distance from 0 on a number line, but in opposite directions. Some other opposites are $^{+}1$ and $^{-}1$, $^{+}6$ and $^{-}6$.

The distance a number is from 0 is referred to as its **absolute value.** $^{+}5$ and $^{-}5$ are both 5 units from 0. So, $|^{-}5|$ and $|^{+}5|$ both equal 5.

> The symbol $|\,|$ means absolute value.

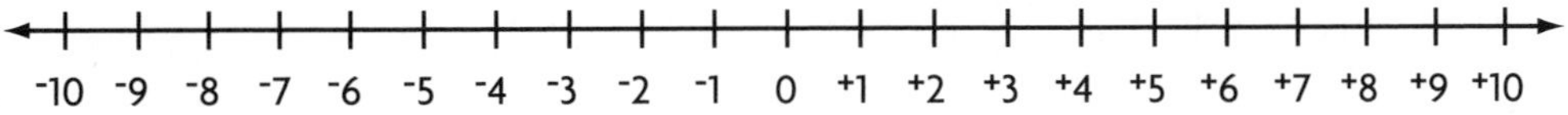

How far from 0 is $^{-}8$? 8 units
So, $|^{-}8| = 8$ because it is 8 units from 0.

Write an integer to represent each situation.

1. an increase in price of $30.00 ______________

2. 10 minutes before school starts ______________

3. 4 feet above ground ______________

Write the opposite of each integer.

4. $^{+}6$ ________ **5.** $^{-}28$ ________ **6.** $^{+}1{,}489$ ________ **7.** $^{-}2{,}000$ ________

Name each integer's absolute value.

8. $|^{+}34|$ ________ **9.** $|^{-}30|$ ________ **10.** $|^{-}235|$ ________ **11.** $|^{+}8|$ ________

Name ____________________

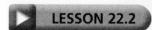

Compare and Order Integers

Integers increase as you move right on a number line and decrease as you move left.

Compare $^{-}7$ to $^{-}8$. Use $<, >$ or $=$.

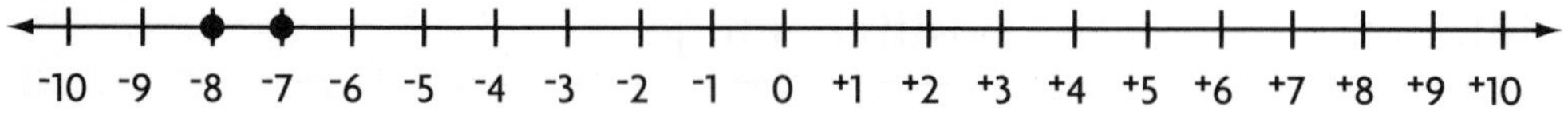

The numbers increase as you move right, and $^{-}7$ is to the right of $^{-}8$. So, $^{-}7 > {}^{-}8$.

Order $^{+}5$, $^{-}5$, $^{-}3$, and $^{+}7$ from least to greatest.

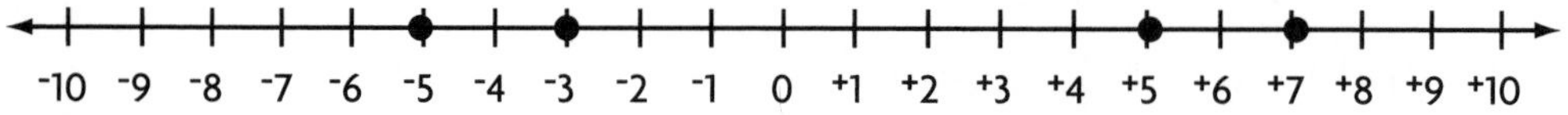

Look at the number line. Since the numbers increase as you move right on the number line, the order from least to greatest is $^{-}5$, $^{-}3$, $^{+}5$, $^{+}7$.

Name the integer that is 1 *less* than $^{-}8$.

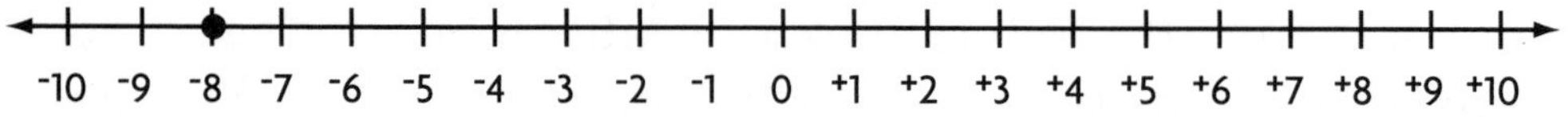

1 less means a decrease, and decreasing amounts move left on a number line. So, 1 to the left of $^{-}8$ is $^{-}9$.

Compare. Write $<$, $>$, or $=$ for each ◯.

1. $^{+}6$ ◯ $^{+}6$ **2.** $^{-}7$ ◯ $^{-}2$ **3.** $^{+}3$ ◯ $^{-}1$ **4.** $^{-}10$ ◯ $^{+}8$

Order each set of integers from greatest to least.

5. $^{-}9$, $^{+}1$, 0, $^{-}4$ ______

6. $^{+}2$, $^{-}5$, $^{+}6$, $^{-}4$ ______

7. $^{+}10$, $^{-}10$, $^{+}1$, $^{-}1$ ______

8. $^{-}4$, $^{+}2$, $^{-}5$, $^{-}1$ ______

Name the integer that is 1 less.

9. $^{+}6$ ______ **10.** $^{-}4$ ______ **11.** 0 ______ **12.** $^{-}21$ ______ **13.** $^{+}25$ ______

Name the integer that is 1 more.

14. $^{-}10$ ______ **15.** $^{+}4$ ______ **16.** $^{-}3$ ______ **17.** $^{+}32$ ______ **18.** $^{-}1$ ______

Name ______________________

Addition and Subtraction of Integers

When you add integers, apply the integer addition rules.

- If the signs of the addends are the same, find the sum and use the sign of the addends.
  Examples: $^{+}4 + ^{+}1 = ^{+}5$ $\quad$ $^{-}6 + ^{-}2 = ^{-}8$
- If the signs of the addends are different, find the difference and use the sign of the number with the greater absolute value.
  Examples: $^{-}5 + ^{+}2 = ^{-}3$ $\quad$ $^{+}8 + ^{-}3 = ^{+}5$

When you subtract an integer from another integer, you add the opposite. Replace the integer being subtracted with its opposite, and change the operation to addition.

Example: Find $^{-}6 - ^{+}2$.

Step 1 Find the opposite of the number being subtracted.
The opposite of $^{+}2$ is $^{-}2$.

Step 2 Add the opposite. Change the operation to addition and replace the number being subtracted with its opposite.
$^{-}6 - ^{+}2 = ^{-}6 + ^{-}2$
So, $^{-}6 + ^{-}2 = ^{-}8$.

Add.

1. $^{-}6 + ^{+}3$ ______ **2.** $^{+}4 + ^{-}5$ ______ **3.** $^{-}8 + ^{-}7$ ______ **4.** $^{+}3 + ^{+}3$ ______

5. $^{-}6 + ^{+}1$ ______ **6.** $^{+}10 + ^{+}4$ ______ **7.** $^{-}4 + ^{+}4$ ______ **8.** $^{-}7 + ^{+}6$ ______

Write each subtraction sentence as an addition sentence and solve.

9. $^{-}5 - ^{+}3$ ______ **10.** $^{-}4 - ^{-}7$ ______ **11.** $^{-}2 - ^{+}8$ ______ **12.** $^{+}7 - ^{-}1$ ______

13. $^{+}2 - ^{+}1$ ______ **14.** $^{+}4 - ^{-}6$ ______ **15.** $^{+}7 - ^{+}3$ ______ **16.** $0 - ^{+}8$ ______

17. $^{-}9 - ^{-}2$ ______ **18.** $^{+}5 - ^{-}5$ ______ **19.** $^{-}2 - ^{-}4$ ______ **20.** $^{-}5 - ^{+}1$ ______

Problem Solving Strategy

Draw a Diagram

Draw a diagram to solve.

PROBLEM: Erik and his friends are practicing scuba diving in a 20-foot-deep, 30-foot-long pool for class. First, they had to go down 15 feet. Then they had to go down 2 more feet to practice clearing the water out of their masks. Then they went up 9 feet and back down 5 feet. At what depth are they now?

When solving problems involving integers, first look for key words to determine the positive and negative numbers. A few key words are listed.

negative (−)	positive (+)
down	up
below	above
drop	raise

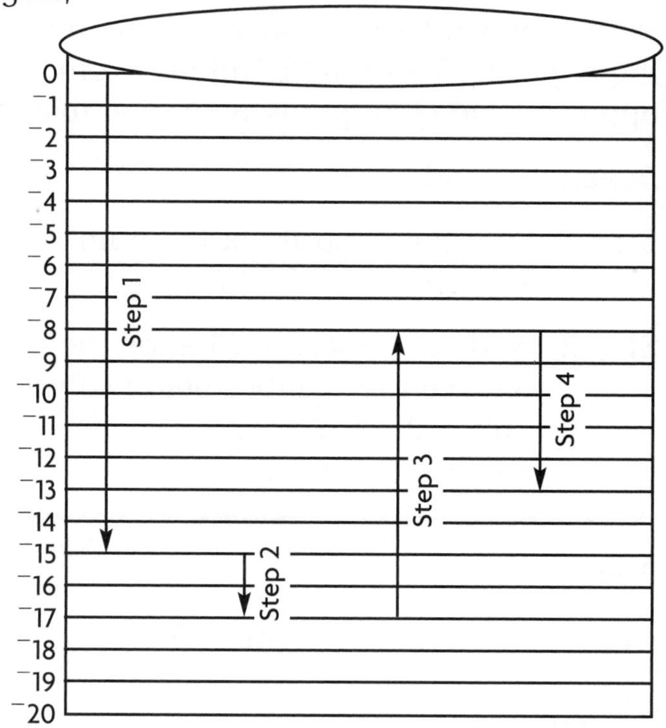

The key words in the problem are *up* (+) and *down* (−). Use the key words to step out the problem.

Step 1 down 15 feet ($^-15$)

Step 2 down 2 more feet ($^-2$)

Step 3 up 9 feet ($^+9$)

Step 4 down 5 feet ($^-5$)

Making or using a diagram will help you visualize the steps to solve the problem. Look at the diagram.

The last step shows that Erik and his friends will go from $^-8$ feet down 5 more ($^-5$) feet. The students are now at 13 feet below the surface, or $^-13$ feet.

Draw a diagram to solve.

1. The next day a new set of divers were practicing in the pool. They began by diving 19 feet. Then they rose 9 feet, went back down 7 feet and up 5 feet. Where are they now?

____

____

2. Jan went swimming. She dove 15 feet, came up 8 feet, went down 1 foot, and came back up 5 more feet. Where is she now?

____

____

Name ________________________________

Graph Relationships

Number of dollars, x	1	2	3	4
Number of rolls of pennies, y	2	4	6	8

Bill put his collection of pennies in $0.50 rolls. Every two rolls held $1. He made a table to show the relationship between number of dollars and number of rolls of pennies.

Bill wrote the data as ordered pairs: (1,2), (2,4), (3,6), and (4,8). Then he graphed the points and drew a line to connect them.

The ordered pair (2,4) means that Bill has $2 if he has 4 rolls of pennies.

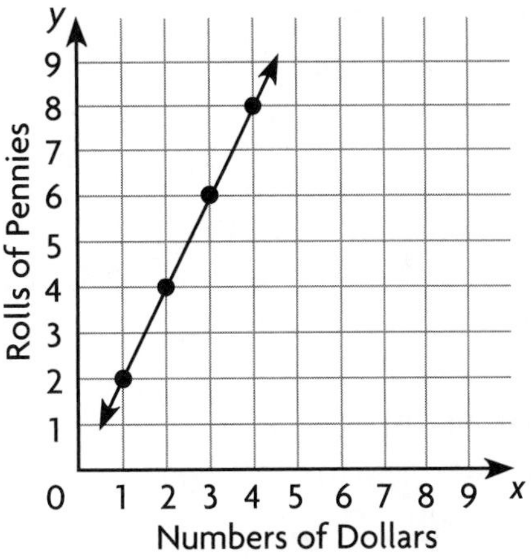

Write the ordered pairs. Then graph them.

1.

Input, x	1	2	3	4
Output, y	4	8	12	16

____

2.

Input, x	8	10	12	14
Output, y	4	5	6	7

____

3.

Input, x	2	4	6	8
Output, y	3	5	7	9

____

4.

Input, x	8	7	6	5
Output, y	6	5	4	3

____

5. In the problem with Bill's pennies, what does the ordered pair (3,6) mean?

____

6. In the problem with Bill's pennies, what would be the next ordered pair?

____

7. How did you decide the answer for problem 6? ________________________________

____

Name ______________________________

Graph Integers on the Coordinate Plane

A coordinate plane is formed by a horizontal number line (x-axis) and a vertical number line (y-axis), which intersect. The point at which the two lines intersect is named by the ordered pair (0,0) and is called the *origin*. The numbers in the ordered pair are called *coordinates*.

For $(^-2, ^+4)$, move 2 units left on the x-axis and 4 units up on the y-axis.

For $(^+2, ^+4)$, move 2 units right on the x-axis and 4 units up on the y-axis.

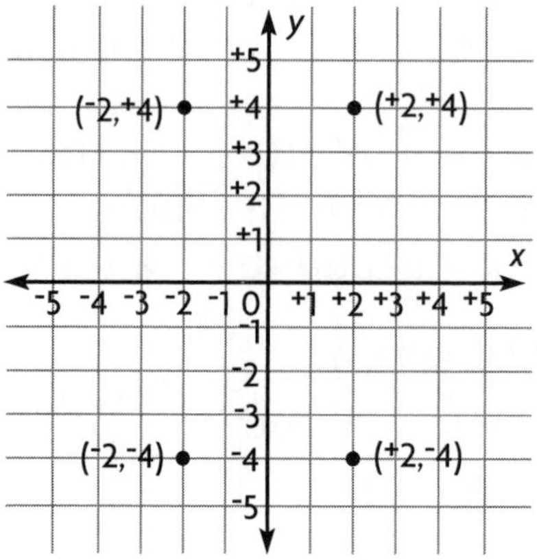

To plot ordered pairs on a coordinate plane, begin at the origin. Positive numbers are to the right and above (0,0). Negative numbers are to the left and below (0,0).

For $(^-2, ^-4)$, move 2 units left on the x-axis and 4 units down on the y-axis.

For $(^+2, ^-4)$, move 2 units right on the x-axis and 4 units down on the y-axis.

Write the ordered pair described. Then plot and label the point on the coordinate plane.

1. Start at the origin. Move right 5 units and up 3 units. ________

2. Start at the origin. Move left 4 units and up 1 unit. ________

3. Start at the origin. Move right 2 units and down 3 units. ________

4. Start at the origin. Move left 1 unit and down 3 units. ________

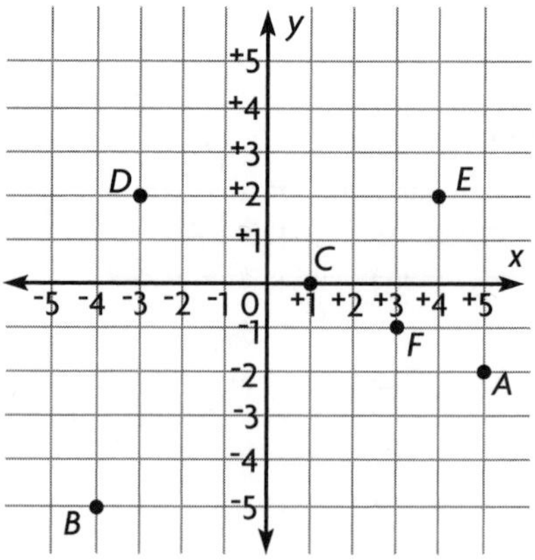

Identify the ordered pair for each point on the coordinate plane above.

5. Point *A* ________

6. Point *B* ________

7. Point *C* ________

8. Point *D* ________

9. Point *E* ________

10. Point *F* ________

Name ______________________________________

LESSON 23.3

Transformations on the Coordinate Plane

When you move a figure, it is called a rigid transformation. A translation is one type of transformation.

When you translate, or slide, a figure on a coordinate plane, the coordinates change. The figure may move up or down, left or right, or both. Here are three examples of translations.

3 spaces to the right

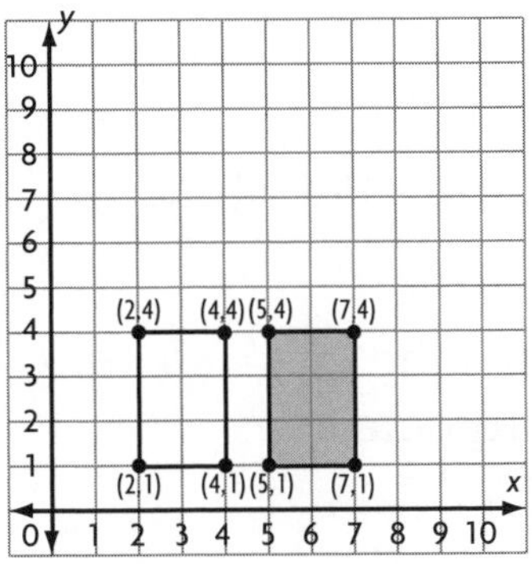

New ordered pairs:
$(^+2, ^+1)$ to $(^+5, ^+1)$,
$(^+4, ^+1)$ to $(^+7, ^+1)$,
$(^+2, ^+4)$ to $(^+5, ^+4)$,
$(^+4, ^+4)$ to $(^+7, ^+4)$

2 spaces up

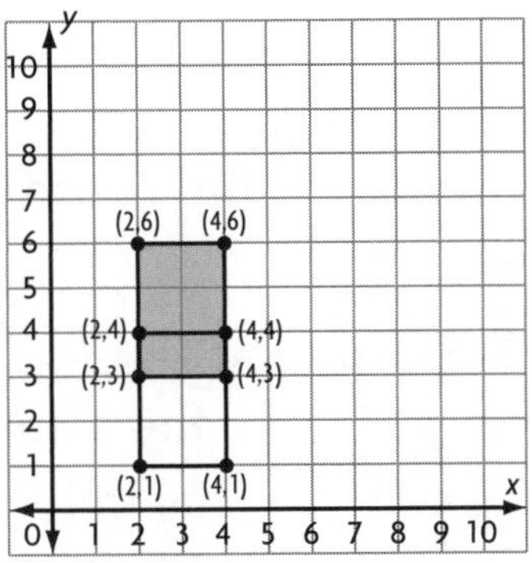

New ordered pairs:
$(^+2, ^+1)$ to $(^+2, ^+3)$,
$(^+4, ^+1)$ to $(^+4, ^+3)$,
$(^+2, ^+4)$ to $(^+2, ^+6)$,
$(^+4, ^+4)$ to $(^+4, ^+6)$

3 spaces to the right and 2 spaces up

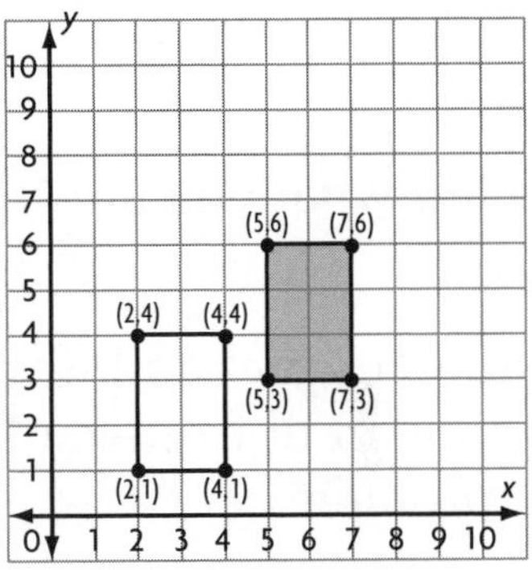

New ordered pairs:
$(^+2, ^+1)$ to $(^+5, ^+3)$,
$(^+4, ^+1)$ to $(^+7, ^+3)$,
$(^+2, ^+4)$ to $(^+5, ^+6)$,
$(^+4, ^+4)$ to $(^+7, ^+6)$

Translate each figure. Draw the new figure with its coordinates. Name the new ordered pairs.

1. Translate the figure 5 spaces to the right and 4 spaces up.

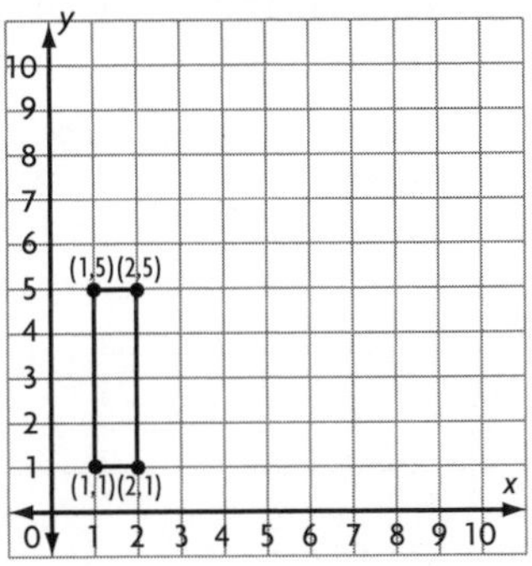

2. Translate the figure 3 spaces to the right and 4 spaces down.

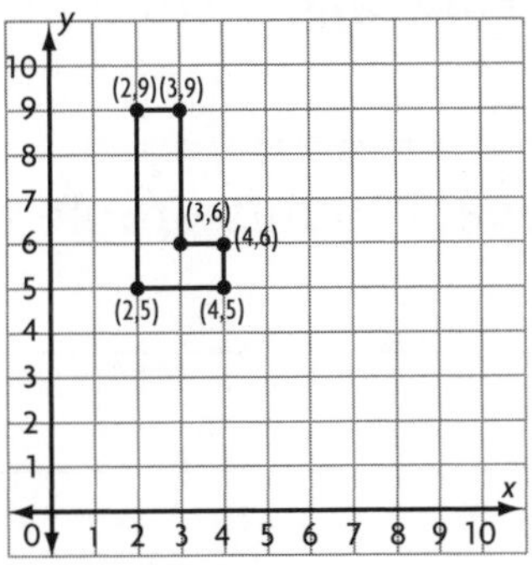

3. Translate the figure 4 spaces to the left and 4 spaces down.

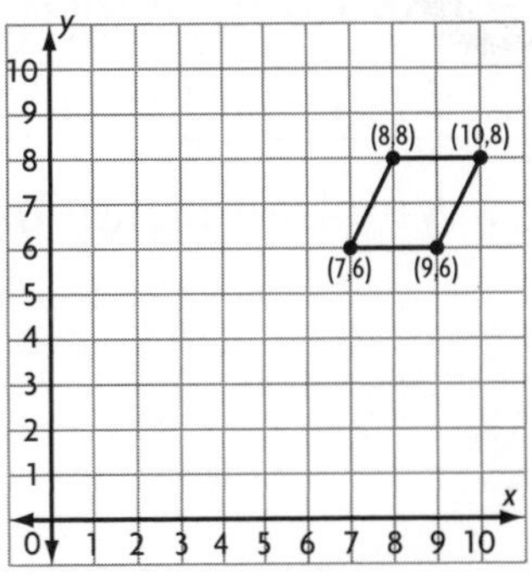

Name ____________________

Problem Solving Skill

Relevant or Irrelevant Information

Jonathan gave a map to his visiting cousin so she would be able to find the places she needs. She is looking for the Pet Store and knows that its x-coordinate is the same as the Food Store's x-coordinate. The Snack Shop is north of the Cinema. Jonathan said that the Pet Store is 4 blocks south of the Toy Store. Can you help her find the Pet Store?

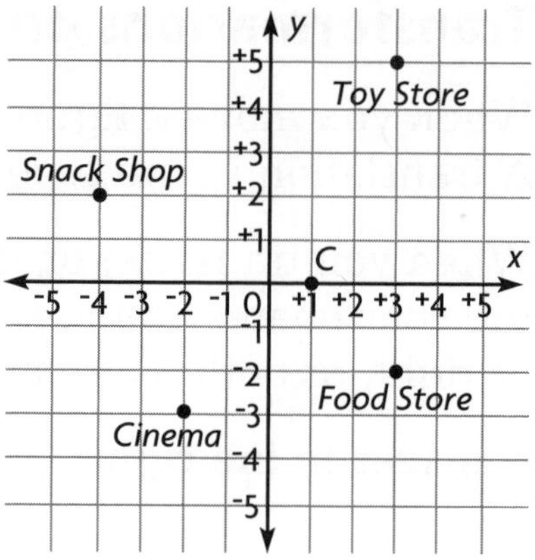

Step 1

Decide what you are trying to find. — the coordinates of the Pet Store

Step 2

Read each fact and decide whether it is relevant or irrelevant to solving the problem.

- The Pet Store has the the same x-coordinate as the Food Store. *relevant*
- The Snack Shop is north of the Cinema. *irrelevant*
- The Pet Store is 4 blocks south of the Toy Store. *relevant*

Step 3

Use the relevant information to solve the problem.

- The Food Store's x-coordinate is $^{+}3$.
- The Toy Store's y-coordinate is $^{+}5$.
- So the Pet Store is at ($^{+}3$,$^{+}1$).

---

1. A group of 72 students visited the science center. One third of them visited the planetarium. One half of that number went to the weather exhibit. The remaining students visited the electricity exhibit. Most of the students liked the science center. How many students saw the electricity exhibit?

____

2. Which information is relevant to this problem?

____

____

____

Name ______________________________

Customary Length

You can measure more precisely by using smaller units of measure.

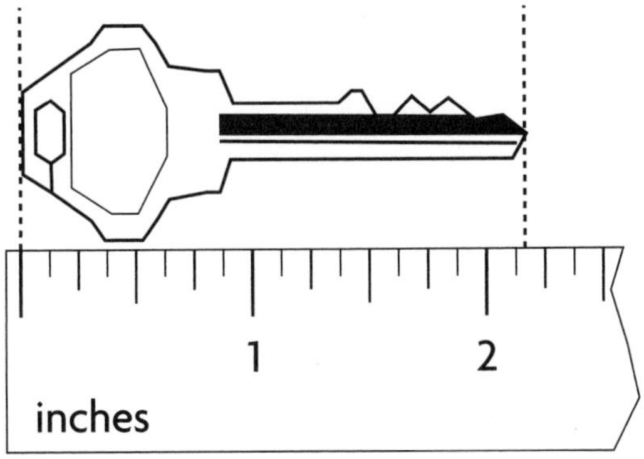

Measured to the nearest inch: 2 in.

Measured to the nearest $\frac{1}{4}$ inch: $2\frac{1}{4}$ in.

Measured to the nearest $\frac{1}{8}$ inch: $2\frac{1}{8}$ in.

So, the measurement to the nearest $\frac{1}{8}$ inch is most precise.

For 1–5, use a customary ruler to measure your textbook.

1. to the nearest inch: height ________ width ________
2. to the nearest $\frac{1}{2}$ inch: height ________ width ________
3. to the nearest $\frac{1}{4}$ inch: height ________ width ________
4. to the nearest $\frac{1}{8}$ inch: height ________ width ________
5. Which is the most precise measure? least precise measure?

____

Tell the best unit and tool for measuring each.

6. length of a car ________________
7. distance from Atlanta to Miami ________________
8. width of your bed ________________
9. height of a vase ________________
10. length of a school playground ________________

Name ______________________________

LESSON 24.2

Metric Length

Use your fingers to help you estimate metric length.

Compare the width of each of your fingers to 1 centimeter.
Is one of your fingers about 1 cm wide?

Use your fingers to help estimate the length of each object. Then use a ruler to measure to the nearest centimeter and millimeter.

1. 

____

2. 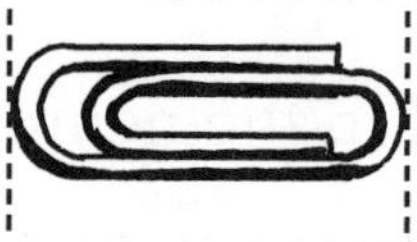

____

3. 

____

4. 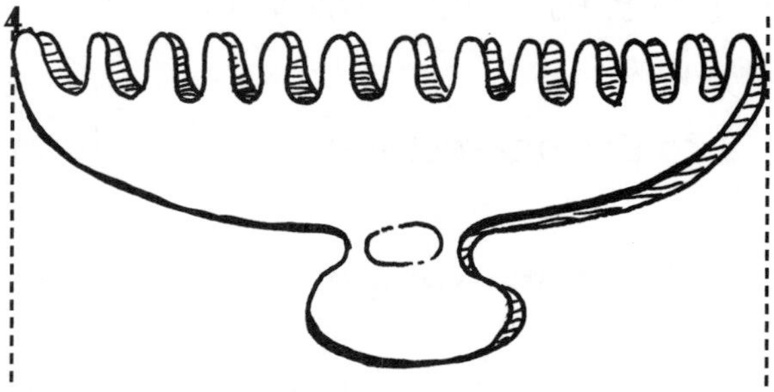

____

5. 

____

6. 

____

Write the appropriate metric unit for measuring each.

7. the length of a driveway

____

8. the width of a window

____

9. the thickness of string

____

10. the height of your backpack

____

11. the distance run in a marathon

____

12. the length of a tennis court

____

Name ______________________________

Change Linear Units

Use a mental image to help you decide whether to multiply or divide when changing linear units.

6 yd = ■ ft

Since each yard has 3 feet, multiply 6 by 3 to find the number of feet in 6 yards.

48 in. = ■ ft

Since each foot has 12 inches, divide 48 by 12 to find the number of feet in 48 inches.

Use a mental image to help you change the units.

1. 3 ft = ______ in. **2.** 12 ft = ______ in. **3.** 15 km = ______ m

4. 36 ft = ______ yd **5.** 80 mm = ______ cm **6.** 36 ft = ______ in.

7. 30 yd = ______ ft **8.** 7 ft = ______ in. **9.** 2 mi = ______ yd

Complete.

10. 3 ft = 2 ft ■ in.

3 ft = 2 ft + ______ ft

= 2 ft + ______ in.

11. 3 km 9 m = 2 km ■ m

3 km 9 m = 2 km + ______ km + 9 m

= 2 km + ______ m + 9 m

= 2 km + ______ m

12. 7 cm 8 mm = 6 cm ■ mm

____

13. 8 mi 30 yd = 7 mi ■ yd

____

Find the sum or difference.

14. 2 ft 3 in.
+4 ft 10 in.

15. 2 ft 1 in.
− 9 in.

16. 8 m 4 cm
− 5 m 80 cm

17. 5 m 13 cm
+ 1 m 5 cm

Name ______________________________

Customary Capacity and Weight

You can change units of weight with multiplication or division.

Change larger units to smaller units by using multiplication.

3 lb = ■ oz

Pounds are larger than ounces, so multiply.

$3 \times 16 = 48$
↑
(16 oz in 1 lb)

So, 3 lb = 48 oz.

Change smaller units to larger units by using division.

48 oz = ■ lb

Ounces are smaller than pounds, so divide.

$48 \div 16 = 3$
↑
(16 oz in 1 lb)

So, 48 oz = 3 lb.

Write *multiply* or *divide*.

Customary Units for Measuring Weight
16 ounces (oz) = 1 pound (lb)
2,000 pounds = 1 ton (T)

1. When I change pounds to tons,

I ______________________.

2. When I change ounces to pounds,

I ______________________.

3. When I change tons to pounds,

I ______________________.

4. When I change pounds to ounces,

I ______________________.

Multiply to solve.

5. 6 lb = __________ oz

6. 15 lb = __________ oz

7. 4 T = __________ lb

8. 1 T = __________ oz

Divide to solve.

9. 20,000 lb = __________ T

10. 128 oz = __________ lb

11. 80 oz = __________ lb

12. 14,000 lb = __________ T

Multiply or divide to solve.

13. 96 oz = __________ lb

14. 20 lb = __________ oz

15. 5 T = __________ lb

16. 12,000 lb = __________ T

Name ______________________________

Metric Capacity and Mass

Use the conversion table to determine whether to multiply or divide to change metric units.

Metric Units of Capacity and Mass
1,000 mL = 1 L
250 mL = 1 metric cup
4 metric cups = 1 L
1,000 liters = 1 kL
1,000 mg = 1 g
1,000 g = 1 kg

Change the unit.

5 liters = ■ metric cups

Think:

1 liter = **4** metric cups

Multiply by 4 to change liters to metric cups.

So, 5 liters = 20 metric cups.

Change the unit.

1. 750 mL= ■ metric cups

250 mL= ________ metric cups

________ by ________ to change mL to metric cups.

750 mL= ________ metric cups

2. 8.5 L= ■ mL

1 L= ________ mL

________ by ________ to change L to mL.

8.5 L= ________ mL

3. 5,000 g= ________ kg

4. 3 kL= ________ L

5. 7 L= ________ metric cups

6. 3,000 mg= ________ g

Name ____________________

Time and Temperature

You can calculate elapsed time by using a clock.

Think of a clock as a circular number line. Count the hours by ones and then count the minutes by fives.

Mark worked from 9 A.M. to 5:15 P.M. How many hours did Mark work?

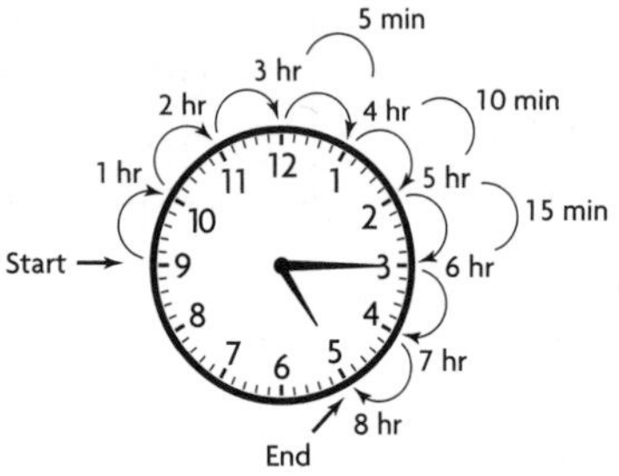

Count the hours and then count the minutes.

So, Mark worked 8 hours 15 minutes.

Use the clocks to determine the missing information.

1. Begin / End

Elapsed time: ____________

2. Begin / End

Elapsed time: ____________

On a thermometer that measures temperature in degrees Fahrenheit, water freezes at 32°F and boils at 212°F. On a thermometer that measures temperature in degrees Celsius, water freezes at 0°C and boils at 100°C.

Choose the temperature that is the better estimate.

3. building a snowman
2°F or 2°C

____

4. a cup of hot chocolate
90°F or 90°C

____

5. a warm spring day
70°F or 70°C

____

6. a good day for the pool
95°F or 95°C

____

7. playing baseball
20°F or 20°C

____

8. wearing a coat
35°F or 35°C

____

Name ______________________________

Problem Solving Skill

Estimate or Actual Measurement

Some problems can be solved by estimating the answer. Other problems need an actual measurement.

Example 1
A can of fruit punch concentrate holds 350 mL. When you add 3 cans of water to the concentrate, will you have more or less than 1 liter of punch?

3 × 350 is about 1 L of water. When you add 350 mL of concentrate, there will be more than 1 L of punch.

Look for key words. The words *more or less* mean that you can **estimate the answer**.

Example 2
A can of fruit punch concentrate holds 350 mL. When you add 3 cans of water to the concentrate, how many liters of punch will you have?

3 × 350 is 1,050 mL of water. Adding 350 mL of concentrate will give 1,400 mL, or 1.4 L, of punch.

Look for key words. The words *how many liters* mean that you should **find an actual measurement**.

Decide whether you need an estimate or an actual measurement. Solve.

1. Ali, Brent, Corey, and Debra are on team A in a tug of war. Ali weighs 53 kg, Brent weighs 62 kg, Corey weighs 58 kg, and Debra weighs 65 kg. The 4 people on team B weigh 210 kg altogether. Which team weighs more?

____

2. Yosef bought 3 pounds of bananas at $0.79 a pound and a gallon of milk for $2.89. He gave the clerk $10.00. How much change did he get?

____

3. Meryl started doing her homework at 4:30 P.M. She spent 20 minutes on math, 15 minutes on English, 12 minutes on science, and 28 minutes on history. What time did Meryl finish her homework?

____

4. Sari's vegetable garden is in the shape of a triangle. The length of the sides are 6 ft 9 in., 7 ft 2 in., and 5 ft 11 in. Does she need more than 20 ft of fencing?

____

Name ______________________

Estimate Perimeter

The **perimeter** of a figure is the distance around the figure. You can use a piece of string to estimate the perimeter of a figure.

Estimate the perimeter of the triangle in centimeters.

Step 1 Lay a piece of string around the figure.

Step 2 Cut the string where it meets itself.

Step 3 Lay the string in a straight line and measure its length with a centimeter ruler.

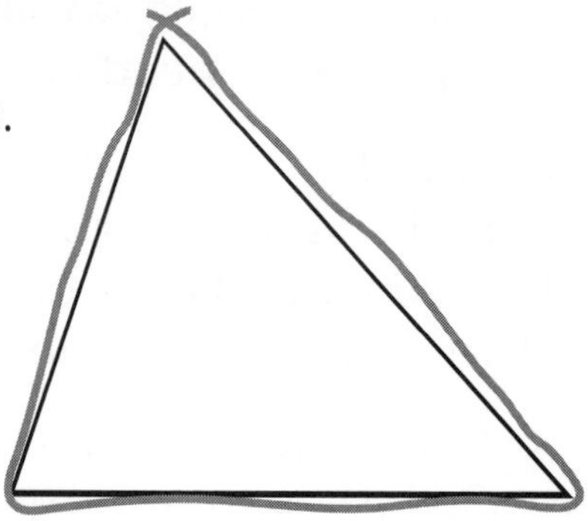

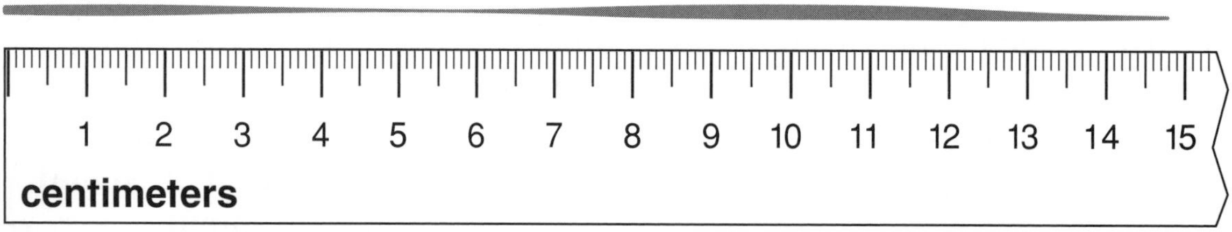

The string is about 15 centimeters long, so the perimeter of the triangle is about 15 centimeters.

Estimate the perimeter of the polygon in centimeters.

1. 

2. 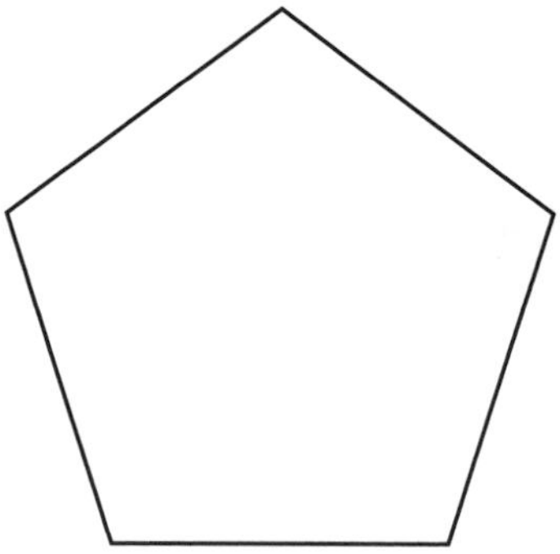

3. 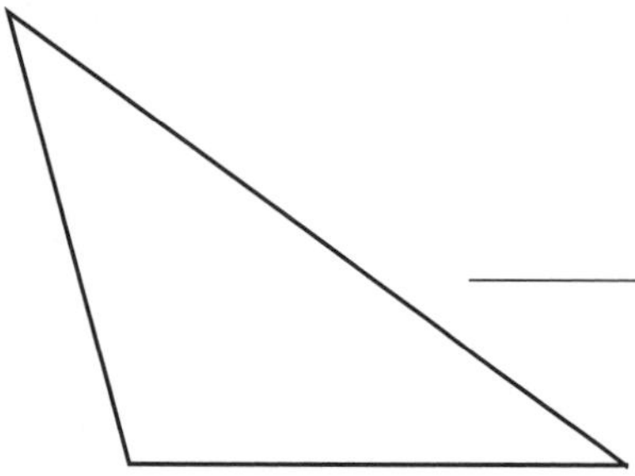

4. 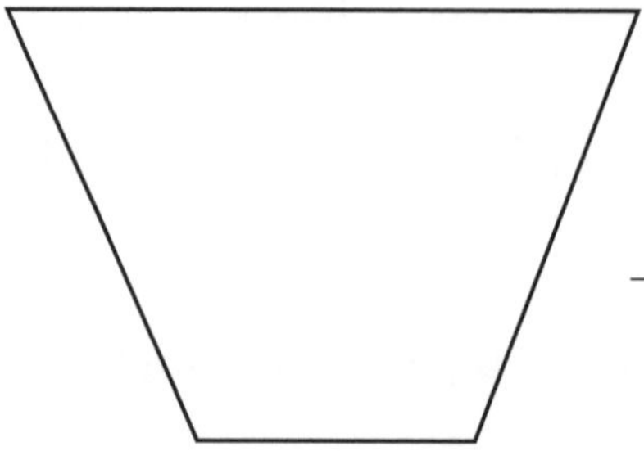

Name ______________________________

Algebra: Find Perimeter

Since opposite sides of a rectangle are equal, you can use a formula to find the perimeter of a rectangle.

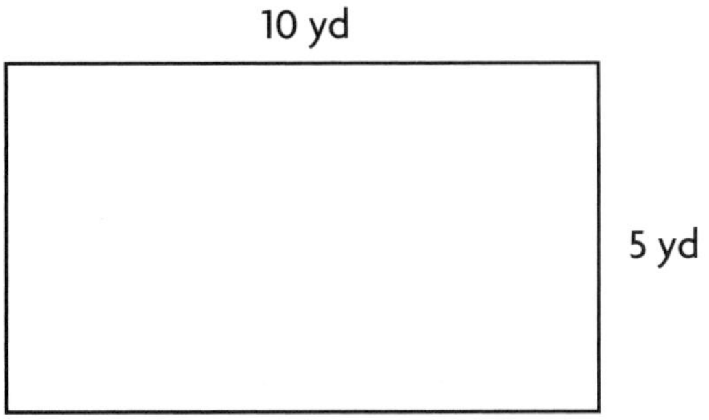

Perimeter (P) $= (2 \times l) + (2 \times w)$
$P = (2 \times 10) + (2 \times 5)$
$P = 20 + 10$
$P = 30$

So, the perimeter of the rectangle is 30 yd.

Since the sides of a regular polygon are equal, you can use a formula to find the perimeter of a regular polygon.

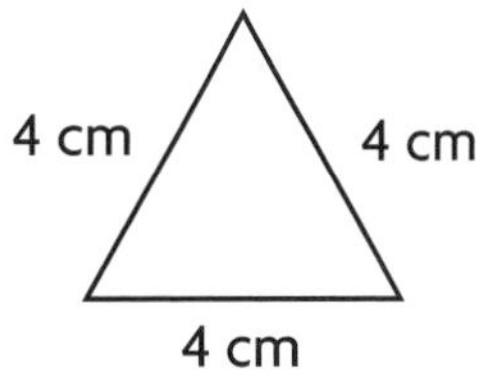

Perimeter (P) $=$ (number of sides) $\times s$
$P = 3 \times 4$
$P = 12$

So, the perimeter of the triangle is 12 cm.

Find the perimeter of each polygon.

1.

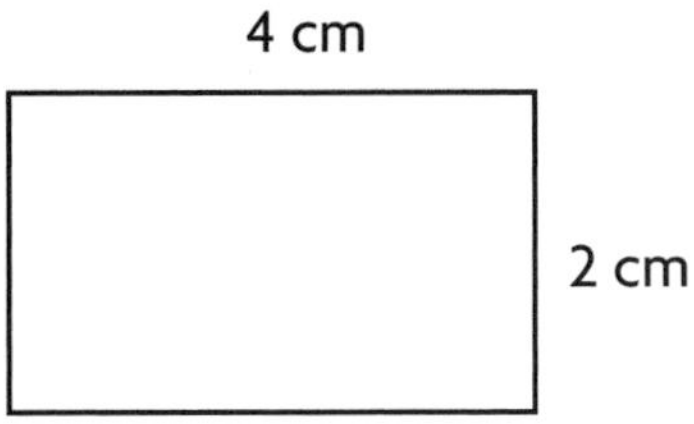

length = ______ width = ______

$P = (2 \times$ ______$) + (2 \times$ ______$)$

$P =$ ______ $+$ ______

$P =$ ______ Perimeter is ______.

2.

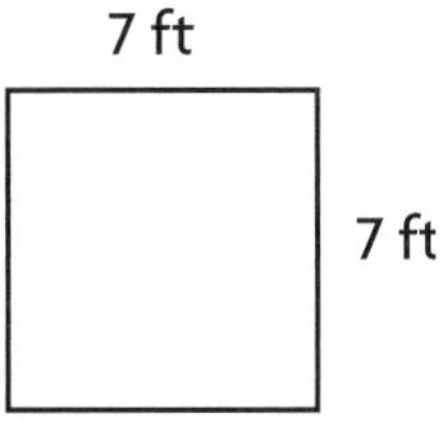

side = ______

$P =$ ______ $\times$ ______

$P =$ ______ Perimeter is ______.

3.

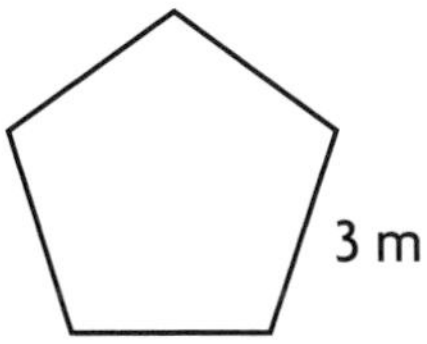

side = ______

$P =$ ______ $\times$ ______

$P =$ ______ Perimeter is ______.

4.

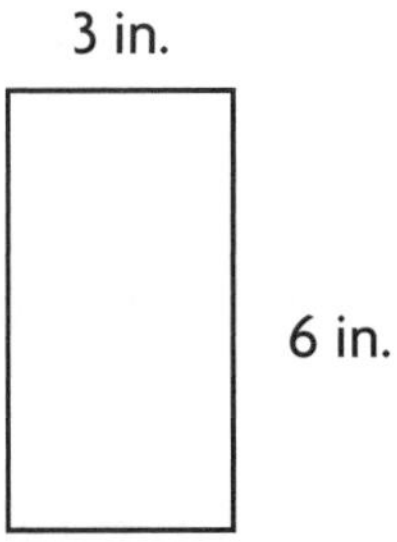

length = ______

width = ______

$P = (2 \times$ ______$) + (2 \times$ ______$)$

$P =$ ______ $+$ ______

$P =$ ______ Perimeter is ______.

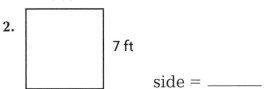

Name ____________________

Problem Solving Skill

Make Generalizations

When you generalize, you make a statement that is true about a whole group of similar situations. Read the following problem.

Jesse is going camping. He will take with him: a box of cereal, paper towels, a flashlight, a soccer ball, and a tent shaped like a teepee. What polyhedrons will Jesse take on his camping trip?

1. Use what you know about each object to make a generalization. You can create a chart.

OBJECT	GENERALIZATION
cereal	Cereal usually comes in rectangular boxes.
paper towels	Paper towels come in a roll, which is a cylinder.
a flashlight	
a soccer ball	
tent	

2. Sort the shapes.

____

____

3. Solve the problem. Which shapes are polyhedrons? Explain.

____

4. Describe the strategy you used.

____

Use what you know about each object to make a generalization. Then solve.

5. Annie takes a book, 2 cans of fruit juice, and a wedge pillow to the beach. What solid figures does she have? How many of these are polyhedrons?

____

____

Name ___________________________________

Algebra: Circumference

The distance around a circular object is called its **circumference.**

A chord that passes through the center of a circle is a **diameter**.

If you know the diameter of a circle, you can find the circumference.

> **Remember. . .**
> The relationship of the diameter to the circumference of a circle, $C \div d$, is about 3.14 and is called *pi*.

Circumference $\approx$ diameter $\times$ 3.14, or $C \approx d \times 3.14$

$\approx$ means "is approximately equal to".

Find the circumference of this circle.

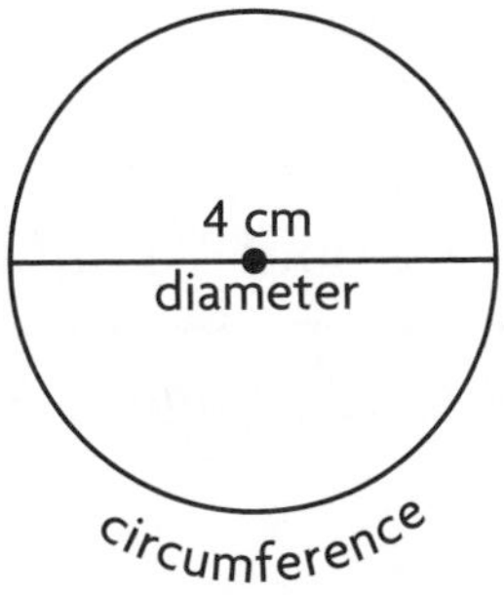

Diameter = 4

Circumference $\approx$ diameter $\times$ 3.14

$\approx 4 \times 3.14$

≈ 12.56

The circumference is approximately equal to 12.56 cm.

The diameter of each circle is given. Multiply the diameter times 3.14 to find the circumference. Round to the nearest tenth.

1.

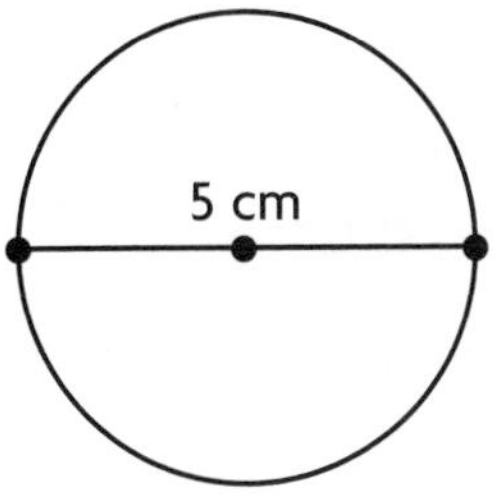

____

2.

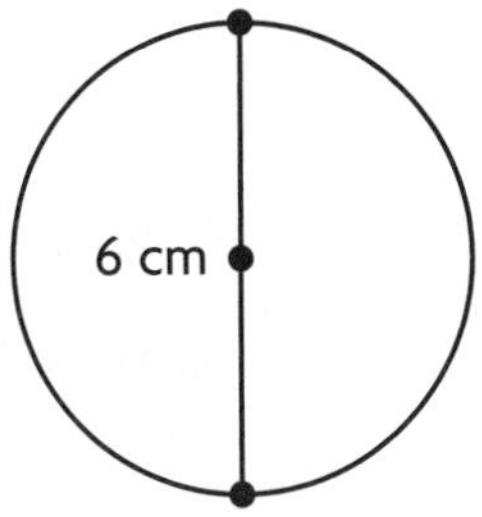

____

3.

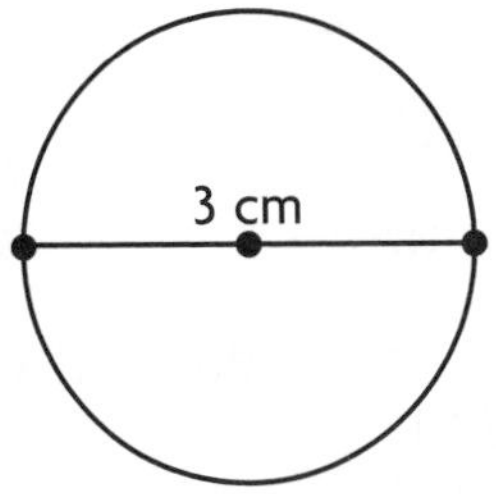

____

4.

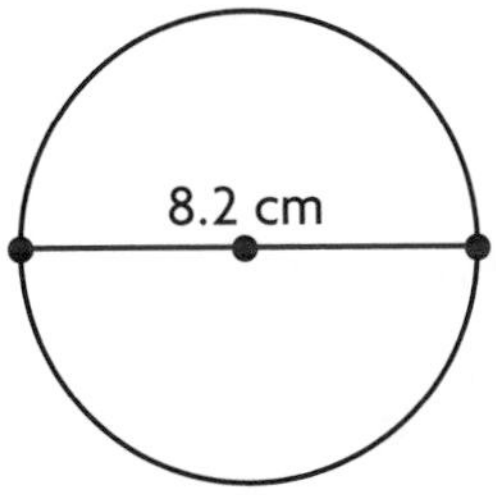

____

5.

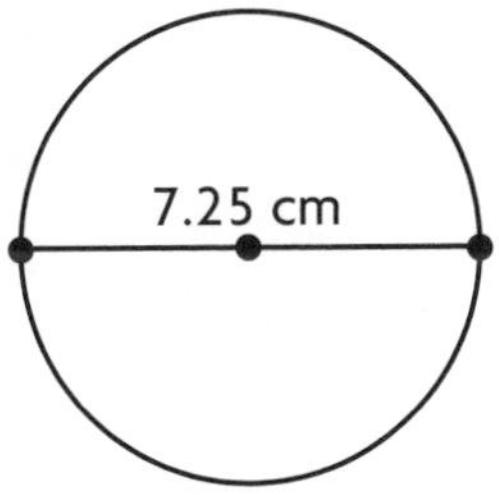

____

6.

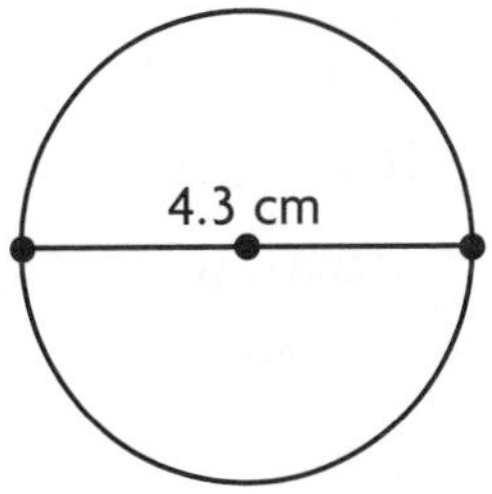

____

Name ______________________________

Estimate Area

Count full and half-full square units to estimate the area of an irregular figure on grid paper.

Count: 8 full squares; 12 half-full squares
Divide: $12 \div 2 = 6$
Add: $8 + 6 = 14$

The area of the figure is about 14 square units.

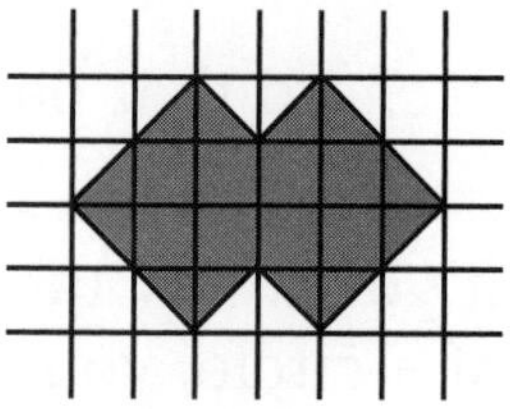

When you have a figure with a curved edge, you need to count full squares, almost-full squares, and half-full squares.

Count: 8 full squares; 2 almost-full squares
6 half-full squares
Divide: $6 \div 2 = 3$
Add: $8 + 2 + 3 = 13$

The area of the figure is about 13 square units.

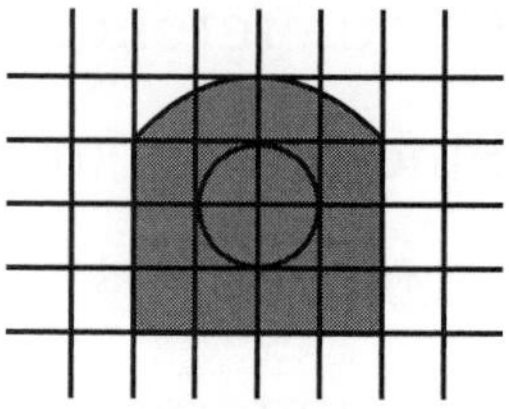

Estimate the area of the shaded figure. Each square on the grid is 1 cm^2.

1.

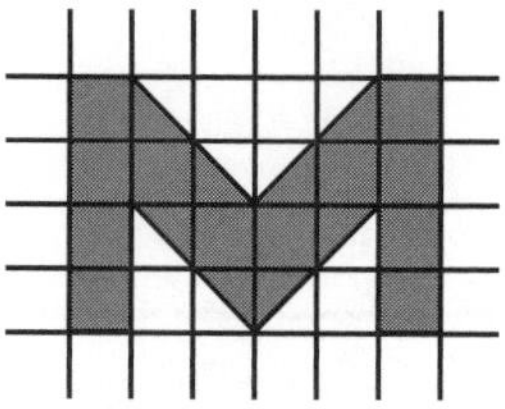

_____ full squares
_____ half-full squares
_____ $\div 2 =$ _____
_____ + _____ = _____
Area is about _____ cm^2.

2.

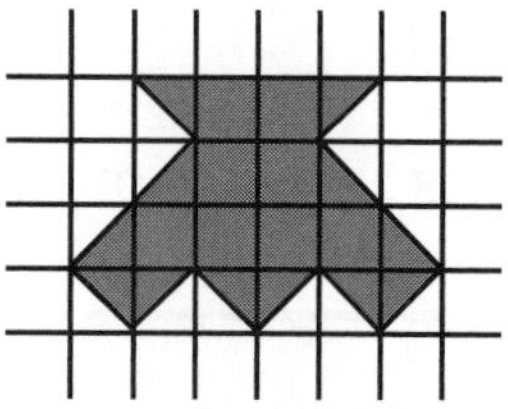

_____ full squares
_____ half-full squares
_____ $\div 2 =$ _____
_____ + _____ = _____
Area is about _____ cm^2.

Estimate the area of the shaded figure. Each square on the grid is 1 $in.^2$

3.

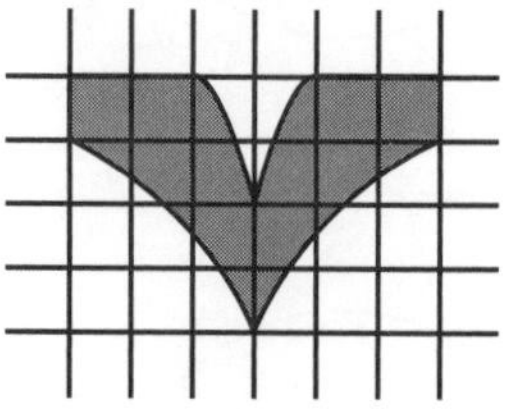

_____ full squares
_____ almost-full squares
_____ half-full squares
_____ $\div 2 =$ _____
_____ + _____ + _____ = _____
Area is about _____ $in.^2$

4.

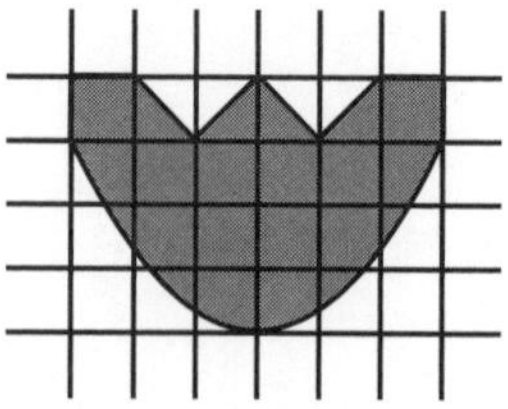

_____ full squares
_____ almost-full squares
_____ half-full squares
_____ $\div 2 =$ _____
_____ + _____ + _____ = _____
Area is about _____ $in.^2$

Name ______________________________

Algebra: Area of Squares and Rectangles

You can use a formula to find the area of a rectangle.

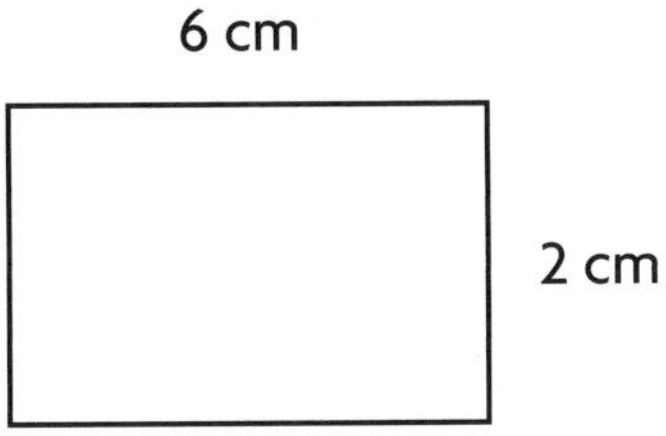

Area $(A) = l \times w$
$A = 6 \times 2$
$A = 12$

So, the area of the rectangle is 12 cm^2.

You can use a formula to find the area of a square.

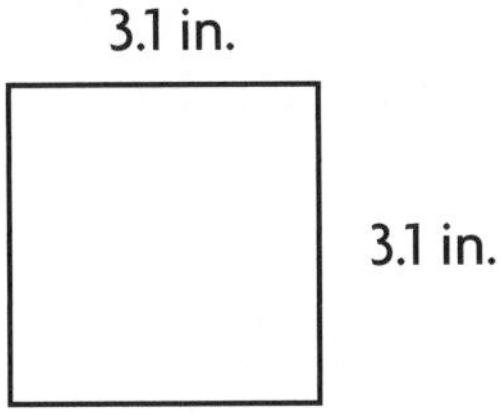

Area $(A) = s \times s$
$A = 3.1 \times 3.1$
$A = 9.61$

So, the area of the square is 9.61 $in.^2$

Find the area of each figure.

1.

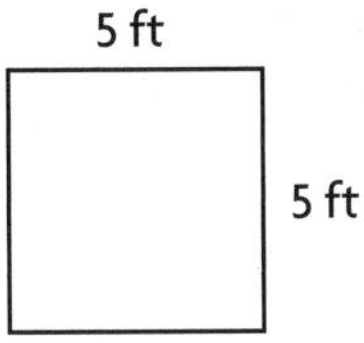

side = ________

A = ________ $\times$ ________

A = ________

Area is ________.

2.

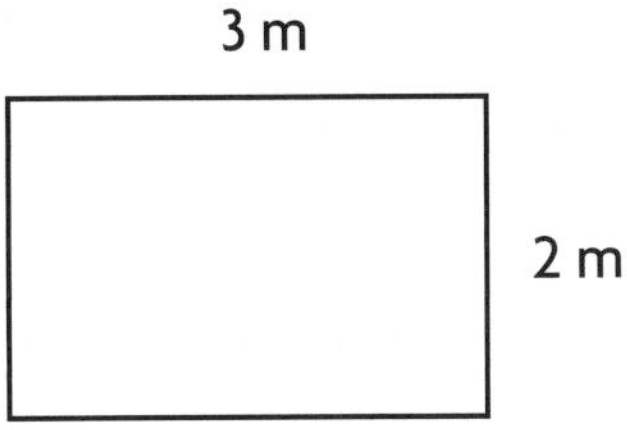

length (l) = ________

width (w) = ________

A = ________ $\times$ ________

A = ________

Area is ________.

3.

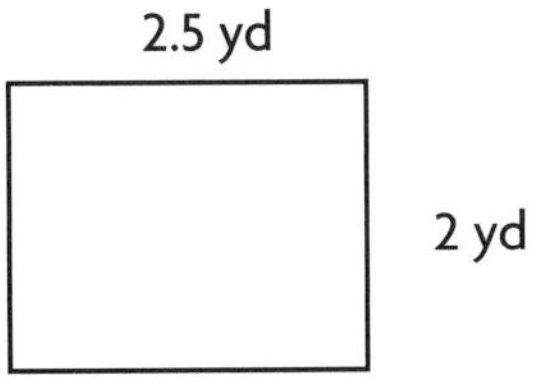

length (l) = ________

width (w) = ________

A = ________ $\times$ ________

A = ________

Area is ________.

4.

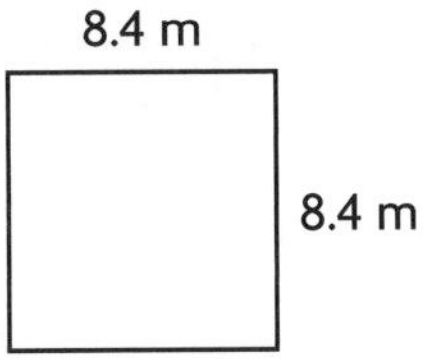

side = ________

A = ________ $\times$ ________

A = ________

Area is ________.

Name ____________________

Relate Perimeter and Area

Rectangles with the same perimeter can have different areas.

Look at the rectangles below. Each rectangle has a perimeter of 24 cm, but their areas are different.

> **Remember...**
> Area (A) = length (l) $\times$ width (w)

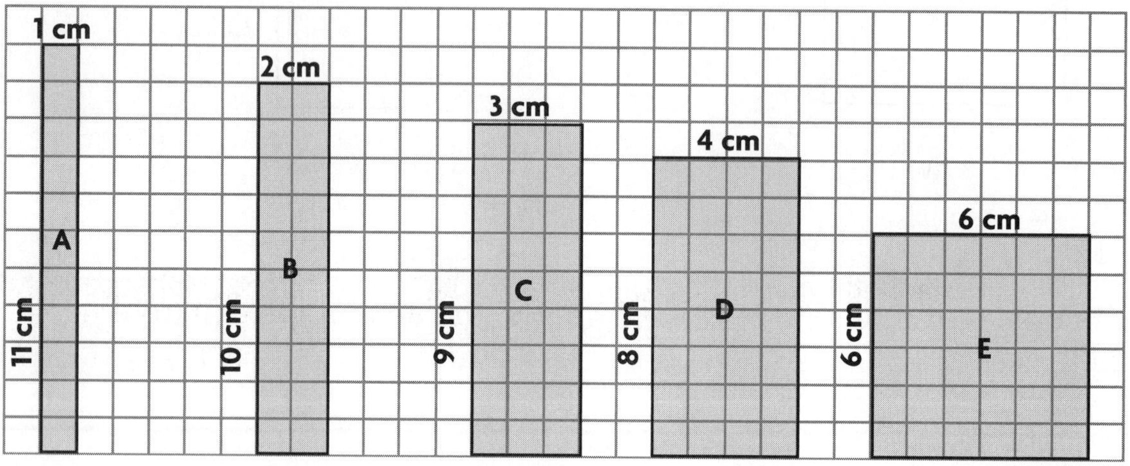

Rectangle A:	Rectangle B:	Rectangle C:	Rectangle D:	Rectangle E:
1 cm $\times$ 11 cm	2 cm $\times$ 10 cm	3 cm $\times$ 9 cm	4 cm $\times$ 8 cm	6 cm $\times$ 6 cm
Area = 11 cm^2	Area = 20 cm^2	Area = 27 cm^2	Area = 32 cm^2	Area = 36 cm^2

Rectangle E is the rectangle with the greatest area, 36 cm^2.

Use the grid to draw rectangles for the given perimeter. Name the length and width of the rectangle with the greatest area.

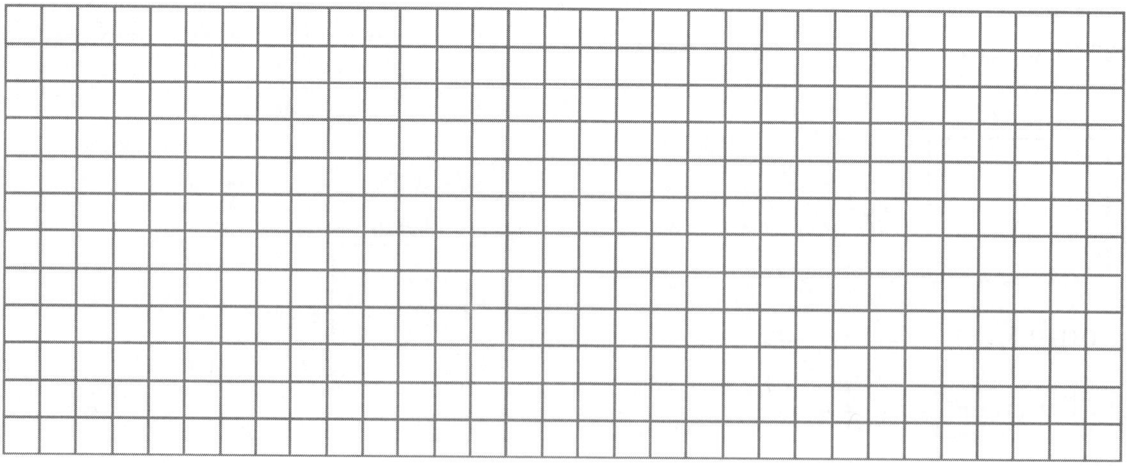

1. Perimeter = 12 cm

____

2. Perimeter = 28 cm

____

Name ______________________________

Algebra: Area of Triangles

Use what you know about the area of a rectangle to find the area of a triangle.

- Area of a rectangle equals length × width. ($A = l \times w$)
- The area of a triangle is half the area of a rectangle with the same base and height. ($A = \frac{1}{2} \times b \times h$)

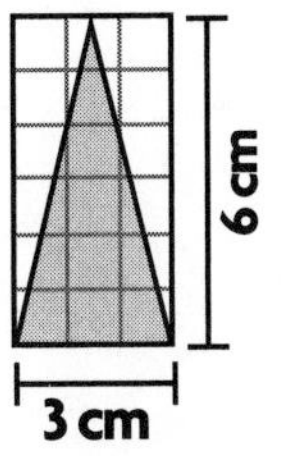

base (b) = 3 cm
height (h) = 6 cm

Area (A) $= \frac{1}{2} \times b \times h$

$A = \frac{1}{2} \times 3 \times 6$

$A = \frac{1}{2} \times 18 = 9$

Area is 9 cm^2.

Find the area of these triangles.

1.

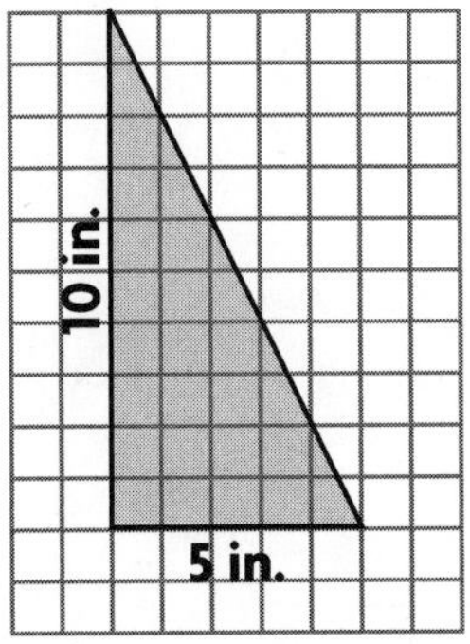

base (b) = ________

height (h) = ________

$A = \frac{1}{2} \times$ ________ $\times$ ________

$A =$ ________ Area is ________.

2.

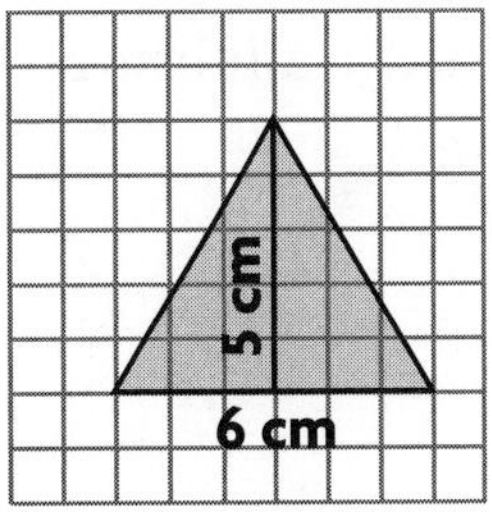

base (b) = ________

height (h) = ________

$A = \frac{1}{2} \times$ ________ $\times$ ________

$A =$ ________ Area is ________.

3.

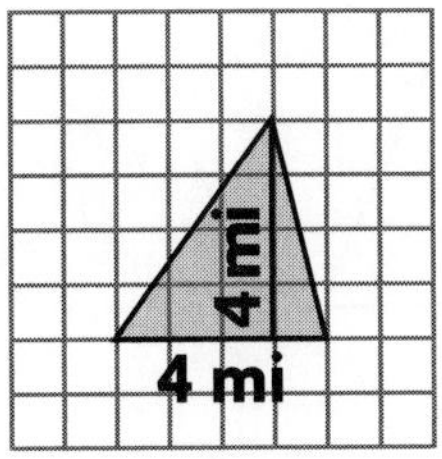

base (b) = ________

height (h) = ________

$A = \frac{1}{2} \times$ ________ $\times$ ________

$A =$ ________ Area is ________.

4.

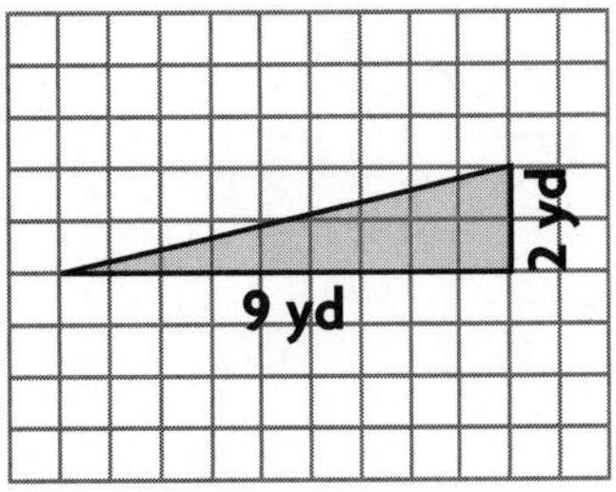

base (b) = ________

height (h) = ________

$A = \frac{1}{2} \times$ ________ $\times$ ________

$A =$ ________ Area is ________.

Algebra: Area of Parallelograms

Use what you know about the area of a rectangle to find the area of a parallelogram.

- Area of a rectangle equals length × width. ($A = l \times w$)
- The area of a parallelogram is equal to the area of a rectangle with the same base (length) and height (width). ($A = b \times h$)

You can use a formula to find the area of a parallelogram.

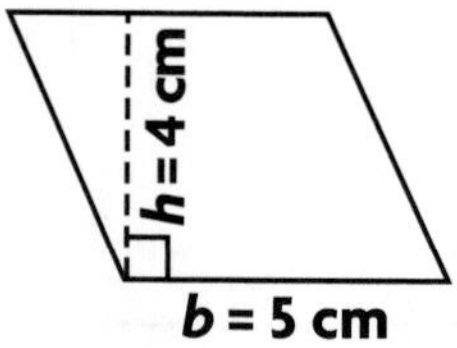

base (b) = 5 cm
height (h) = 4 cm

Area (A) = $b \times h$
$A = 5 \times 4$
$A = 20$
Area is 20 cm^2.

Find the area of these parallelograms.

1.

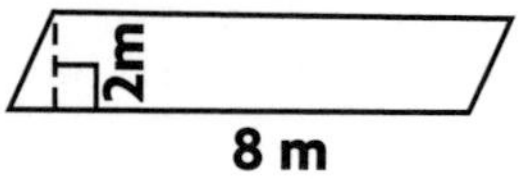

base (b) = ________
height (h) = ________
A = ________ × ________
A = ________ Area is ________.

2.

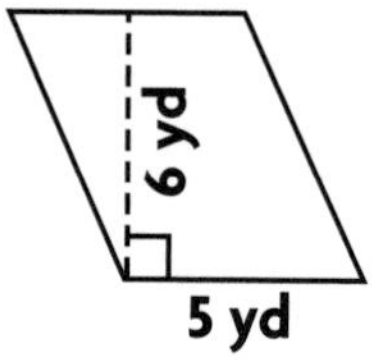

base (b) = ________
height (h) = ________
A = ________ × ________
A = ________ Area is ________.

3.

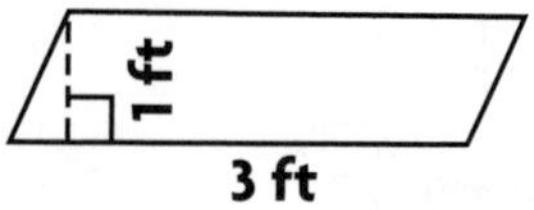

base (b) = ________
height (h) = ________
A = ________ × ________
A = ________ Area is ________.

4.

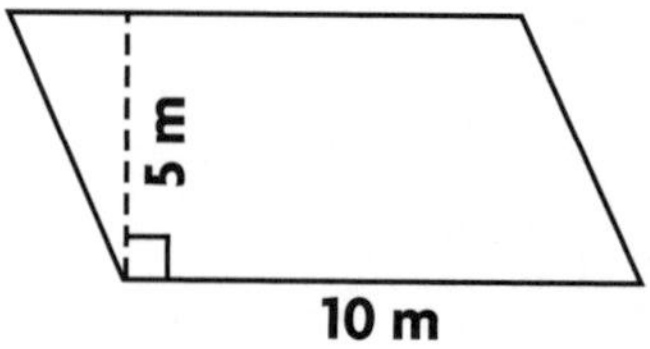

base (b) = ________
height (h) = ________
A = ________ × ________
A = ________ Area is ________.

Name ______________________________

Problem Solving Strategy

Solve a Simpler Problem

Peter wants to paint a triangle with red paint on the playground. The height of the triangle will be 20 meters and the base 5 meters. Each container of red paint covers 10 square meters. How many containers of red paint will Peter need to paint his whole triangle?

Step 1

What does the problem ask? It asks how many containers of paint Peter will need.

Step 2

Find the area of the triangle.

Area $(A) = \frac{1}{2} \times$ base $(b) \times$ height (h)

$A = \frac{1}{2} \times 5 \times 20$

$A = 50$ The area is 50 m^2.

Step 3

Identify the number of 10 m^2 containers needed to cover 50 m^2.

Divide.

$50 \div 10 = 5$

So, Peter needs 5 containers of paint to paint the triangle on the playground.

Break these problems into simpler steps to solve.

1. Frank's house needs new carpet. The living room is 12 feet long and 13 feet wide. The dining room is 15 feet long and 11 feet wide. How many square feet of carpet will be needed?

   ____

2. Tom is laying new sod in his yard. His front yard is 20 yd by 15 yd, and his backyard is 20 yd by 20 yd. Sod is sold by the square foot. How many square feet of sod does Tom need?

   ____

Name ______________________________

Nets for Solid Figures

A **net** is a two-dimensional pattern for a three-dimensional prism or pyramid.

Look at the net at the right.

- It has 1 triangular base.
- It has 3 other triangular faces.

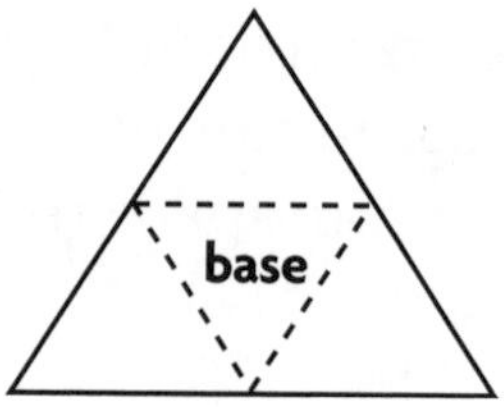

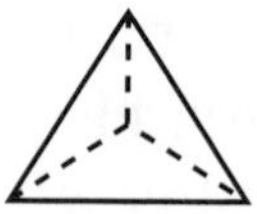

Think about how you could fold it to make a solid figure.

- It folds into a triangular pyramid.

Look at the second net at the right.

- It has 2 rectangular bases.
- It has 4 other rectangular faces.

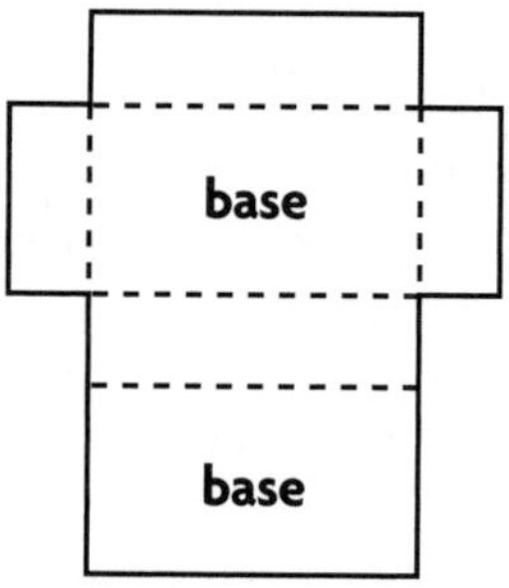

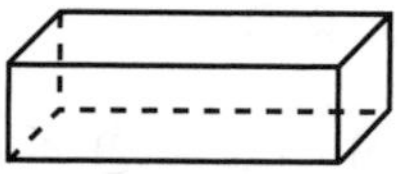

Think about how you could fold it to make a solid figure.

- It folds into a rectangular prism.

Match each solid figure with its net.

1.

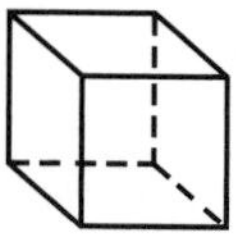

____

2.

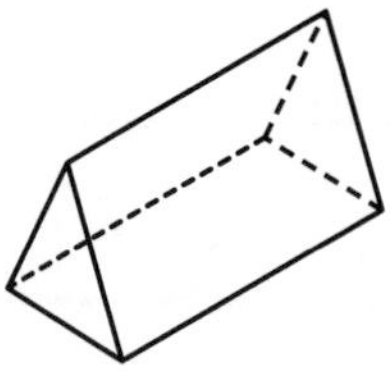

____

3.

____

a.

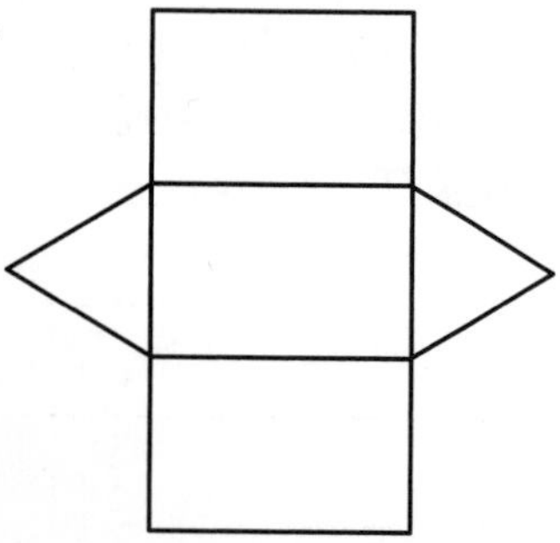

b.

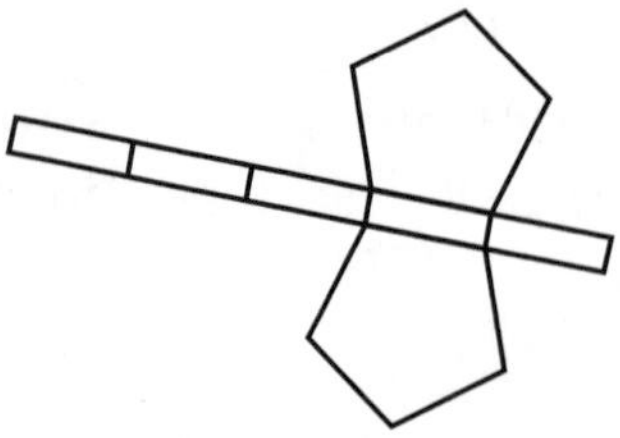

c.

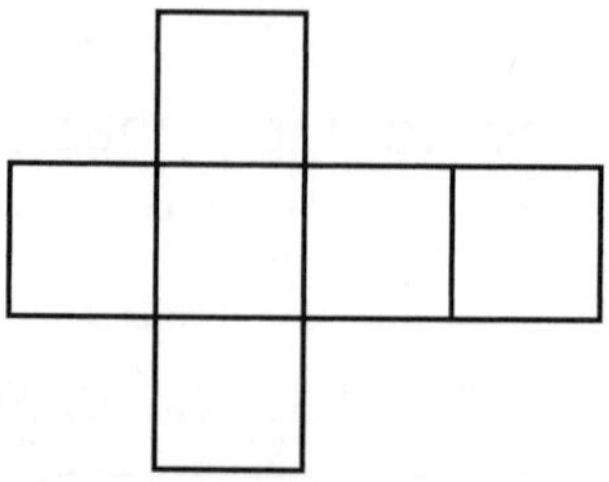

Name ______________________________

Surface Area

The surface area of a solid figure is the sum of the areas of its faces. To find the surface area of a box, add the areas of the 6 faces.

Use the net to find the area of each face in cm^2. Then add the areas.

Face	Area
Top (C)	$5 \times 4 = 20\ cm^2$
Bottom (E)	$5 \times 4 = 20\ cm^2$
Left (A)	$4 \times 7 = 28\ cm^2$
Right (F)	$4 \times 7 = 28\ cm^2$
Front (D)	$5 \times 7 = 35\ cm^2$
Back (B)	$5 \times 7 = 35\ cm^2$
Total Area	$166\ cm^2$

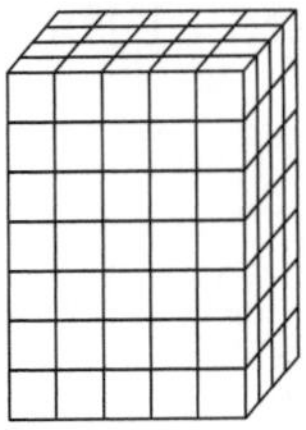

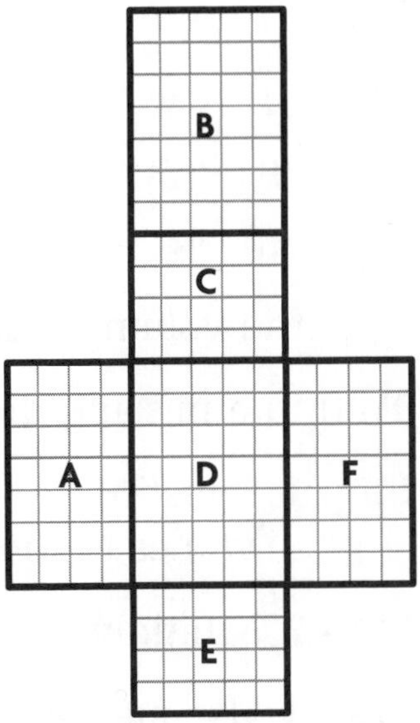

Use the net to find the area of each face in $in.^2$ Then find the surface area of each box.

1.

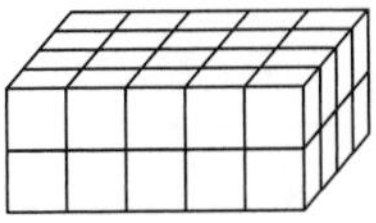

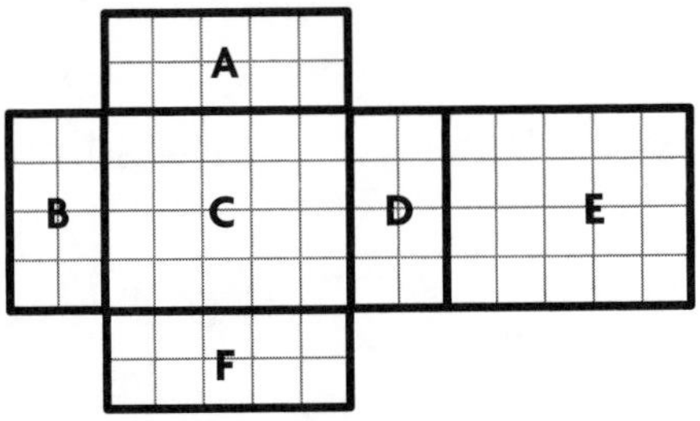

Face	Area
Top (C)	$5 \times 4 =$
Bottom (E)	
Left (B)	
Right (D)	
Front (F)	
Back (A)	
Total Area	

2.

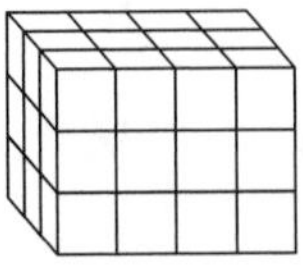

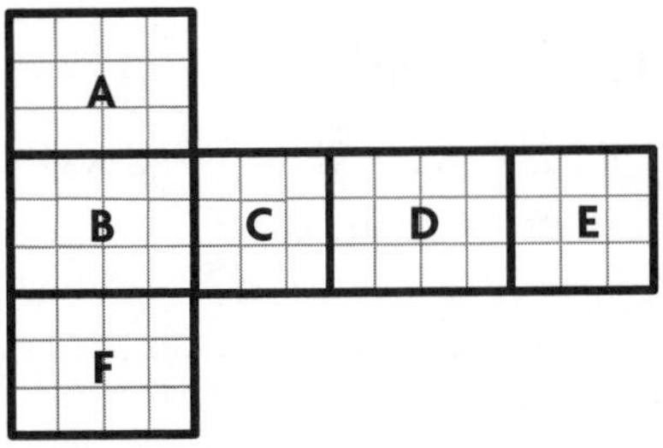

Face	Area
Top (B)	$4 \times 3 =$
Bottom (D)	
Left (E)	
Right (C)	
Front (F)	
Back (A)	
Total Area	

Name ______________________________

Algebra: Estimate and Find Volume

Volume is the amount of space a solid figure occupies or can hold. The formula for volume is:

Volume = length × width × height

Look at the rectangular prism at the right.

$V = l \times w \times h$

$V = (8 \times 5) \times 6$

$V = 40 \times 6 = 240$

So, the volume is 240 cm^3.

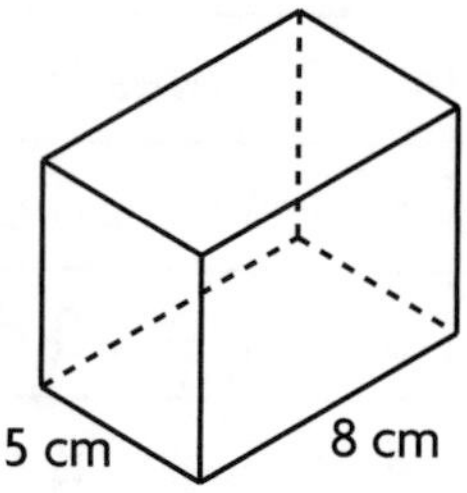

To find a missing dimension, use the formula for volume.

Step 1 Substitute the known values in the formula. $V = l \times w \times h$; $200 = (10 \times 4) \times h$

Step 2 Multiply. $200 = 40 \times h$

Step 3 Use mental math. Think: 40 times what number equals 200? $200 = 40 \times 5$; $5 = h$

So, the height is 5 ft.

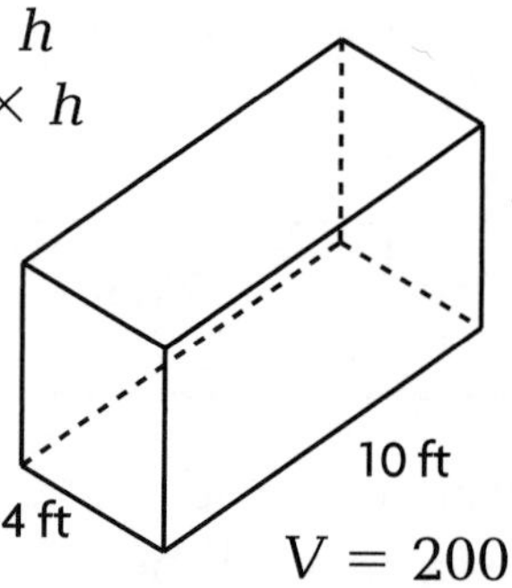

Find the volume.

1. l = 12 yd, w = 2 yd, h = 6 yd

   V = ____________

2. l = 7 m, w = 12 m, h = 2 m

   V = ____________

3. l = 11 cm, w = 7 cm, h = 3 cm

   V = ____________

Find the missing dimension.

4. length = 6 in.
   width = 8 in.
   height = ________
   Volume = 240 $in.^3$

5. length = ________
   width = 5 m
   height = 2 m
   Volume = 150 m^3

6. length = 10 ft
   width = ________
   height = 9 ft
   Volume = 270 ft^3

7. length = 4 ft
   width = 5 ft
   height = ________
   Volume = 120 ft^3

8. length = 6 cm
   width = ________
   height = 12 cm
   Volume = 216 cm^3

9. length = ________
   width = 14 in.
   height = 7 in.
   Volume = 1,960 $in.^3$

Name ______________________________

Measure Perimeter, Area, and Volume

Keywords can help you decide upon the appropriate unit of measure.

- Use *linear units* to measure the length of or distance around an object.

  Keywords: around, length, height, distance, perimeter

- Use *square units* to measure the area of an object.

  Keywords: cover, area, surface area

- Use *cubic units* to measure the volume of an object.

  Keywords: volume, capacity, fill, space

Substitute *inches, meters,* and so on for *units* when you are given specific measurements.

Underline the keywords and tell the appropriate units to measure each. Write *linear, square,* or *cubic.*

1. capacity of a mug ____________

2. paper to cover a box ____________

3. length of a room ____________

Underline the keyword and write the units you would use to measure each.

4. surface area of this cube

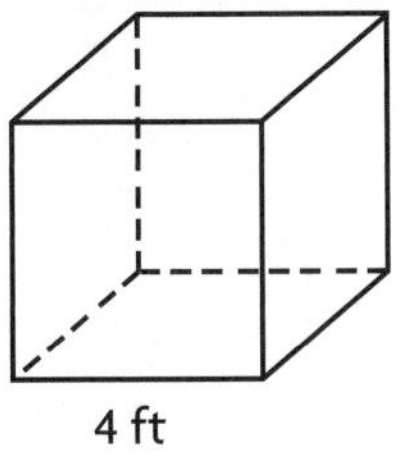

____

5. perimeter of this square

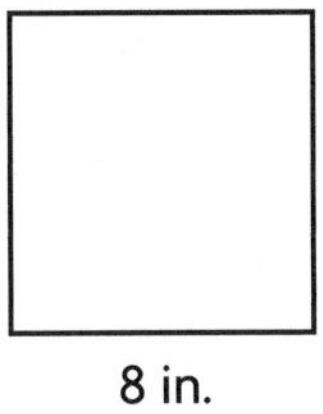

____

6. volume of this prism

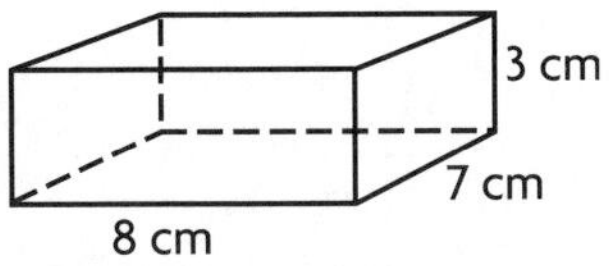

____

7. area of this parallelogram

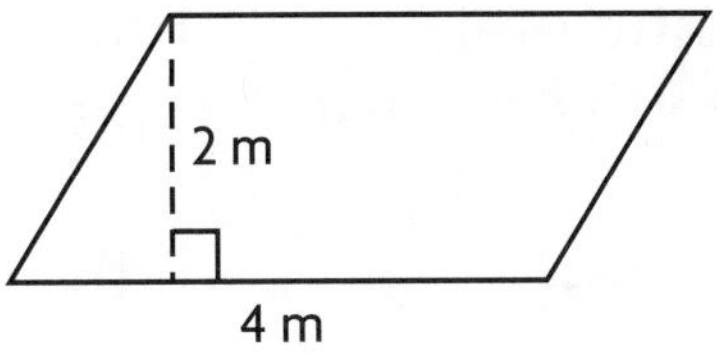

____

Name ____________________

Problem Solving Skill

Use a Formula

Paul wants to send some things to his brother at camp. He finds a box in his garage that is 12 inches long and 10 inches wide. It has a volume of 1,200 cubic inches. Paul wants to pack a container that is 14 inches high. Will the container fit in the box?

To answer the question, you need to find the height of the box.

Use the formula for volume. $V = l \times w \times h$

- Substitute. $1{,}200 = 12 \times 10 \times h$
- Multiply. $1{,}200 = 120 \times h$
- Use mental math. $1{,}200 = 120 \times 10$

The height is 10 inches. The answer is *no*, the container will not fit in the box. $h = 10$

Use a formula and solve.

1. Rita wants to put a wallpaper border around her room. Her room is 11 ft by 13 ft. How many ft of border does she need to do the job? How many sq ft of carpet are required to carpet the room?

____

____

2. Matthew needs to return a lamp that measures 15 inches by 12 inches by 8 inches. He has a box that is 16 inches long and 13 inches wide. It has a volume of 2,080 cubic inches. Is the box big enough for the lamp?

____

____

3. Mark needs to ship 500,000 cubic centimeters of peanuts. The shipping crate is 90 centimeters by 80 centimeters by 70 centimeters. Is it large enough to ship the peanuts? Explain.

____

____

4. How many square feet of carpet do you need to cover a 12-foot by 15-foot room? how many square yards?

____

____

Name ____

Understand Ratios

You can use decimal models to help find ratios. Ratios compare two quantities. There are three types of ratios.

Part to Whole

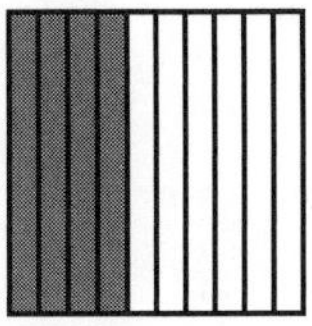

Shaded parts: 4

Total parts: 10

So, the ratio of part to whole is 4 to 10.

Whole to Part

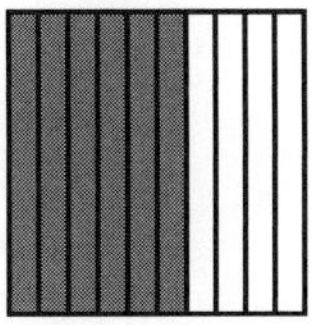

Total parts: 10

Shaded parts: 6

So, the ratio of whole to part is 10 to 6.

Part to Part

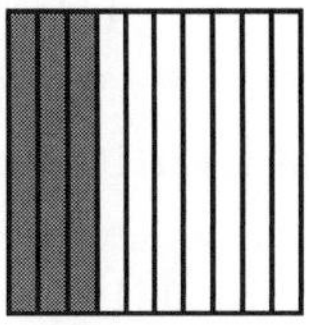

Shaded parts: 3

Unshaded parts: 7

So, the ratio of part to part is 3 to 7 or 7 to 3.

Complete the ratios.

1.

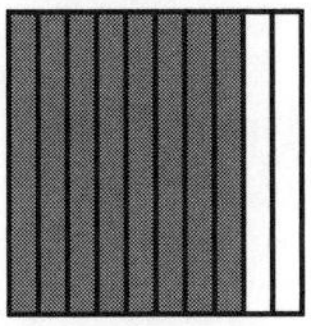

shaded parts: __________

total parts: __________

part to whole ratio __________

2.

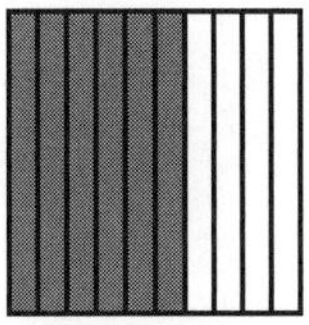

shaded parts: __________

unshaded parts: __________

part to part ratio: __________

3.

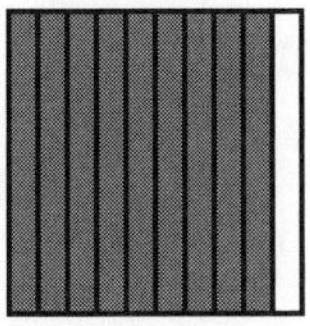

part to whole ratio: __________

whole to part ratio: __________

part to part ratio: __________

4.

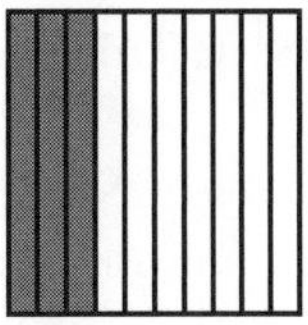

part to whole ratio: __________

whole to part ratio: __________

part to part ratio: __________

Tell which type of ratio is expressed.

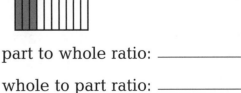

5.

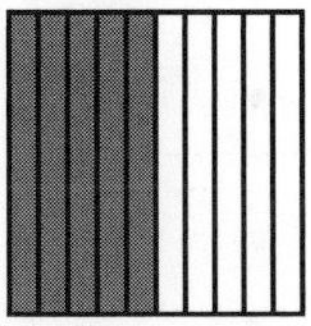

5 to 5 ______________________________

10 to 5 ______________________________

Name ______________________________________

Express Ratios

You can write ratios in three ways.

A **part to whole** ratio can be written:

6 to 10   6:10 $\frac{6}{10}$

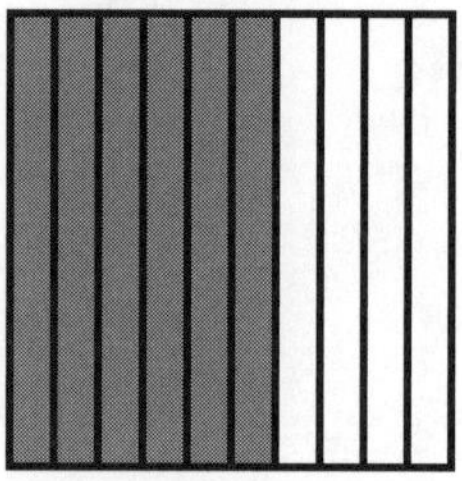

A **whole to part** ratio can be written:

10 to 6   10:6 $\frac{10}{6}$

A **part to part** ratio can be written:

6 to 4   6:4 $\frac{6}{4}$

Write each ratio in three ways. Then name the type of ratio.

1. 4 red counters to 3 green counters

____

2. 12 pencils to 6 pens

____

3. 2 soccer balls out of 11 balls

____

4. 16 of 24 students are boys

____

Circle *a, b,* or *c* to show which ratio represents each comparison.

5. 3 red apples out of 8 apples

a $\frac{3}{8}$ **b** 8:3   **c** 3 to 11

6. 7 boys to 8 girls

a $\frac{8}{7}$ **b** 7:8   **c** 7 to 15

7. 8 baseballs to 13 basketballs

a 21:8   **b** 13 to 8   **c** $\frac{8}{13}$

8. 1 month out of 12 months

a 1:11   **b** 12 to 1   **c** 1 to 12

Write each ratio in two other ways.

9. 3:5 ______________

10. 11 to 13 ______________

11. 28 to 47 ______________

12. 14:6 ______________

13. $\frac{21}{4}$ ______________

14. $\frac{7}{19}$ ______________

Name ______________________________

Ratios and Proportions

You can use pictures to show equivalent ratios.

This shows the ratio 3:4.

□□□
△△△△

This shows an equivalent ratio, 6:8.

□□□ □□□
△△△△ △△△△

You can also use fractions to show equivalent ratios.

$$\frac{3}{4} = \frac{6}{8} = \frac{9}{12} = \frac{12}{16} = \frac{15}{20} = \frac{18}{24}$$

Write two fractions that are equivalent to each ratio.

1. $\frac{4}{5} =$ ______ = ______

2. $\frac{9}{2} =$ ______ = ______

3. $\frac{11}{12} =$ ______ = ______

4. $\frac{6}{10} =$ ______ = ______

5. $\frac{8}{6} =$ ______ = ______

6. $\frac{3}{7} =$ ______ = ______

Write two ratios that are equivalent to each ratio.

7. 2:3 ______________

8. 3 to 4 ______________

9. 8 to 12 ______________

10. 5:7 ______________

11. 11:9 ______________

12. 16 to 4 ______________

13. 1:6 ______________

14. 2 to 10 ______________

15. 7:11 ______________

16. 2:6 ______________

Draw pictures to determine if the ratios are equivalent. Then write *yes* or *no*.

17. 1:2 and 3:6 ______

18. 3:4 and 4:6 ______

19. 2:3 and 3:5 ______

20. 2:5 and 4:10 ______

Name ______________________________

Scale Drawings

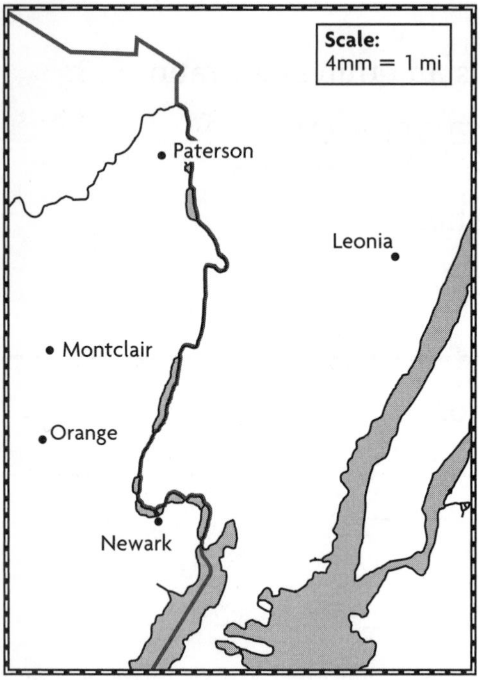

You can use map scales and equivalent ratios to determine actual distances.

In this map of New Jersey, the scale is 4 mm = 1 mi. So, the ratio of millimeters to miles is 4:1.

The map distance from Paterson to Leonia is about 36 mm. What is the actual distance in miles?

Use equivalent ratios.

$$\frac{4}{1} = \frac{36}{n} \qquad \begin{matrix} \longleftarrow 4 \times 9 = 36 \\ \longleftarrow 1 \times 9 = 9 \end{matrix}$$

Since $4 \times 9 = 36$, you would multiply 1×9.

So, the distance from Paterson to Leonia is 9 miles.

Use the map scale above and equivalent ratios to find the actual distance.

1. The map distance from Paterson to Newark is 48 mm.

   What is the distance in miles? __________

2. The map distance from Montclair to Orange is 12 mm.

   What is the distance in miles? __________

3. The map distance from Paterson to Orange is 42 mm.

   What is the distance in miles? __________

Use a map scale of 1 cm = 15 mi and equivalent ratios to complete the table.

4. Watertown to Belmont	6 cm	________
5. Arlington to Bedford	4 cm	________
6. Belmont to Avon	11 cm	________
7. Franklin to Millis	3.5 cm	________

Name ______________________________

Problem Solving Skill

Too Much/Too Little Information

Sometimes you have *too much* or *too little* information to solve a problem. When you are given *too much* information, you must decide what information to use to solve the problem. When you are given *too little* information, you can't solve the problem.

Read the table carefully. Look at the question and decide if you have *too much* or *too little* information.

What is Jared's ratio of rainbowfish to tetras?

Jared's Fish Populations Fish to Types of Fish	
fish : catfish	5:1
fish : rainbowfish	25:3
fish : tetras	25:5

What information you **Know:**

- You know Jared's ratio of fish to rainbowfish is 25:3.
- You know Jared's ratio of fish to tetras is 25:5.

What information you **Don't Need:**

- You don't need the information on catfish.

You have too much information, so you can solve the problem. Jared's ratio of rainbowfish to tetras is 3:5.

Use the table to complete each problem.

1. How many red rainbowfish does Jared have for every one rainbowfish?

   ____

   What you Know:

   ____

   What you Don't Need:

   ____

   What you Need to Know:

   ____

2. How many fish are there for every one tetra?

   ____

   What you Know:

   ____

   What you Don't Need:

   ____

   What you Need to Know:

   ____

Name ______________________________

Understand Percent

You can represent part of the whole by using a percent. **Percent** means "per hundred." 100 percent is the whole.

The 10 × 10 grid has 100 squares. Each square represents 1 percent.

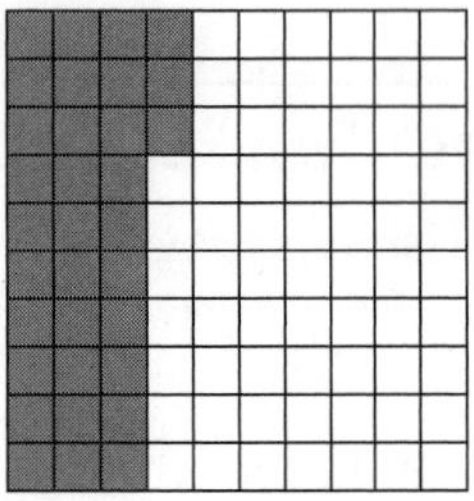

33 squares are shaded.
So, 33% of the squares are shaded.
67% of the squares are unshaded.

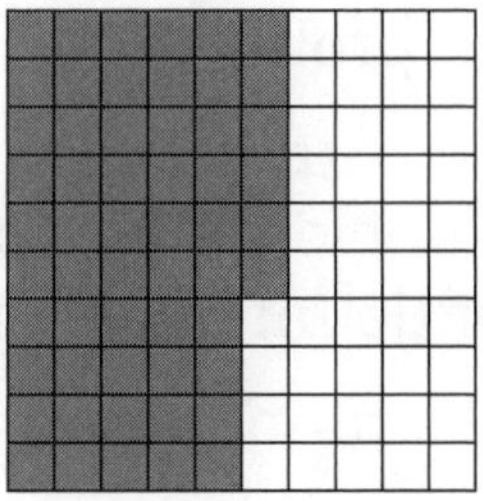

56 squares are shaded.
So, 56% of the squares are shaded.
44% of the squares are unshaded.

Write the percents for the shaded and unshaded squares.

1.

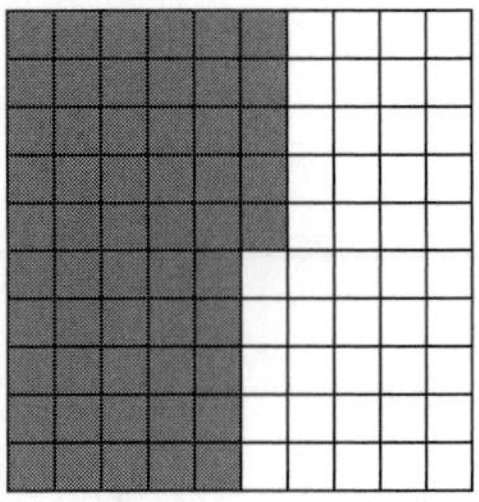

Percent shaded _____

Percent unshaded _____

2.

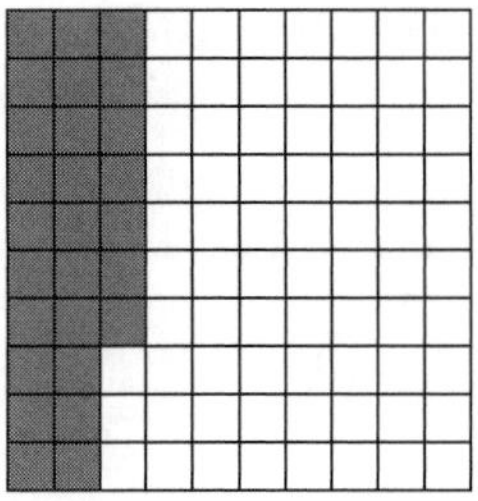

Percent shaded _____

Percent unshaded _____

3.

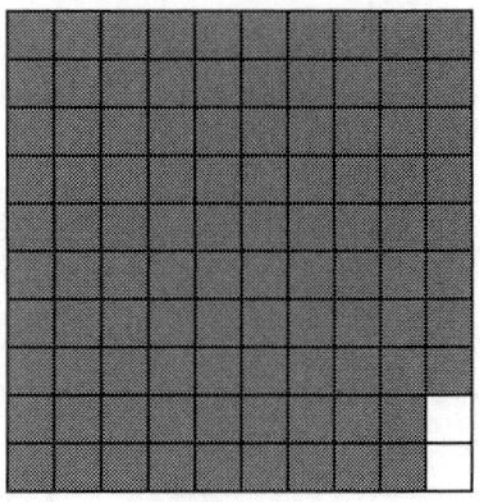

Percent shaded _____

Percent unshaded _____

Shade the 10 × 10 grid to show the percent.

4. 34%

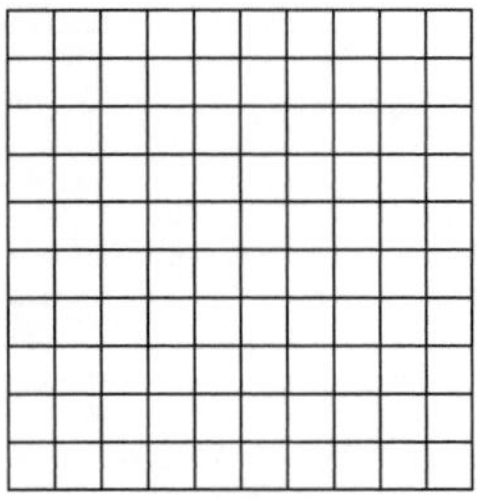

5. 69%

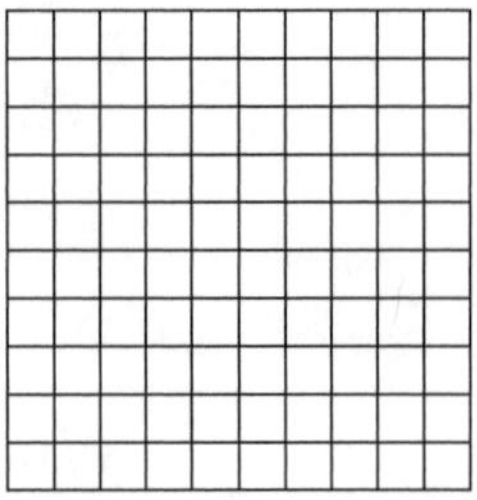

6. 82%

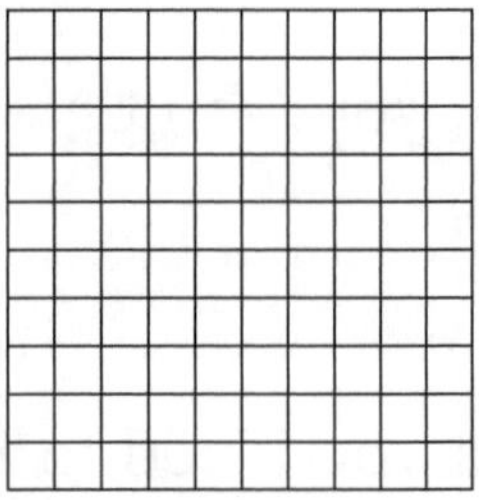

Name ______________________________

Relate Decimals and Percents

Percents and decimals both represent a part of a whole, or of 100.
You can use money to compare percents and decimals.

	Quarter	Dime	Nickel	Penny
Decimal:	$0.25	$0.10	$0.05	$0.01
Read:	twenty-five hundredths	ten hundredths	five hundredths	one hundredth
Ratio:	25 out of 100	10 out of 100	5 out of 100	1 out of 100
Percent:	25% of a dollar	10% of a dollar	5% of a dollar	1% of a dollar

---

Write a decimal and a percent to describe each total amount.

1. 1 quarter, 2 dimes

decimal ________

percent ________

2. 1 quarter, 1 dime, 1 penny

decimal ________

percent ________

3. 3 quarters, 3 pennies

decimal ________

percent ________

4. 8 dimes, 3 nickels, 2 pennies

decimal ________

percent ________

5. 12 nickels, 4 pennies

decimal ________

percent ________

6. 3 pennies

decimal ________

percent ________

Write the number as a decimal and as a percent.

7. forty-five hundredths

____

8. twenty-one hundredths

____

9. eighty-four hundredths

____

10. seventy-two hundredths

____

Name ______________________________

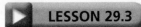

Fractions, Decimals, and Percents

Percents can be written as decimals, or as fractions with 100 as the denominator.

- 45% means forty-five hundredths, or 0.45.
- 45% also means $\frac{45}{100}$.

To write a fraction in simplest form, divide the numerator and the denominator by the same number. Keep doing this until 1 is the only common factor.

- $45\% = \frac{45}{100} = \frac{45 \div 5}{100 \div 5} = \frac{9}{20}$

So, $45\% = 0.45 = \frac{9}{20}$.

To write a fraction as a percent, write a fraction with the percent as the numerator and 100 as the denominator.

- $\frac{37}{100} = 37\%$, or 0.37
- $\frac{3}{4} = \frac{3 \times 25}{4 \times 25} = \frac{75}{100} = 75\%$, or 0.75

Complete. Write each as a decimal, a percent, and a fraction in simplest form.

1. $0.35 = 35\% = \frac{35}{100} = \frac{35 \div 5}{100 \div 5} =$ ______

2. ______ $= 25\% = \frac{}{100} = \frac{}{100 \div 25} =$ ______

3. ______ $= 20\% = \frac{}{100} = \frac{}{100 \div } =$ ______

4. $0.90 =$ ______ $= \frac{}{100} = \frac{}{100 \div } =$ ______

5. $0.16 =$ ______ $= \frac{}{100} = \frac{}{100 \div } =$ ______

6. $0.49 = 49\% = \frac{}{100} = \frac{}{100 \div } =$ ______

Complete. Write as a decimal and as a percent.

7. $\frac{1}{20} = \frac{}{100} =$ ______, or ______

8. $\frac{3}{10} = \frac{}{100} =$ ______, or ______

9. $\frac{11}{100} = \frac{}{100} =$ ______, or ______

10. $\frac{6}{25} = \frac{}{100} =$ ______, or ______

11. $\frac{2}{5} = \frac{}{100} =$ ______, or ______

12. $\frac{3}{4} = \frac{}{100} =$ ______, or ______

Name ____________________

Compare Fractions, Decimals, and Percents

To compare or order fractions, decimals, and percents, write each fraction or percent as a decimal. Then compare the decimals.

Compare $\frac{1}{4}$ and 14%

Step 1 Write $\frac{1}{4}$ as a decimal. ---→ $\frac{1}{4} = 1 \div 4 = 0.25$

Step 2 Write 14% as a decimal. ---→ $14\% = 0.14$

Step 3 Compare the decimals. ---→ $0.25 > 0.14$

So, $\frac{1}{4} > 14\%$.

Order 0.7, 65%, and $\frac{2}{3}$ from least to greatest.

Step 1 Write 65% as a decimal. ---→ $65\% = 0.65$

Step 2 Write $\frac{2}{3}$ as a decimal. ---→ $\frac{2}{3} = 2 \div 3 = 0.667$

Step 3 Compare the decimals. ---→ $0.65 < 0.667$, $0.667 < 0.7$

Step 4 Order from least to greatest. ---→ 0.65, 0.667, 0.7

So, the order from least to greatest is 65%, $\frac{2}{3}$, 0.7.

Compare. Write <, >, or = for each ◯.

1. 0.4 ◯ 40%

2. $\frac{4}{5}$ ◯ 54%

3. 0.38 ◯ $\frac{3}{8}$

4. $\frac{11}{20}$ ◯ 55%

5. 109% ◯ 1.9

6. 0.088 ◯ 88%

7. $\frac{9}{4}$ ◯ 225%

8. 500% ◯ $\frac{5}{5}$

9. 0.65 ◯ 6.5%

10. 0.02 ◯ $\frac{1}{20}$

11. 1.5% ◯ 1.5

12. $\frac{1}{6}$ ◯ 0.12

Order from least to greatest.

13. $\frac{3}{25}$, 10%, 0.2 ____________

14. 72%, 0.68, $\frac{3}{4}$ ____________

15. 0.6, $\frac{5}{8}$, 58% ____________

16. $\frac{5}{3}$, 153%, 1.5 ____________

Find a Percent of a Number

You can make a model to find a percent of a number.

Find 40% of 30.

Step 1

Use pieces of paper to represent 30.

Step 2

Separate the pieces of paper into 10 equal groups. Each group represents 10%.

Step 3

Separate 4 groups from the rest. These 4 groups represent 40%.

Since each group has 3 pieces of paper, 4 groups have 12 pieces of paper.

So, 40% of 30 equals 12.

You can find a percent of a number by changing the percent to a decimal and multiplying.

Step 1

Change the percent to a decimal.

$40\% = 0.40$

Step 2

Multiply the number by the decimal.

$0.40 \times 30 = 12$

So, 40% of 30 equals 12.

Use a decimal to find the percent of the number.

1. 10% of 30 ____________

2. 20% of 50 ____________

3. 15% of 40 ____________

4. 20% of 60 ____________

5. 25% of 40 ____________

6. 3% of 18 ____________

Name ___________________________________

Problem Solving Strategy

Make a Graph

You can make a graph to display percent data.

Step 1 Review your data. If your data show the relationship of parts to a whole, you can use a circle graph.

Step 2 Divide a circle into 10 equal sections.

Step 3 Label the number of sections that show each percent.

1 section represents 10%.

2 sections represent 20%.

There are three 20% sections.

3 sections represent 30%.

Step 4 Label the percents and title the circle graph.

FAVORITE MAGAZINES	
Magazine	**Percent**
Sports for Kids	20%
Around the World	30%
Media Talk	10%
Buy Smart	20%
Puzzle Power	20%

FAVORITE MAGAZINES

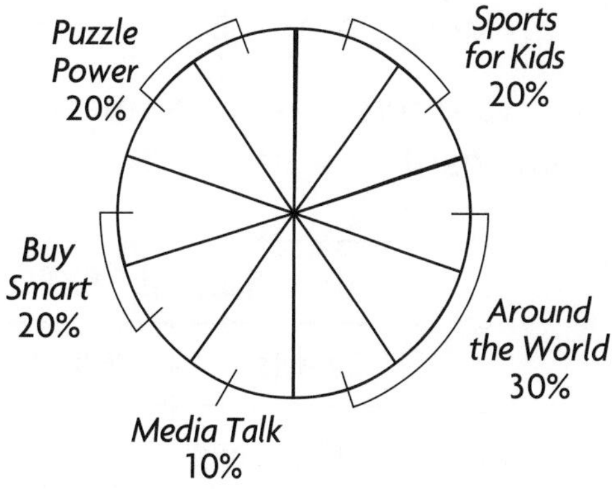

Use a 10-section circle and the data in the table to make a circle graph.

1.

FAVORITE VACATIONS	
Vacation Place	**Percent**
National Park	20%
Beach	20%
Amusement Park	40%
Foreign Country	10%
Famous City	10%

2.

FAVORITE HOBBIES	
Hobby	**Percent**
Painting	20%
Collecting Stamps	10%
Making Models	30%
Collecting Stuffed Animals	30%
Other	10%

Name ____________________

Probability Experiments

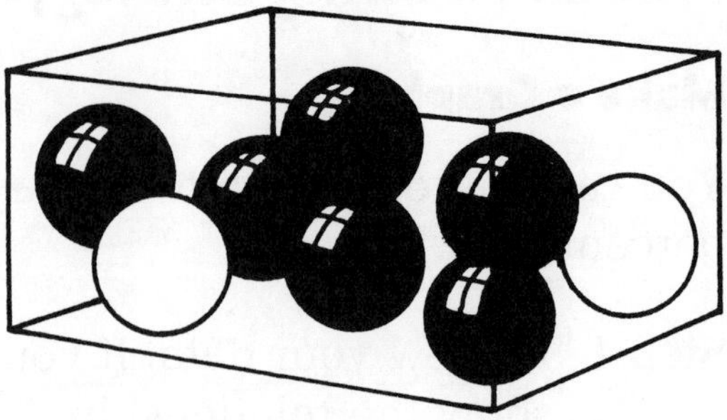

A box contains 6 black marbles and 2 white marbles.

Experiment: Shake the box, and pull a marble. Record the color; then replace the marble.

There are two possible **events** for this experiment.

- The marble is black. The probability of pulling a black marble is 6 out of 8.
- The marble is white. The probability of pulling a white marble is 2 out of 8.

Tom conducts the experiment 16 times. He records the actual results in a table.

MARBLE EXPERIMENT		
Events	**Black**	**White**
Frequency	𝍸 𝍸 |	𝍸

1. What were Tom's results after 16 trials?

____

2. Based on the results of Tom's experiment, what is the probability of pulling a white marble?

____

Tom adds 3 red marbles to the box.

3. What is the probability of pulling a black marble?

____

4. What is the probability of pulling a marble that is **not** black?

____

Name ____________________

Probability Expressed as a Fraction

You can predict the **probability**, or chance, that an event will happen.

Ben has a spinner with six sections. The possible outcomes are blue, red, yellow, and green. What is the probability of spinning blue?

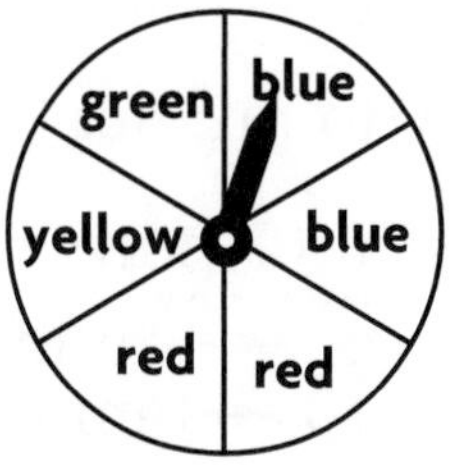

Probability of spinning blue $= \frac{\text{number of blue sections}}{\text{total number of sections}} = \frac{2}{6}$

So, the probability of spinning blue is $\frac{2}{6}$, or $\frac{1}{3}$.

For Problems 1–4, use spinner A. Write a fraction for the probability of each event.

1. blue ____________
2. red ____________
3. green ____________
4. yellow ____________

A

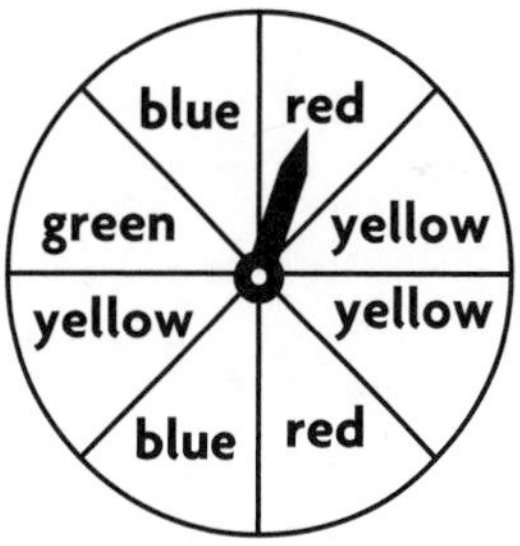

For Problems 5–8, use spinner B. Write a fraction for the probability of each event.

5. 1 ____________
6. 2 ____________
7. 3 ____________
8. 4 ____________
9. 5 ____________

B

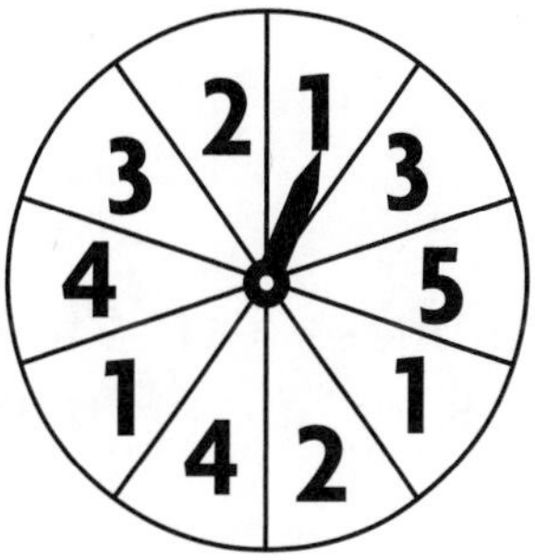

Name ______________________________

Probability and Predictions

The **experimental probability** of an event can be found by comparing the number of times an outcome actually happens to the total number of times the event is performed.

Andrew won 3 out of his 5 last tennis matches.

$$\text{Experimental probability} = \frac{\text{number of times outcome actually happens}}{\text{total number of times event is performed}} = \frac{3}{5}$$

You can use the experimental probability to predict future events.

How many of his next 10 tennis matches can Andrew expect to win?

Write a proportion and solve.

$$\frac{3}{5} = \frac{x}{10} \begin{array}{l} \leftarrow \text{tennis matches won} \\ \leftarrow \text{tennis matches played} \end{array}$$

$$\frac{3 \times 2}{5 \times 2} = \frac{6}{10} \quad \textbf{Think: } 5 \times 2 = 10$$

$$x = 6$$

So, Andrew can expect to win 6 of his next tennis matches.

The probability of winning is $\frac{4}{5}$. Predict the number of wins.

1. in 15 games ______

2. in 45 games ______

3. in 70 games ______

4. in 25 games ______

5. in 65 games ______

6. in 100 games ______

Express the experimental probability as a fraction. Predict the same event in future trials.

7. 2 losses in 5 games
15 more games
______

8. 2 heads in 3 tosses
12 more tosses
______

9. 3 red marbles in 4 pulls
24 more pulls
______

10. 8 wins in 10 games
40 more games
______

11. 4 tails in 8 losses
16 more tosses
______

12. 5 green tiles in 10 pulls
4 more pulls
______

Name ______________________________

Tree Diagrams

Your cafeteria offers a choice of tuna, turkey, or veggie sandwiches. You can also choose between white and wheat bread. What are your possible choices?

A **tree diagram** shows you all the possible choices.

Breads	Sandwiches	Choices
white	tuna	tuna sandwich on white bread
	turkey	turkey sandwich on white bread
	veggie	veggie sandwich on white bread
wheat	tuna	tuna sandwich on wheat bread
	turkey	turkey sandwich on wheat bread
	veggie	veggie sandwich on wheat bread

So, you have 6 possible choices.

---

1. Amanda must choose swimming a 25-meter, 50-meter, or 100-meter race. She can swim in either the freestyle or backstroke division. How many choices does Amanda have? Complete the tree diagram.

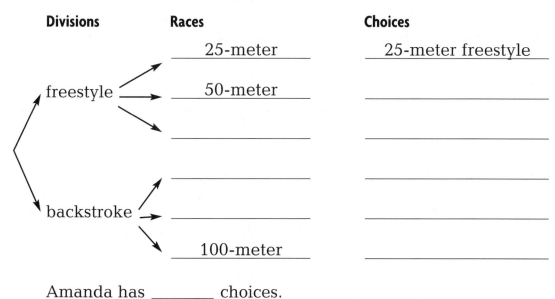

Divisions	Races	Choices
freestyle	25-meter	25-meter freestyle
	50-meter	____________
	____________	____________
backstroke	____________	____________
	____________	____________
	100-meter	____________

Amanda has ________ choices.

2. Brian's parents are buying a new car. They can choose a sedan or a minivan. Both cars are available in red or white. How many choices do they have? __________

Name ____________________

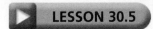

Arrangements and Combinations

An **arrangement** of a set of items lists all the possible outcomes. In an arrangement, the order of the items is important.

Example 1

Ron bought three wooden letters that represent his initials. The letters he bought are **R**, **M**, and **W**. List all the different arrangements that are possible for his initials.

- The possible arrangements starting with **R** are **RMW** and **RWM**.
- The possible arrangements starting with **M** are **MRW** and **MWR**.
- The possible arrangements starting with **W** are **WRM** and **WMR**.

So, there are 6 possible arrangements of Ron's initials.

A **combination** is a selection of items that are arranged in no particular order.

Example 2

Pencils with the school logo are sold in 3 colors: **purple**, **blue**, and **black**. Alyssa wants to buy 2 pencils of different colors. How many combinations can she make? **Think:** there are fewer combinations than arrangements because the order is not important.

- **Purple** and **blue** is the same combination as blue and purple.
- **Blue** and **black** is the same combination as black and blue.
- **Purple** and **black** is the same combination as black and purple.

So, there are 3 combinations of two pencils.

Use the letters A, N, D.

1. List the three-letter arrangements that are possible.

____

2. Find the probability that the letter A is in the middle position for any of the three-letter arrangements chosen at random.

____

3. List all the two-letter arrange-ments that are possible.

____

4. List all the combinations, or choices, of two letters that are possible.

____

Name ______________________________

Problem Solving Strategy

Make an Organized List

Making an organized list can help you determine the possible outcomes of a probability experiment.

Sharon has a coin and a spinner divided into two sections: red and yellow. She will toss the coin and spin the spinner. What are the possible outcomes? How many are there?

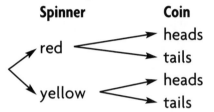

Spinner	Coin	Outcomes
red	heads	red and heads
	tails	red and tails
yellow	heads	yellow and heads
	tails	yellow and tails

So, there are 4 possible outcomes.

Make an organized list to solve.

1. Jereme is conducting a probability experiment with a coin and a bag of marbles. He has 3 marbles in the bag: 1 red, 1 purple, and 1 brown. He will replace the marble after each turn. How many possible outcomes are there for this experiment? What are they?

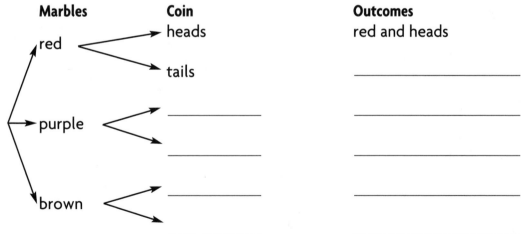

Marbles	Coin	Outcomes
red	heads	red and heads
	tails	____________
purple	____________	____________
	____________	____________
brown	____________	____________
	____________	____________

There are ________ possible outcomes.

2. Sarah has 10¢. How many different combinations of coins could she have? ______________________________